GO GREEN, $AVE GREEN

A Simple Guide to Saving Time, Money,
and GOD'S Green Earth

NANCY SLEETH

Tyndale House Publishers, Inc.

Carol Stream, Illinois

Visit Tyndale's exciting Web site at www.tyndale.com

TYNDALE and Tyndale's quill logo are registered trademarks of Tyndale House Publishers, Inc.

Go Green, Save Green: A Simple Guide to Saving Time, Money, and God's Green Earth

Interior designed by Jennifer Ghionzoli

Published in association with the literary agency of Daniel Literary Group, Nashville, TN.

All quotations from *Serve God, Save the Planet* as well as the energy audit worksheet are used with permission of Chelsea Green Publishing, White River Junction, Vermont 05001.

All quotations take from *It's Easy Being Green* by Emma Sleeth. Copyright © 2008 by Emma Sleeth. Used by permission of Zondervan, www.zondervan.com.

All Scripture quotations, unless otherwise indicated, are taken from the HOLY BIBLE, NEW INTERNATIONAL VERSION®. NIV®. Copyright © 1973, 1978, 1984 by International Bible Society. Used by permission of Zondervan. All rights reserved.

Scripture quotations marked NLT are taken from the *Holy Bible*, New Living Translation, copyright © 1996, 2004, 2007 by Tyndale House Foundation. Used by permission of Tyndale House Publishers, Inc., Carol Stream, Illinois 60188. All rights reserved.

Scripture quotations marked NKJV are taken from the New King James Version® Copyright © 1982 by Thomas Nelson, Inc. Used by permission. All rights reserved. *NKJV* is a trademark of Thomas Nelson, Inc.

Scripture quotations marked KJV are taken from *The Holy Bible*, King James Version.

Library of Congress Cataloging-in-Publication Data

Sleeth, Nancy.
    Go green, save green : a simple guide to saving time, money, and God's green earth / Nancy Sleeth.
        p. cm.
    Includes bibliographical references.
    ISBN 978-1-4143-2698-6 (sc)
    1. Sustainable living. 2. Simplicity—Religious aspects—Christianity. 3. Human ecology—Religious aspects—Christianity. I. Title.
    GF78.S58 2009
    640—dc22   2008052203

Printed in the United States of America.

15   14   13   12   11   10   09
 7   6   5   4   3   2   1

To my dear and loving husband, Matthew

"If ever two were one, then surely we.
If ever man were lov'd by wife, then thee."

Foreword

"How can I get my electricity bill down to the $20 range?"

"Can I feed my family, support local agriculture, and spend less money?"

"What does the Bible say about simple living, frugality, and generosity?"

"What should I do if my spouse won't stop buying stuff we don't need?"

These are just a few of the practical questions that Nancy and I have been asked while speaking at churches and schools throughout the country. A growing number of people are being inspired by their faith to cut back on spending and live more spirit-filled, less materialistic lives, yet they don't know where to start.

Over and over we are told, "Okay, you've convinced us that we need to take better care of what God has given us, but we need to know how."

Go Green, Save Green provides the down-to-earth, practical advice that is so urgently needed. The first faith-based guide for green living, this book will help you save time and money while leaving a healthier environment for your children and future generations. Filled with ideas for greening up your home, workplace, school, and church, this book will help you put your faith into action—immediately. You'll learn how to accumulate less stuff while building more community; how to spend your holiday, travel, and entertainment times in ways that honor God; and how to create a rhythm of Sabbath rest in the midst of your fast-paced lives. In the pages that follow, you'll find strategies to tangibly show your love for God by caring for his creation—today, this week, this month, and this year.

Go Green, Save Green, however, is not about making do with less; it's about doing *more* with less. It's about spending more time with family, friends, and God—and less time taking care of things. It's about acknowledging that it all belongs to God, and learning to be better stewards of his blessings.

We live in uncertain times. Real estate and stock markets fluctuate widely. Jobs and grocery prices are no longer stable. Yet it is possible to have a security that cannot be shaken, no matter how volatile our economy. That security is found not in the global economy, but in God's economy.

Earth stewardship is based on sound theology. From Genesis to Revelation, we are told that God wants us to love what he loves. He sent his Son to die for the whole world; God loves all of creation. We should love and show respect for everything created by God's hand.

Those who follow Jesus are told to be humble and meek. We are taught not to store up our treasures on earth, but in heaven. We are instructed to help the orphans and the widows. Living like Christ is not only good for our souls; it is good for the planet. It is a strategy that will enable your family to thrive, especially in difficult times.

Go Green, Save Green is based on real life—our family's life. The stories and advice Nancy shares are not abstract; they are rooted in years of frugal living, simplicity, and generosity. In practical terms, these lifestyle choices have made it possible for us to carry out our ministry while sharing God's love.

Nancy and I do not believe in living big, except in one area: hospitality. When Abraham welcomes the strangers at his tent, when Rebecca waters the camels at the well, when Mary anoints Jesus with oil, they are demonstrating extravagant hospitality. What distinguishes Christian frugality from other money-saving strategies is that instead of focusing on self, it extends to sharing with others. When we save money, it gives us more to share with our neighbors. It allows us to be generous and to help those who have much greater physical needs than we do. It frees us up to answer God's call.

Christian frugality means that when someone knocks, you are free to open the door and give your very best.

One of the most important questions we have ever been asked occurred at a public forum. We were speaking at a Christian college in the Bible Belt. The girl who raised her hand was one of the youngest in the audience, only twelve or thirteen years old. Her query was the elephant in the room, the question everyone wanted—but was afraid—to ask: "Is it too late?"

The answer is no, it is not too late, but we do need to make changes—quickly. A lot of small actions by a lot of people make a big difference. Science, government, and business will provide some of the answers, but the church offers something that these institutions cannot: hope.

With God, together we can move mountains. But we all need to pick up a spade and start shoveling. This book will show you how.

For the glory of God,
Your brother in Christ,

J. Matthew Sleeth, MD

Acknowledgments

THE PARABLE OF THE TEN LEPERS teaches us to give thanks to those who give us life. "Thank you" is a mere shadow of the gratitude I feel for the family and friends who gave life to this book.

Matthew: You are the love of my life. Thanks for thirty years of love, friendship, walks, and laughter. You helped me see the Creator and his creation with new eyes. Most of all, thank you for bringing Jesus into my life.

Emma: I can think of no greater peace than having you rest on my arm. Thank you for cooking dinners last summer and reminding me to have fun. You make being green not only easy, but beautiful. I will always be your "me-mommy."

Clark: You are the least materialistic, most humble person I know. Thank you for setting an example for us all, and for the privilege of being your mother.

Emily: God brought the perfect researcher back into my life just when I needed her most. Thank you for the walks to the river, and for walking with me through life. To say that I could not have done this without you is an extreme understatement. I pray for a shower of blessings as you return to Tanzania to continue God's good work. I will miss you.

Greg: This book wouldn't have happened without you. Some people have friends. Others have agents. We are blessed to have both in you.

Lisa: I love you too. Not just because you are the editor from heaven. Not just because you let me use sentence fragments, when (and only when) they add meaning. I love you because you are extraordinarily patient, kind, beautiful, and wise. Thank you for making *Go Green* at least a zillion times better than it would have been without you.

Becky and Carol: The moment we first met when you drove to Kentucky I knew we would be friends for life. Thank you for being my sisters in Christ and for putting together the Tyndale dream team. Thank you for biking to work, and for using cloth shopping bags. Thank you for believing. It's been a match made in heaven.

Jen, Jenn, and Bonne: Jen Ghionzoli, your design genius makes *Go Green* infinitely easier to read and inviting. Jenn and Bonne, thank you for being my second sets of eyes and catching my many mistakes. I am grateful.

The Tyndale Team: To Ron Beers, Maria, Kendra, the indefatigable copyeditors and proofreaders, the national sales team, and all the other people who made *Go Green* possible—thank you for honoring Christ in everything you do and say. It's pure joy to work with you.

Becky, Felice, Johnny Dogmatic, Mary, and Stephanie: You have been my resident experts. Thank you for volunteering your time, energy, and considerable knowledge. You are angels, truly heaven-sent.

Will: Thanks for taking a chance with us. You are an answer to prayer. With you by our side, we shall fly.

Mom and Dad: You give new meaning to "unconditional love."

Thank you for nearly five decades of warm hugs and shared lives. You are the best cheerleaders a daughter could ask for. I love you both dearly.

Margie and Leslie: "Friends may come and go, but sisters are forever." Thanks for always being there. Richard: I miss you. We all do. Very much.

The Spicers: You are our second family. Thank you for your counsel, friendship, faith, and generosity. God put you into our lives for a reason, which reveals itself more clearly with each passing day. You model what it means to live as Christians, on call for God and his broken people, 24-7.

Communality: You are my heroes. Thank you, Geoff and Sherry, for providing pastoral care to your flock. You live among and love the least among us, just as Jesus calls us to do. Special thanks to the beautiful and wise women in our Wednesday night Bible study: you fill my well.

Linda, Peg, Terre, and Mattie: Laughter and tears; prayers and thanksgiving; grief and joy. Our Saturday morning women's group feeds me, physically and spiritually. It would be a lonely journey without you.

All the friends who allowed me to share their stories, the people who invite us into their churches and lives, and the Wilmore Creation Care Group: This book is for you.

God: Thank you for being who you are—Creator and Sustainer, Artist and Inventor, Gardener, Shepherd, The Rock. Thank you for putting your Son by my side as I walked down the mountain at dusk on that drizzly Sunday when I gave my life to Christ. Thank you for never leaving me. You are the author of my life, my friend, my Savior.

Introduction

*You see that his faith and his actions were working
together, and his faith was made complete
by what he did.*

JAMES 2:22

IT ALL BEGAN WITH TWO SIMPLE QUESTIONS.

A few years back, my husband was a well-respected physician at
the top of his career—director of emergency services and chief of
medical staff. He loved taking care of patients, and I loved caring
for our family. We lived with our children, Clark and Emma, in
a picture-perfect town in a three-story New England house, complete with library, guest suite, and four bathrooms. Our kids took
sailing lessons in the summer and skied in the winter. We ate lob-
ster fresh from the wharf. We were enjoying the good life and living out the American dream.

But something was missing. We had all the nice *things* that were
supposed to make us happy, yet at the core we still felt hollow.

Then, during the course of one week, Matthew admitted three
different women to the hospital—all in their thirties, all with breast
cancer, all destined to die. One woman seized uncontrollably, and
Matthew could not stabilize her. He had to go out to the waiting

room and tell her husband, who had a toddler on one hip and a little girl holding his hand, that his wife was gone. Matthew did what any compassionate doctor would do: he hugged the young dad, and they cried together.

That night, Matthew came home visibly upset. He told me about the young women with breast cancer, and then asked, "What are the odds?" We looked in his textbook from medical school, which said that one in nineteen women had a lifetime chance of getting breast cancer. The updated version of that same textbook said one in nine women. The incidence now, just a few years later, is nearly one in six.

Matthew said that it was time to stop "running for the cure" and start looking for the cause.

Around this time, we went on a family vacation to a barrier island off the coast of Florida. The island is idyllic—no cars, no roads, no stores—just sun and surf and beautiful sunsets. After playing in the ocean all day and running around trying to catch geckos, the kids went to bed early, exhausted. Adult time, at last! Matthew and I relaxed on the upstairs deck, watching the palm trees waving in a cool breeze and enjoying the silence of the stars.

We stayed like that, just sitting in the tropical moonlight, for a long time. I couldn't help but compare the peacefulness of the night air with the busyness of our lives back home. So rarely did we have time to stop and think, to discuss the big questions of life. Our conversation rambled from art and music, to books we were reading, to the state of the world.

And then I asked two questions that would change our lives forever.

"What do you think is the biggest problem facing the world today?"

I could just about see the wheels whirling in Matthew's head: *Hunger? Poverty? War? AIDS?* There was no shortage of potential answers.

After a few minutes, Matthew offered a reply that I was not expecting: "The world is dying."

He explained his reasoning. "There are no chestnuts left on Chestnut Lane, no elms on Elm Street, no caribou in Caribou, Maine. The oceans are just about fished out, and the songbirds are disappearing. Rainforests the size of North Carolina are being cut down each year—and more than twenty thousand species go extinct annually."

Matthew took a long sip from his glass, and then sighed. "For the first time in history, the amount of living matter on earth is actually decreasing—there's no good ending to this story. If we don't have a healthy planet to sustain humanity, none of the other problems will matter."

It didn't take much to convince me that Matthew was right— our planet is indeed dying. I could see the changes in my own lifetime. As a child, I remember frequently stopping to help turtles cross the road—and seeing frogs and fireflies, honeybees and butterflies everywhere. Seemingly endless flocks of birds would fly overhead every spring and fall. But in just a few decades, nearly all of this wildlife had disappeared. The meadow behind my childhood house had been replaced with ChemLawn green grass and cookie-cutter McMansions. When I approached the nearest major city, I saw a dome of smog covering its inhabitants. Without clean air, clean water, and healthy soil our children would face a turbulent future, with people struggling for increasingly scarce resources.

The more we talked about the demise of the planet, the more depressing it all felt. The problems seemed so overwhelming. But Matthew is a big-picture thinker, a problem solver, a man of action.

That's when I asked the second, more difficult, question:

"If the planet is dying, what are we going to do about it?"

My husband did not have a ready answer. But when we got back from vacation, he did not stop thinking about the challenge. A couple of months later, he finally did get back to me—with an answer I wasn't prepared to hear:

"I'll quit my job," he said, "and put all my energy toward saving the planet."

"Are you sure we need to do *that* much?" I replied.

I had always thought of myself as a good environmentalist. I understood why recycling was important. And picking up litter. I was even okay being the only mom on our block without a family van, making do with a more fuel-efficient sedan. But giving up a career that my husband clearly loved, as well as the prestige, steady income, and security that came along with it, to "save the planet"?

The thought terrified me. My stomach turned inside out just thinking about what we might lose—our beautiful home, our harborside neighborhood, our vacations, not to mention health benefits and a retirement plan. It wasn't like Matthew had a meaningless job—he was employed by a nonprofit hospital, healing the sick and taking care of the poor. And he was extremely good at his work: Matthew had a gift for diagnosis and a talent for putting his patients at ease in even the most trying circumstances.

The selfish part of me began to whine: What about the three years of undergraduate school, four years of medical school, and three years of residency we had gone through together? Wouldn't he be wasting all that training? And then there were practical concerns: The kids were approaching their teen years. College was just around the corner. How would we possibly save enough money to pay for their education if our income dropped suddenly to zero? How, for that matter, would we put food on the table?

Each of my arguments sounded logical on its own. In the material world, my husband's sudden career change made no sense. Walking in faith may sound good in theory—when it happens to other people and everything turns out okay in the end—but I was terrified to take even the first step. What followed was a tense time, full of anxiety, fear of change, and conflicting desires.

People ask us if we had any arguments. Of course we did! I'd be lying if I said that there were no raised voices or sleepless nights.

But gradually I came, if not to peace, at least to acceptance of the new direction our life would take.

The transition—as much emotional and spiritual as physical—took a couple of years. One of the very first things we did was to take an accounting—a measure of our ecological footprint. We had always thought of ourselves as environmentally aware—using cloth diapers, recycling, never driving a car with more than a four-cylinder engine. But when we actually calculated our total use of resources, we found ourselves exactly average for Americans: not bad for a physician's family—since in general the more income people have, the more resources they consume. Yet, we were clearly using more than our fair share on a global scale: *six times* more energy than our neighbors around the world!

Providentially, as we embarked on our environmental journey, we also began a faith journey. It seemed—at least to us—that the two were inseparable. Coming from two different faith backgrounds, Matthew and I began reading a range of sacred texts—including Hindu, Buddhist, and Hebrew. We listened to the Ramayana on tape together, read parts of the Book of Mormon, and even worked through the beginning of the Koran—but still we did not seem to find any satisfactory answers.

One slow night in the hospital, Matthew picked up an orange Gideon's Bible in the waiting room. He read through one of the Gospels. A light came on. Here were the answers we had been seeking.

Matthew brought the Bible home. One by one, each of us became believers—first Matthew, then Clark, then me, and finally Emma. And that changed everything. Suddenly, the whole family was working off the same page. We had a clear purpose: to love God with all our heart, mind, soul, and strength, and to love our neighbors as ourselves. One way that we could show our love for the Creator, and for our global neighbors, was to start taking better care of the planet.

To learn what the Bible had to say about earth stewardship,

Matthew read through the entire Old and New Testaments, underlining in orange pencil everything that had to do with nature, creation, and how we are to instructed to care for the earth. We found that Matthew 7:3-5 seemed to speak directly to our family: "And why worry about a speck in your friend's eye when you have a log in your own? How can you think of saying to your friend, 'Let me help you get rid of that speck in your eye,' when you can't see past the log in your own eye? Hypocrite! First get rid of the log in your own eye; then you will see well enough to deal with the speck in your friend's eye."

We took Jesus' advice and began cleaning up our own act before worrying about cleaning up the rest of the world. Over the next couple of years, we downsized our lifestyle, giving away half of our possessions and moving to a house the size of our old garage. Contrary to my earlier fears, we found that the more we "gave up" in material things, the more we gained in family unity, purpose, and joy. Eventually, through many small changes, we reduced our electricity usage and trash production by nine-tenths and our fossil fuel usage by two-thirds.

After we had our own house in order, we felt called to share our journey. Matthew wrote a book called *Serve God, Save the Planet: A Christian Call to Action*. Using stories from our family's life and the ER, he relayed why we made these changes and inspired others to do the same.

People liked the book—a lot. It's an easy book to read, but hard to ignore. Letters poured in from readers who felt called to change but didn't know where to start. Invitations to speak, preach, and lead workshops came from Washington, D.C. to Washington State, from every denomination and faith, from churches with ten members to tens of thousands. People were inspired to change; now they wanted to know *how*.

In *Go Green, Save Green*, I will share what worked, what didn't, and what we learned in the process. Some steps came easily; others required a new way of thinking or a change of habits. I don't offer a one-size-fits-all plan; each family must decide which changes work best for them, and then keep doing a little bit better every year.

What if someone in your household is not on board? Our daughter Emma, reluctant at first, ended up writing a book for teens called *It's Easy Being Green* and becoming a leader of the next generation's Christian environmental movement.

Regardless of where you and your family members are on the journey, this book will provide practical advice on everything from household cleaners, gardening, and fast food—to tips for Christmas shopping, giving away money, and finding quiet time with God.

This is not, however, just a book about practical ways to save time, energy, and money. This is a personal journey of hope. If someone like me can do it, I know you can too!

Years ago, back on that island in Florida, two questions— prompted by God—launched our family on this journey.

Today, when making any choice, purchase, or decision, we ask ourselves two new questions: Does this bring me closer to God? And, does this help me love my neighbor?

The answers always lead us down the right path.

Dear heavenly Father, Creator, and Sustainer, please open my heart to the beauty of your creation. Teach me to value your sustaining gifts and to steward them wisely. I beseech you, gracious and loving God of the universe, to create a thirst in my heart for change: Give me a thankful heart, and free me from my wasteful habits. Teach me to rely on your strength alone, for I know that real and lasting transformation can only come through you.

The changes we have made will not earn our way into heaven, but they do two important things for our souls: They connect us with the family of humanity around the globe, and, more important, they bring us closer to God. If he asks us to give up everything we have and follow him, I now know with certainty that each member of my family would gladly do so. This lack of attachment to things, rather than the size of our home, brings us priceless freedom and allows us to hear his call.

—*Serve God, Save the Planet*

They say home is where the heart is—and home is also the best place to start in making our lives greener. In offering lots of suggestions for making your home more earth-friendly, my point isn't to make you feel guilty about all the things you should be doing differently. My point is to help you see that there are so many ways—some very simple, some a little tougher—to have a positive impact on the environment. We all have the ability to change the world, one choice at a time.

—*It's Easy Being Green*

1

Home

Small Changes, Big Results

Heaven is my throne, and earth is my footstool:
what house will ye build me?

ACTS 7:49, KJV

THE DAY I TURNED FORTY, my older sister called. "Forty is okay," she reassured me. "It's a couple years from now that the body really starts to slide downhill."

And she was right. Within a couple of years, I couldn't read the road signs quite as easily, especially at night. The arches of my feet started to ache if I didn't wear shoes with good support. And my clothes seemed to shrink all at once—or was that my waistline growing?

A new prescription for my glasses and a pair of good insoles took care of the first two problems, but what about the extra inches? One of the perks of my new teaching job at an independent boarding school was free food for my entire family: three meals a day, seven days a week. And this was no ordinary cafeteria—we had a wealthy international boarding population among our students, and they expected the best. Eggs made to order, homemade waffles, pancakes with fresh fruit every morning. At lunch, a choice of several hot entrées was served alongside a wrap and sandwich line—you tell the cafeteria workers what you want and they make it. Dinner was my favorite meal, especially since at the end of a ten-hour day, the last thing I felt like doing was cooking a big meal for my family—and there were no dishes to clean up! Best of all, there was a dessert bar—I could always count on the intensely rich chocolate layer cake to keep me buzzed for another couple hours of grading papers.

And did I mention that *the entire family* could have *as much food as we wanted*? Three meals a day? Seven days a week? And that it was all *free*? I began to understand why my petite friend Cindy gained 7 pounds every time she went on a cruise!

One October morning, I headed to the school gym before morning chapel, climbed down two flights of stairs, wriggled into my long-disused bathing suit, and eased into the pool. Even though the pool was indoors, the water was cold—no wimpy swimmers in northern New England. After I swam a few laps, my eyes started to sting—I had forgotten that my eyes are unusually sensitive to pool water. And that's when Mr. Golden, the boisterous, lovable art teacher, paddled over to my lane. Mr. Golden (yes, that's his real name!) wore a big float around his waist and used a kickboard to cruise around the pool. He was known throughout campus for attending every home game of every sport for something like forty years. He was a big, burly man with a heart as big as his bellowing voice.

> *I love your sanctuary, Lord, the place where your glorious presence dwells.*
>
> PSALM 26:8, NLT

"Come back tomorrow," Mr. Golden said. "My ears are bad—I can't go underwater anymore—I've got a great pair of goggles you can use."

But I wasn't so sure that I *wanted* to get up a half hour early the next day. And the water was so cold! Yet how could I refuse this thoughtful offer?

So I came back the next day. And the next. And the next.

Exercising in the morning makes me hungry, so I started eating a healthy breakfast and less at lunch and dinner. After New Year's, I gave up chocolate, except on Sundays. When my daughter, Emma, was assigned the same lunch period as me, we began picking up a couple of veggie wraps from the cafeteria and eating together in the quiet oasis of my classroom—where no monster chocolate chip cookies could tempt me! At dinner, I started gravitating toward the salad bar instead of the dessert line. When the days grew warmer, I went on long walks while the kids finished their after-school activities.

By the time summer vacation arrived, my new eating and exercise habits were well established—and the extra inches around my middle had disappeared.

> " I [God] did not intend my creatures to make themselves servants and slaves to the world's pleasures. . . . They owe their first love to me. Everything else they should love and possess, as I told you, not as if they owned it but as something lent them. —*Catherine of Siena (1347–1380)*, The Dialogue "

Suddenly, my forties didn't look so bad.

Matthew, my brilliant doctor-husband, has developed a medically proven, no-fail plan for patients who want to lose weight: eat less, exercise more. As a concerned mom, I offer an equally simple plan for people who want to start greening their homes: consume less, save more.

The basic principles of nutrition and health are a lot like the principles behind green living: Just as we need to be good stewards of the physical body God gave us, we need to take care of the physical planet that sustains all life. Both require some measure of discipline. Both result in major improvements when small changes are made over a period of time. And both bring joy—to us and our Creator.

Will the process always be easy? convenient? popular with other members of your family or neighborhood? No, I'd be lying if I said that the green way has been hassle free for our family. But the Bible does not promise us an easy life—just a purpose-filled one.

At first, some of the changes in this chapter may seem about as inviting as a cold pool on a New England winter morning. But if you persist, making small changes over the course of a year or more, I promise that you will find yourself living in a healthier, more joy-filled home with less baggage weighing you down and more time for family, friends, and God.

And suddenly your future, and your children's future, will look a little brighter.

Getting Started: Simple No-Cost Changes

The energy costs of two families living in *exactly* the same house can differ as much as 100 percent. This means you can *halve* your energy costs by changing a few simple behaviors.

- Turn down the temperature on your water heater to 120 degrees. (Look for a little metal box on the side of the water heater.)

- Do laundry in cold water and you can save up to $63 per year!

- Turn your refrigerator and freezer to the warmest setting. (We've done it for years, with no adverse health effects!)

- Activate the "sleep" mode on your home office equipment. Use laptops rather than desktops when possible.

- Turn the thermostat up three degrees in summertime and down three degrees in wintertime—saving $200 per year!

- Turn off lights, TVs, stereos, and computers when leaving the room.

- Hang clothes on the line to dry. (Even once a week helps!)

- Reduce shower time by at least two minutes.

- Close curtains at night during the winter and on hot days in the summer.

- Only do full loads when using the dishwasher, clothes washer, and dryer.

THROUGHOUT THE HOUSE
Weighing In

When we need to shed a few pounds, doctors advise us to start by stepping on the scale. The same principle applies to lightening our impact on the planet. We need to see where we are, set goals, and measure our progress.

In Appendix A, you'll find the energy audit worksheet that our family used to begin our environmental journey. Take a few minutes to fill it out now. Once you have a baseline, you can set goals and make changes needed to live a less consumeristic, more God-centered life.

If you want to go one step further, contact your local utility provider to see if they offer energy audits. For a small fee (it's $15 in our area), they will come to your house and check windows, doors, insulation, and appliances, and leave you with a personalized action plan for saving energy, including estimates of how much the upgrades may cost and how much you can expect to save.

Tools

Several organizations offer interactive tools for home energy check-ups on their Web sites. Many offer instant feedback.

- The Alliance to Save Energy (http://www.ase.org/section/_audience/consumers/homecheckup)
- The U.S. Department of Energy (http://hes.lbl.gov)
- The U.S. Environmental Protection Agency and the U.S. Department of Energy (http://www.energystar.gov/index.cfm?fuseaction=home_energy_yardstick.showStep2)

GO GREEN
Twenty-three percent of the new homes in America are more than 3,000 square feet. The bigger the house, the more resources it consumes.

The Upside of Being Downwardly Mobile

When we moved to our 1960s ranch house, I left behind a stable full-time teaching position for a part-time, adjunct job at a Christian college, which paid a whopping $8,000—the only income our family could count on that year. As my husband, Matthew, likes to say, we were the poster family for the downwardly mobile. He had already left his ER position four years earlier, and we were in an economic free fall once again. Needless to say, we did not have a lot of extra money to spend on home improvements. Instead, we first invested in inexpensive projects that had the quickest payback (making insulated curtains for windows, fixing leaky faucets and toilets, changing lightbulbs), and then we used the savings to pay for longer-term investments such as attic insulation and energy-efficient windows. (We took advantage of tax incentives that helped us pay for these larger energy-saving home improvements.) Since then, our electric bills have plummeted, and the savings go on year after year.

SAVE GREEN

Take that first step! An audit can help you save up to 30 percent on your energy bills.

Thermostat

We struggle with the thermostat settings in our family. Moving to Kentucky has made my life much easier because I'm the one who gets cold, but it's made Matthew's life more difficult since he has a hard time functioning in heat. We keep the heat low in winter—usually around sixty degrees during the day, and completely turned off at night. On very cold nights, I open the sink cabinet doors before I go to bed to be sure the pipes don't freeze. In the morning, I dress in multiple layers, brew a pot of hot tea, and use a small electric heater in my home office to take off the chill. In summer, we watch the weather closely—opening windows at night to cool the house down. The humidity in our area seems to increase significantly in the late afternoon and evening, so that's when we briefly run the air conditioner.

In general, turn down the thermostat at night during the winter and when you're away from home; in the summertime, turn up the thermostat. Contrary to some common myths, it won't take any more energy to bring your house back to the desired temperature than it would to leave it at your optimum temperature all day. A programmable thermostat gives you much more flexibility to control your home's climate, and it pays for itself in one season. Adjusting your thermostat just three degrees year-round will save about $200 on your heating and cooling bills.

Green Power

More and more public utilities are offering a green power option that supports renewable resources. Most of our electricity comes from coal. Coal mining destroys mountains and creates far more pollution than any other energy source (mercury, sulfur dioxide,

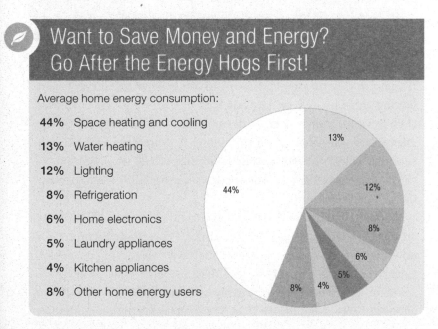

Want to Save Money and Energy? Go After the Energy Hogs First!

Average home energy consumption:

44% Space heating and cooling

13% Water heating

12% Lighting

8% Refrigeration

6% Home electronics

5% Laundry appliances

4% Kitchen appliances

8% Other home energy users

nitrous oxides, or particulates). Call your local electricity provider to see if green power is available in your area, and make the switch. It will cost a bit more, but you will be showing love for our global neighbors and allowing your children and your children's children to breathe more freely.

This year, our April electricity bill was $14. When our May bill came, Matthew was disappointed that it had gone up to $18. But then I pointed out that our public utility had just added the green power option, and we had elected to pay an extra $5 per month to promote alternative energy sources for our electricity. So our May bill energy usage was actually lower ($13, including mandatory transmission fees and taxes), and we were more than offsetting our 122 kWh (kilowatt-hour) electricity usage for under $20 per month. Conservation pays!

> **GO GREEN**
>
> Loving our neighbors? Americans make up 5 percent of the world's population but use 26 percent of its energy.

Lighting

It's a myth that turning lights on and off uses more electricity than leaving them on. We taught our kids to turn lights off whenever they leave a room. Energy-efficient bulbs use one-quarter of the energy and last seven to ten times longer. Watch out for torchères (upright lamps). They often use lightbulbs of 300 watts or more—the equivalent of thirty or more energy-saving bulbs—and present dangerous fire hazards.

About 95 percent of the electrical current for standard lightbulbs creates heat rather than light. This makes energy-saving bulbs not only vastly more efficient, but also much safer. According to an EPA Energy Star fact sheet, if every American home replaced just one standard lightbulb with an energy-efficient bulb, we would save enough energy to light more than 3 million homes, retain more than

$600 million in annual energy costs, and prevent greenhouse gases equivalent to the emissions of more than 800,000 cars. Changing our lightbulbs also saves thousands of lives lost due to respiratory illnesses and asthma attacks, especially among children and senior citizens—the very people God tells us to care for.

Green Light to Savings

Matthew has always been obsessed with light; our family has been the guinea pig of lighting technology. We have tried every new kind of lightbulb on the market, going back more than twenty years to those first energy-saving bulbs that buzzed and gave off a harsh light. When we moved the last time, a friend jokingly suggested that we start a Museum of Lightbulb History.

If you have been reluctant to buy energy-saving lightbulbs because you think they give off an unflattering light, give the new "soft" and "warm" bulbs a try. Their light is indistinguishable from regular lightbulbs—and the wide selection of bulbs available today makes it possible to find the right energy-saving bulb for every fixture.

I've often been asked about people who need extra reading light, especially our growing elderly population. Matthew just turned fifty, but he's had some medical problems with his eyesight that go beyond the normal aging process. No worries! Lightbulbs are available in every imaginable wattage; the last time we went to the hardware store, we saw 300 watt–equivalent compact fluorescent (CFL) bulbs—enough for even the most extreme lighting needs. They also now come in different base sizes. Our son Clark's apartment for medical school came with wall sconces that use candelabra bulbs. We considered buying new sconces, but then found CFL bulbs that screw right in. Several lightbulb manufacturers even make CFLs designed for use on dimmer switches.

Energy-saving bulbs do cost more initially, but the average payback in energy savings is less than a year, even sooner if you use rebates or find them on sale. Conventional bulbs use the most energy, followed by halogens, then compact fluorescents, and the least energy users of all (but not widely available yet), light-emitting diode (LED) bulbs. The current LED bulbs do not give off as much light, so we use them in areas that don't require bright lighting—two in the basement and two outside—but need to be on frequently. Dimming your lights also can cut back on electricity bills.

GO GREEN

Energy-saving lightbulbs use about one-quarter the energy of standard lightbulbs and last up to ten times longer.

Windows

We waited nearly two years until we could afford to replace the single-paned, aluminum-framed windows that came with our 1960s house. Matthew gave the two window installers an extra $50 each so that they would beef up the insulation around each

What about Mercury?

One of the most common questions we get on the road is about the mercury in CFL bulbs. It's true: a CFL bulb contains a minuscule amount of mercury (5 mg), about one-fifth of the mercury found in the average watch battery and less than 1/600th of the mercury found in a home thermostat. However, if you do the math, the tiny amount they contain is dwarfed by the extra amount of mercury that coal-burning power stations emit to power the much-less-efficient incandescent bulb. A power plant will emit 10 mg of mercury in order to produce the amount of electricity needed to run an incandescent bulb compared to emitting only 2.4 mg of mercury to run a CFL for the same length of time.

Those signs you see when you go fishing, warning children and pregnant women to avoid eating the catch, are not because of toxins dumped into the water. The concern is primarily because of the mercury emitted from coal-fired power plants that settles in our rivers and lakes. To properly dispose of your burned-out CFL, just drop it off at a local Home Depot or IKEA store, or check out http://www.earth911.org for other safe disposal options. Bottom line: using compact fluorescents cuts back on your electric bill and is safer for the environment.

of the windows and seal them extra tight. The new windows have made a *huge* difference—our house is quieter and much more comfortable—with lower energy bills than ever. Before selecting an installer, we made sure that the company routinely recycled all of the window glass and aluminum.

In general, double- or triple-pane high-efficiency windows can save your family $340 each year, depending on climate. They also improve comfort in both winter and summer. If you can't afford to replace windows right away, install storm windows or consider temporary fixes for your leaky windows, such as plastic film kits that act like an interior storm window.

> The creation is quite like a spacious and splendid house, provided and filled with the most exquisite and the most abundant furnishings. Everything in it tells us of God.
> —*John Calvin (1509–1564)*, Institutes 1:14

Curtains

Cut heat transfer by one-third by hanging heavy, lined curtains. In summer, keep the curtains closed during the day, and open both curtains and windows at night for natural ventilation. In winter, closing the curtains at night and opening them on sunny days can have a huge impact on your energy bill, especially if you use insulated curtains.

Lined curtains do an amazing job of keeping the heat in during the winter and out in the summer. According to *The Green Book*, if we all hung curtains for extra insulation, it would save the same amount of energy that the entire country of Japan uses.

Awnings

Remember awnings? Yes, they are an investment, but they will keep your home so much cooler during summertime, especially if you do not have energy-efficient windows. When speaking at a college in North Carolina, I noticed that all of the older homes still had beautiful, practical awnings, while not one of the newer homes did—

our grandparents knew best! Other energy-saving summer options include fabric patio covers and solar window screens. Do a little research to see whether or not these are available in your area.

Energy monitoring

How low can you go? You can get a real-time reading of your home energy use by purchasing an energy monitoring device such as The Energy Detective (TED), which costs about $140 (http://www.theenergydetective.com). After being hooked up to your circuit breaker box by a handy homeowner or electrician, TED provides a small display that shows your household electricity usage in real time, and then projects your monthly bill. Just as the energy-consumption display on our Toyota Prius has taught me to adjust my driving habits, TED claims that real-time energy feedback can help reduce your energy consumption by as much as 15 to 20 percent, translating into savings of hundreds of dollars. And it can be a fun way to get the whole family on the energy-saving bandwagon. The bottom line: if you can measure it, you can manage it. Make small adjustments throughout the day and see how quickly the savings add up. If you want to know exactly how much energy your appliances use, including when they are "off," you can purchase a Kill A Watt Electricity Usage Monitor for about $20 (available at Amazon.com and other Internet stores). Just plug the appliance into the meter, and it will help you see where your energy dollars are going. Spread the savings: offer to lend the watt meter to your church facility manager, extended family, and neighbors. For instance, a side-by-side refrigerator will almost always use more energy than a refrigerator with a freezer on the top or bottom

> *So don't be dismayed when the wicked grow rich and their homes become ever more splendid. For when they die, they take nothing with them. Their wealth will not follow them into the grave.*
>
> PSALM 49:16-17, NLT

How Much Energy Do You Use?

The amount of energy that appliances use varies widely from model to model, so be sure to compare the yellow energy-use tags and look for Energy Star models. However, keep in mind that a product receives an Energy Star rating only because it uses less energy than others *in its class.*

The table below will help you identify the energy guzzlers in your home; remember that many electronic components, such as stereos, DVD players, and TVs, continue to burn watts even when turned off.

APPLIANCE	AVERAGE WATTS USED PER HOUR
Fluorescent lightbulb	13
Conventional lightbulb	60
Exhaust fan	75 (turn it off as soon as you can)
Laptop computer	50
Stereo	100
Television	100 (High Definition uses more!)
VCR/DVD player	22
Refrigerator/freezer	800 (biggest overall user because it is left on 24-7)
Desktop computer	150 (many families leave them on 24-7)
Hair dryer	1,200 (hair appliances are energy intensive)
Microwave	750 (saves energy when used to precook)
Vacuum cleaner	800
Toaster	1,000
Iron	1,000
Dishwasher	1,200–2,400 (higher when using heat dry option)
Small portable heater	1,000
Clothes dryer	1,800–5,000
Electric stove (1 burner)	1,300
Large portable heater	2,000 (size does matter!)
Oven	2,150
Electric stove (everything on)	11,500

of equivalent size. And size does count—in general the smaller the appliance, the less energy it will use.

One Step Forward, Two Steps Back

Green living leads to green savings, and a less consumeristic lifestyle leads to more time with family, friends, and God.

When I talk with other moms about practical ways to save money and green up our lives, our discussions often lead us to even deeper, more basic questions: living in an age of great wealth and physical ease, why do we feel lonelier and less content than ever before?

The answer, I believe, begins at home. Just think about all the electronic devices that did not exist when our grandparents were born: clothes dryers, clock radios, blow-dryers, TVs, microwaves, toaster ovens, blenders, cell phones, computers, iPods, printers, VCRs, DVD players, Xbox . . . the list goes on and on. With all of these gadgets in our homes, Americans now consume more than twice as much as they did fifty years ago. The average house size in the United States has more than doubled since the 1950s to 2,350 square feet—but this consumer frenzy doesn't seem to be making us happy. In fact, it's making us less happy. According to Gary Gardner, senior researcher at Worldwatch Institute and author of *Inspiring Progress: Religions' Contributions to Sustainable Development*, as a country, our national happiness peaked in the 1950s, and our contentedness continues to decline as household incomes increase.

Our houses are filled with labor-saving devices, but we have less time for families, friends, and God. We work longer and longer hours, but no one is home to enjoy our wealth. In those rare times when families are in the house together, we separate ourselves with TVs, headphones, and computers, sharing only a few minutes a day of meaningful conversation with our spouses or children.

All of this focus on materialism comes at a huge cost—financially, spiritually, relationally, and environmentally. Yet there is great hope: little changes made by a lot of people can make a big difference. We don't need to give up all modern conveniences, shivering in unheated rooms; however, we do need to change wasteful practices and bring our lifestyles more in line with our values. Practicing the Christian disciplines—sacrificing a bit of comfort to honor God's creation—will bring joy to your family while drawing you closer to him.

Stewardship is a journey, not a destination. When I compare my life to the meek and humble example that Jesus set, I know that I have only taken the first few steps. Yet having an eternal benchmark gives purpose to my journey. If we can reduce our impact by 10 percent a year, we are on the right road.

IN THE KITCHEN
Refrigerator

Your refrigerator is the biggest energy-using appliance in the kitchen because it is on 24-7. For the last ten years, we've kept our refrigerator and freezer on the warmest-possible setting, with no problems beyond slightly softened ice cream. Matthew is a doctor, so I trust he would tell me if there were serious health ramifications in doing this!

Eight Low-Cost, High-Payback Home Improvements

- Purchase a programmable thermostat and use it to turn on heat or a/c just before you wake up or come home.

- Replace furnace and air-conditioning filters at least three times a year.

- Caulk between window frames, door frames, and walls.

- Add storm windows or use plastic film kits to improve single-pane windows.

- Insulate water heater and pipes, and turn water heater down to 120 degrees.

- Install motion sensors, dimmers, and timers for indoor and outdoor lighting.

- Install ceiling or other fans to cut down on air-conditioning costs.

- Change lightbulbs to compact fluorescent bulbs

Consider these other energy-saving ideas for your refrigerator:

- Decide what you want before you open the door—refrigerator gazing can cost $30–$60 per year.
- Put hot food in a cold water bath or place it outside in cold weather before refrigerating, so less energy is required to keep it cool.
- Keep your refrigerator and freezer full. Doing so uses less energy because less cooling is lost each time you open the refrigerator.
- Defrost food in the refrigerator; it will keep the refrigerator cooler.
- Make sure the seals are in good shape. Try this quick test: Shut the fridge and freezer door on a dollar bill. If you can pull it out easily, your door seals are damaged and need to be replaced.
- Give your refrigerator room to breathe. Do not jam the refrigerator against the wall, and keep at least 3 inches clear above it in order to allow for proper airflow.
- Unplug extra refrigerators (such as those in your garage or basement) when not in use.
- Disconnect automatic ice makers, which add heat to the freezer to release the cubes.

> **SAVE GREEN**
>
> Nearly 20 percent of homes have at least two refrigerators. The older the model, the more energy it uses. Consider giving your second refrigerator to a family in need. In addition to helping someone out, you will also be saving up to $100 per year on your electricity bill.

Sink

Most modern faucets have aerators (wire mesh attachments). If yours does not, you can install one pretty easily. These inexpensive aerators or flow valves, found at your local hardware store, can reduce your water flow by half without reducing water pressure.

Dish washing

There's quite a bit of controversy over which method uses more water and energy: hand washing or the dishwasher. The average dishwasher uses more than 10 gallons of water; energy-efficient dishwashers use about half that. My family washes dishes by hand, using 3–5 gallons a day. We try to wash the cleaner dishes first, turning off the tap while we scrub and rinsing with cold water. Most of the year we collect that water in a tub and reuse it to refresh our garden.

In addition to using more water, dishwashers also require electricity to run the motor; hand washing does not. Think about it: it takes energy to power your dishwasher for forty-five minutes per cycle, whereas children who regularly participate in washing and drying dishes require *zero* electricity. Some of Emma's and Clark's fondest memories are when they've been making up silly songs as they do the dishes together.

Dishwashers use anywhere from 331 (Energy Star) to 1,000 (conventional) kWh per year. Washing by hand can save $100 per year on your electricity bill—and it can teach your children the value of working cooperatively.

Have Money, but No Time?

Hire an energy-performance contractor. The Department of Energy and EPA have started a program called Home Performance with Energy Star. These specially trained contractors conduct a whole-house energy audit and make specific recommendations for saving energy in your home. For an additional fee, some contractors will then implement the suggestions that you approve. What a great example of the growing green economy and job market! To see if the program is available in your state, visit http://www.energystar.gov/index.cfm?c=home_improvement.hm_improvement_hpwes_partners.

If you do use the dishwasher, run full loads and avoid prerinsing before putting dishes in—you could save up to 20 gallons of water per load or 7,300 gallons per year—as much as the average person drinks in a lifetime. Turn the dishwasher completely off when the cycle is finished. To save even more, avoid using the boosted cleaning and heated dry options and air dry the dishes instead.

Detergent

While the government no longer permits phosphates in laundry detergents, they do allow them in automatic dishwasher soaps. When phosphates end up in rivers and coastal areas, they can "fertilize" algae populations, leading to large algal blooms, which in turn can choke out plant and animal life in aquatic ecosystems and contribute to aquatic dead zones. But there is good news: store-brand, environmentally friendly cleaning products now cost about the same as standard cleaning products. Back when we still used a dishwasher, we squirted about one teaspoon of phosphate-free dishwashing liquid into the detergent dispenser instead of dishwasher powder, and the dishes always came out sparkling clean.

> " The seriousness of the ecological issue lays bare the depth of man's moral crisis. . . . Simplicity, moderation and discipline, as well as a spirit of sacrifice, must become a part of everyday life.
>
> —*Pope John Paul II (1920–2005)*, Peace with God the Creator, Peace with All of Creation "

Paper products

Our family uses an average of one roll of paper towels every two to three years. Rather than paper, we use cloth towels for cleaning up. We drain bacon on paper grocery bags. When we do purchase paper products, we make sure they are made from recycled paper. We purchase our 100 percent recycled toilet paper in bulk from an office supply store—it's cheaper than "regular" toilet tissue and oh-so-much better for the forests.

For parties, draft a couple of teens to wash and dry dishes so you don't have to rely on paper products. We fed fifty teenagers lasagna for Clark's birthday party last year, with Emma and her roommate keeping a fresh supply of clean dishes available all night. Don't have enough plates? Ask friends to bring their own, or borrow a set from a neighbor.

Cleaning products

America has become bacteria-phobic—and the overuse of antibacterial soaps is leading to an unhealthy rise in resistant bacteria. Matthew, an ER doctor, always joked around the house that he did not believe in the germ theory of disease. In reality, he did not want his kids to become the stereotypical obsessive-compulsive, hypochondriac doctor's kids, so we've always taken a rather laid-back attitude toward germs—and our kids are healthier for it.

Look for cleaning products that are nontoxic, biodegradable, and made from renewable resources (not petroleum). Green cleaning products are now readily available at grocery, office supply, and home improvement stores—even Clorox now offers a green cleaning product line! The cheapest solution? I've found that baking soda or vinegar mixed with warm water can handle almost any cleaning job. Baking soda also works great as a scouring powder

Hugging Trees for Jesus

From Genesis to Revelation, it is clear that God loves trees.

Trees are mentioned one thousand times in the Bible, more than any living thing other than humans. The symbol of God is the tree of life, Abraham met the Lord under the oaks of Mamre, Moses heard God speak from a bush that would not burn, and Deborah held court under palm trees.

Before his ministry started, Jesus worked with trees; at the end of his ministry, he stretched out his calloused carpenter hands for our salvation and hugged a tree—the cross he bore for us. Using recycled paper is one way of showing that we love what God loves!

in sinks and on pans. (Use on stainless steel, copper, and iron pans but not on aluminum pans—baking soda can make shiny aluminum pans oxidize or discolor a bit.)

Pest control

The first step to reducing pests and insects in the kitchen is to remove the source that is attracting them. Don't allow food scraps to linger on counters or floors. Dripping faucets and soaking dishes can also serve as a water source, enticing insects into the kitchen. Keep food staples that insects find attractive—such as flour, pasta, and cornmeal—in airtight containers or in the refrigerator.

There are many natural remedies you can use to control pests. If ants are a problem, follow the trail to see where they are entering and sprinkle chili pepper, dried peppermint, or borax to deter them. Roaches can be eliminated by sprinkling four parts borax, two parts flour, and one part sugar or cocoa in infested areas—

Green Cleaning

INSTEAD OF	USE THIS
Glass cleaner and paper towels	White vinegar and lint-free cloth
Powder bleach	Borax
Carpet cleaner	Cornstarch or baking soda
Scrubbing powder (like Ajax)	Baking soda
All-purpose cleaner	Liquid castile soap and baking soda or borax. Dilute for floors, walls, and counters.
Drain opener	Try plunging before chemicals. If plunging does not work, pour one cup of baking soda down the drain, followed by one cup of vinegar. One minute later, add one pint of hot water. (Stand back because the liquid can come back up toward you.)

For more nontoxic cleaning recipes, visit http://www.greenerchoices.org.

roaches will carry the mixture back to their nests and die. Use under the sink and in back of cabinets to prevent further infestations. Borax is available in the grocery store alongside laundry soaps. Be sure to keep borax away from children.

Garbage disposal
Compost your waste instead of using energy to run the disposal. If you must run the disposal, use cold water. Disposal waste can cost you money by clogging pipes and septic systems and can disrupt water and soil ecosystems.

Trash bags
Reuse grocery bags to line your trash cans. When we occasionally forget to bring cloth bags into the store, we ask for paper and use them under the sink for trash. Many grocery stores are now offering to recycle plastic bags rather than having them clutter the landscape and pollute the seas. Some cities and countries are even outlawing them.

Kitchen remodeling
If you decide to remodel, avoid particle board (unless it is one of the new *green* particle board products), vinyl, and laminates. Make sure you include space for a pantry (saves trips to the store) and a recycling center (close to the hub of activity). Post your old cabinets, countertops, and appliances on classified advertising Web sites like http://www.freecycle.org or http://www.craigslist.org, so someone else can give them another life. We have even given away used drywall on Freecycle to someone building a shop in his backyard!

Energy Star appliances

When it's time to replace appliances, look for the bright yellow tags that provide annual energy-usage comparisons and the Energy Star symbol. Buy the smallest appliance to meet your needs. If you can only replace one kitchen appliance, replace the refrigerator.

IN THE BATHROOM

Shower

If you tried a low-flow showerhead years ago and were not satisfied—try again. They've improved dramatically. Readily available at hardware and home improvement stores, low-flow showerheads cost less than $10, and installation is about as simple as screwing in a lightbulb. Standard showerheads use 4–6 gallons per minute. Water-efficient showerheads cut that back to 1.5–2 gallons. In one year, a family of four can save up to 18,200 gallons of water as well as the energy used to heat that water. Reduce even further: shower every other day in winter, cut back on your shower time by a couple of minutes, or turn off the water flow while you shampoo and shave.

Use a water-resistant cloth shower curtain instead of vinyl, or consider a glass door system. Plastic curtains and liners are not recyclable and end up in landfills.

> **SAVE GREEN**
>
> About 25 percent of the water supplied to the average American home is used for showers. Installing a low-flow showerhead can save a family of four 350 gallons of water each week—about $73 per year.

Bath

In general, baths use three times more water than showers. If you do take a bath, plug the drain before you turn on the faucet. The average tub faucet runs 3–5 gallons per minute, so savings add up fast. And scoop up the water afterward to use on your garden or indoor plants.

> **GO GREEN**
>
> If every American used one gallon less of water per day, we would save more than 100 billion gallons per year. That's enough to supply the entire population of Mozambique with water for five years.

Toilet

When Matthew was speaking at a seminary, one woman from a rural village in South Korea confessed that the biggest surprise to her when coming to the United States was not the big grocery stores or the fast-food restaurants; it was the fact that she had to empty her bladder into drinking water.

The 1960s home we purchased has two original standard toilets that use 3.5 gallons per flush. We immediately cut that in half by inserting bricks and a one-gallon milk jug filled with water (clean one-liter soda bottles work too) into the toilet's water tank, thus reducing the amount of water the toilet uses each time the tank fills up.

Modern high-efficiency toilets use less than 2 gallons per flush. Even better are dual flush toilets—one button for big flushes (1.6 gallons) and one for small (.9 gallon).

If your toilet is leaking, get it fixed. A leaky toilet can waste 200 gallons of water every day.

> **GO GREEN**
>
> Toilets are the biggest water users in the home. Only 3 percent of the earth's water is fresh, yet Americans are flushing 4.8 billion gallons of freshwater down the drain every day. As much as 40 percent of our drinking water is flushed down toilets. Flush once less per day and you will save as much water as the average person in Africa uses all day for drinking, cooking, bathing, and cleaning.

Sink

Turn off the faucet while brushing your teeth. Savings for an average family of four? A whopping 48 gallons a day—as much as $70 per year!

> **GO GREEN**
>
> The average U.S. household consumes more than seventy times as much water every year as the average home in Ghana.

Shaving

Only turn on the water when rinsing the razor, or try rinsing the razor in a cup filled with warm water.

Alternative: brush your teeth while you wait for the water to warm up for your shave. Water savings: up to 1,825 gallons per year, enough to fill the bathtub thirty-five times.

Matthew keeps a pitcher by the bathroom sink and collects the water that runs while he's waiting for it to turn warm, then he uses that water for rinsing dishes or watering plants.

Instead of using shaving cream, our son, Clark, shaves with old-fashioned shaving soap and a brush. He saves money while keeping aerosol cans out of the landfills.

Speaking of landfills: stop using disposable razors. Seek out a more permanent replacement. Best bet: single-blade razors with no plastic packaging.

> **GO GREEN**
>
> Two billion disposable razors end up in landfills annually.

Health-care products

The average American spends about $600 per year on soaps, toiletries, and cosmetics. Some hair products, shampoos, deodorants, and perfumes contain active ingredients that are dangerous in high doses. Many cosmetics and health-care products contain known carcinogens—others are simply untested. There is no universal safety test for health-care products. Used in small amounts, many may be harmless, but when washed down the drain, their cumulative effect rivals that of agrochemicals.

Good news: health-food chain stores are carrying natural product alternatives (store brands), so you can protect your family's health without spending a lot more. Before purchasing, make sure that containers can be recycled by checking for the triangular recycling symbol on the bottom.

Because I work at home now, I rarely wear makeup. When I do, my whole routine takes less than five minutes. I keep it simple—one tube that acts as foundation and concealer, one tube for lip and cheek color, and a little mascara along the tips of my lashes. If I'm going someplace fancy, I wait until my hair is 90 percent dry, and then I style it quickly with a blow-dryer. For everyday, my "style" is a low-key wash-and-wear—why fight nature? It helps to have a husband who supports a low-maintenance look: on my last birthday, when Matthew wrote me a card listing the forty-seven reasons why he loves me, number six was "You don't dye your silver hair."

> **GO GREEN**
>
> Of the many thousands of synthetic chemicals used in health-care items, less than 20 percent have been tested for acute effects and less than 10 percent have been tested for reproductive, mutagenic, or chronic effects.

IN THE BEDROOM
Bedding

Buy quality products that don't have to be replaced every few years. We pile on extra blankets in the winter so we can turn the heat off at night. Wear layers if you—like me!—get colder than your spouse. If you can afford it, purchase organic cotton bedding—you will be resting your head eight hours each night on bedding with fewer chemicals and protecting future generations from the high cost of chemical-intensive agribusiness. Looking for a cost/benefit compromise? Try bedding with "transitional cotton"—made from fields that have committed to organic growing practices but have not yet completed the organic certification process.

Closets

When it comes to clothing, less is more. My husband is the ultimate example of wardrobe simplicity. Before going on a speaking engagement, he asks me if he should wear Outfit A (the suit) or Outfit B (khaki pants, white shirt, tie, and blue sports jacket). In very casual settings, he opts for Outfit B–minus (Outfit B, minus the tie or jacket).

Alas, it's not so simple for women. I try to stick to classic fashions and colors that work for me and consciously avoid fashion magazines so I don't get sucked into the latest trends. I'm only too happy to accept hand-me-downs from friends and relatives. In fact, most of what's in my closet is secondhand.

Matthew has gotten me in the habit of cleaning my closet out at least once a year. I always enlist my daughter, Emma, to help—if I haven't worn an item in the last year, she makes sure I pass it along to someone who can make good use of it through a refugee organization, Goodwill, St. Vincent de Paul, or the Salvation Army.

> The family needs a home, a fit environment in which to develop its proper relationships. *For the human family, this home is the earth*, the environment that God the Creator has given us to inhabit with creativity and responsibility. We need to care for the environment: it has been entrusted to men and women to be protected and cultivated with responsible freedom, with the good of all as a constant guiding criterion.   —*Pope Benedict XVI, (1927–)*, The Human Family, A Community of Peace

Shopping

Bring an accountability friend (or daughter) when shopping and help each other say no to any impulse purchases. Never shop just for fun; always have a purpose, and stick to it. Try to buy used whenever possible, and always combine trips. If you are considering a major purchase, wait a month. In most cases, you'll find that you forgot about it, or can do without.

GO GREEN

After food, clothing has the highest environmental impact of any consumer activity. Nearly 40,000 gallons of water are used in the production and transport of new clothes bought by the average American household—each year!

Fabrics

When Matthew and I first married nearly thirty years ago, I tried to buy cotton fabrics because I assumed they were more natural. Not necessarily so. Although synthetics such as nylon, polyester, and Lycra are made from fossil fuels, natural fibers are not always the best answer. I've since learned that cotton is the most chemical-intensive crop—each pound of cotton uses ten to eighteen applications of herbicides, insecticides, and fungicides and 3,800 gallons of water. Wool requires even more water—22,400 gallons of water per pound—and causes soil compaction and habitat loss due to fertilizer-dependent pastures. And hybrid fabrics, such as poly-cotton blends, are impossible to recycle.

What to wear? When possible, look for chemical-free organic cotton, linen, wool, and hemp fabrics. Even in discount stores, you can now find clothing made from "transitional cotton."

GO GREEN

Globally, one-quarter of all pesticides are used on cotton crops.

Secondhand clothes

Jesus told us to be more like the birds and the lilies; it's what's *in* us—not *on* us—that matters. Our family buys a large portion of our clothes from secondhand stores. Buying used means less land must be used to grow crops for clothing, and new items don't need to be manufactured and transported. Look for quality items that will stay in style and last a long time.

I rely on polar fleece (mine is made from recycled pop bottles) for warm layering. As I write this, I'm wearing my $5 polar fleece from Goodwill, which has kept me toasty for years and still looks nearly new.

Unless the Lord builds a house, the work of the builders is wasted.
PSALM 127:1, NLT

At a recent faith and environment conference, I looked at our daughter, Emma, and realized that everything we both were wearing was from a secondhand store. I unashamedly tell people that the majority of the clothes in my closet are from Goodwill, including my favorite traveling dress, which happens to be an Ann Taylor design.

Layers

Before clothes became a fashion statement, people wore layers to survive in a world with no artificial heat or air-conditioning. Clothes are the most efficient form of insulation. If you live in a colder climate, warm your body, not your entire house. Each morning, I check the weather and dress accordingly.

Goodwill/God's Will

Do not conform any longer to the pattern of this world, but be transformed by the renewing of your mind. Then you will be able to test and approve what God's will is—his good, pleasing and perfect will. —ROMANS 12:2

Emma and I usually go Goodwill shopping together—mother/daughter bonding time. But recently I needed another church dress, so I did something very rare: I went shopping *alone*.

I stopped at the store on my way home from a meeting in Lexington. It took me about ten minutes to sift through the dresses, try a few on, and decide on a real "find" that would travel well and be great for both meetings and church.

That's when I made my mistake. Though I didn't *need* anything else, I thought it wouldn't hurt to look at the shirts while I was there. Then I gravitated toward the sweaters and lightweight jackets—I always need to wear layers around the house because we try to use the heat as little as possible. So shopping a bit longer would be the environmentally sensible thing to do—right?

Wrong. One hour and eight additional items later, I headed for the cash register. The monetary cost was negligible, as was the environmental cost—these were used clothes, after all, and I hadn't driven even a foot out of my way to get here. But the "too much stuff" weight was immense. When I got home, I tried on my purchases for Emma. She helped me, as she usually does in the store, to say no to all but the dress and one shirt. It's not that the other clothes didn't look okay or fit right—I just didn't need them. And so, when my work calls me back to Lexington in a few days, I will swing by Goodwill and give back all but these two items. And I will feel much lighter. Consider it a $12 donation to a good cause and a very cheap reminder about confusing wants with needs.

I had forgotten an important lesson: the problem lies not in us owning things, but in things owning us.

What Did Jesus Own?

What did Jesus own? A robe, some sandals, maybe a walking stick—we'll never know for sure, but the Bible is pretty clear that he and his disciples did not have lots of material things weighing them down.

When I look at all the stuff in my closets, the parable of the rich young man who was unwilling to give up his possessions to follow Christ hits uncomfortably close to home (Luke 18:18-23).

What does Nancy own? Too much to list! Maybe it's time to start a new campaign: I Clean Closets for Jesus!

Furniture

Like secondhand clothing stores, secondhand furniture also can save resources used in the manufacturing and transportation process. Check out http://www.craigslist.org for local furniture listings. When buying new, look for furnishings with labels saying that they are made from sustainably harvested wood or recycled materials rather than from veneer-covered particle board, which can cause indoor air pollution through noxious off-gassing (the evaporation of volatile chemicals that you may continue to breathe in for years).

At this moment I am writing at the oak desk that Matthew and I found in a used furniture store when we first got married. Matthew, a carpenter at the time (how handy!), refinished the desk, and I've been using it now for nearly three decades—with the hope of enjoying it for three more. It's been through nine moves with us and has endured a myriad of projects—college and graduate school papers, Matthew's medical school applications, bills, the kids' homework, manuscripts, and paperwork for our nonprofit organization, Blessed Earth. This desk has been central to every season of our lives together. It's more beautiful than ever—the water glass rings just add a bit more character (and fond memories) to the wood someone first planed a century or more ago. Our dining room table and chairs, Matthew's desk, Clark's bed—they all have similar stories. Most of the other furniture in our house was handmade by a friend who manages his wood lot using draft horses—the least harmful way to harvest lumber—ensuring that his land will be both beautiful and financially productive for generations to come.

Floor coverings

Nearly all carpet is petroleum based, with the exception of wool. Carpet making is water and chemical intensive, even before the dyeing process creates millions of gallons of polluted wastewater. But the worst part of carpet manufacturing is the volatile organic compounds in the adhesives—benzene and toluene. These are well-recognized health hazards, adding to indoor air pollution. In addition, because of mold and dust mites that are impossible to fully remove no matter how often you steam clean, doctors advise that people with allergies or asthma avoid carpeting their homes.

Better options? Area rugs that can be vacuumed on both sides and shaken out, wool carpet, and carpet made from recycled materials. Even better, use bamboo, cork, wood, or other natural materials. Look for labels indicating that these materials were grown sustainably.

One of the things that motivated us to select our 1960s ranch-style home was its real oak floors. We removed the stained carpet in two bedrooms and revealed the wood floors beneath—they look great and will last several more lifetimes.

Fans

We have ceiling fans in the three main bedrooms of our home, as well as in the family room/kitchen area. When the fan in the family room needed to be replaced, we chose an Energy Star model.

The Green Room

Want to shop for sustainable furniture online? These sites will get you started:

- http://www.ecobedroom.com
- http://www.greenerlifestyles.com
- http://www.pristineplanet.com
- http://www.steelcase.com
- http://www.vivaterra.com

Always be sure to check for the Forest Stewardship Council seal of approval, which certifies the use of sustainably grown lumber. This seal ensures that the wood was harvested from a healthy forest, and not clear-cut from a tropical rainforest or the ancestral homelands of forest-dependent indigenous people.

> **SAVE GREEN**
>
> Stay cool all night for less—consider installing a ceiling fan over your bed. It costs sixteen times more to run a room air conditioner than a ceiling fan; it costs forty-three times more to run a central air conditioner than a ceiling fan.

Electronics

We made a rule long ago—no TVs or computers in the bedrooms. Placing TVs and computers in children's bedrooms promotes separation, not unity. Falling asleep with the TV running is a huge waste of energy.

> **GO GREEN**
>
> Most video recorders and cable boxes stay on 24-7. Even in standby mode, they consume 85 percent of the power that they use while turned on.

IN THE FAMILY ROOM

Fireplace

Only open the fireplace damper when you are using the fireplace. If possible, burn wood from a sustainably managed wood lot—we get our wood supply from fallen trees. Let your neighbors know that you are happy to saw (or hire someone to saw) their fallen trees as well. When a storm knocked over our neighbor's maple last week, it resulted in a one cord windfall for us!

> **SAVE GREEN**
>
> An open damper can allow 8 percent of your home's heat to go up the chimney. In summer, an open damper can add about $100 to your cooling costs. Adding a chimney balloon could save you $200 or more on energy costs.

Because a chimney damper is frequently heated and cooled, it can warp or break over time, causing cold drafts to enter your home and heat to escape. An inflated chimney balloon, also called a chimney pillow, prevents this heat loss by acting as a plug, saving you money, heat, and comfort. Google "chimney balloon" and "chimney pillow" to learn more about sources and proper sizing.

Wood-burning stoves are far more efficient than open fire-places. If you have a fireplace that is never used, close the damper and stuff it loosely with fiberglass batting, or insert a balloon especially designed for this purpose. Either option will allow some air movement while still preventing major heating or cooling losses.

Matches

Use matches instead of lighters. About 1.5 billion disposable lighters end up in landfills and incinerators each year. The plastic casings and butane fuel from lighters are made from petroleum products. Petroleum products are finite—and are quickly becoming scarcer, as evidenced by rising fuel prices.

If you do use a lighter, invest in one that can be refilled.

Junk mail

You can reduce the amount of junk mail you receive by registering at https://www.dmachoice.org. (It costs $1 if you register by mail; it's free if you register online.) I reregister every couple of years and also whenever we've moved. If a company sends me a catalog, I call the toll-free number and ask them to unsubscribe me. We recycle the junk mail we do receive, including envelopes with plastic windows.

For more ways to reduce junk mail, visit http://www.new dream.org.

Paper

Purchase recycled paper. Paper that contains 30 percent postconsumer waste costs about the same as regular paper; 100 percent recycled will cost a bit more, but saves trees for your children to enjoy. Just as important—recycling your paper uses much less water and energy than making new paper.

Printers

Refilled ink cartridges cost far less than new ink, with identical results. Many offices and schools now collect used ink cartridges as fundraisers. If you aren't recycling your ink cartridges, try http://www.fundingfactory.com, which has already doled out $10.5 million to schools and nonprofit organizations. Funding-Factory can help you recycle cell phones for profit as well.

Just Say No to Junk

More than 100 million trees' worth of bulk mail arrives in American mailboxes each year.

About 6 million tons of catalogs and other direct mailings end up in the U.S. municipal solid waste stream—enough to fill over 470,000 garbage trucks.

California's state and local governments spend $500,000 each year collecting and disposing of AOL's direct-mail disks alone.

The production and disposal of junk mail consumes more energy than 2.8 million cars.

Computers

Our family has made the switch to laptop computers because they use significantly less energy than desktops. Kick the habit of leaving the computer on all day, and always be sure to shut the computer down completely at night.

Phantom loads

That little green or red light emitted by your TV, DVD player, stereo, or computer means that the system is still partially on, thereby causing what is known as a phantom load (energy consumed by products even when they are turned off). About 5 percent of a household's energy is wasted on phantom loads, costing U.S. consumers about $8 billion annually. Even in standby or sleep mode, appliances can be using up to 85 percent of their full power. In fact, audio equipment in America actually uses more energy when it is off than when it is on. When you are not listening to music (most of the time!), your equipment is still partially powered; even a little bit of energy being used 24-7 adds up to a lot. Avoid phantom loads by purchasing smart power strips that allow you to turn the power completely off at the source. Unplug infrequently used electronics.

Throws

We keep two heavy polar fleece blankets in the family room to stay warm and cozy even when the heat is turned down. Remember—the point is to warm your body, not your whole house.

> **GO GREEN**
>
> Need another reason to invite friends over during the winter? Each person in your home generates the same amount of warmth as a 100-watt heater.

Our Old Kentucky Home

When we moved from New Hampshire to Kentucky, it gave us the opportunity to simplify by giving away a lot of stuff that was still cluttering our lives. Clothes went to the Salvation Army, art supplies to a kindergarten teacher, books to libraries hit by a hurricane, and tools to a church friend starting a second career as a carpenter.

Since moving in, we've made a number of cost-effective simple changes or additions to our new, old house. The first thing we did was change all the lightbulbs in the house to compact fluorescents. Matthew also put our stereo and our son's computer on a power switch, eliminating the phantom loads.

We needed to purchase a new washing machine and a refrigerator. At the local home center, I picked out a front-load washer. Using the Energy Star comparison tags, I also found a standard refrigerator that uses 445 kWh per year, much more efficient than others in its class. Matthew lowered the energy use of our new refrigerator even more by turning off the automatic ice maker—ice makers run a heating element so that the ice slides out easily.

We chose not to purchase a clothes dryer. Instead, Matthew restrung an abandoned clothesline in the backyard. Friends helped us dismantle an unsafe, rickety porch on the back of the house, and Matthew and our son, Clark, built a new one using decking made of recycled soda bottles, thus eliminating the need for toxic stains or paints.

I joined the local http://www.freecycle.org and found a free composting bin for the backyard, which eliminates the need to power a garbage disposal in the sink and makes an organic soil booster for the garden. I also used Freecycle to give away our moving boxes and some extra building materials. Thanks to Freecycle, whatever we didn't need was used by someone else— including the former deck stairs and extra lumber from the deck, which prevented scrap from going into the landfill.

Next Matthew got busy on the glamorous part of conservation, changing a leaky float valve in the toilet and cutting the water used per flush in half by inserting several bricks and a milk jug filled with water into the toilet tanks. He also changed the showerhead to a low-flow model (purchased at the hardware store for about $5), turned the water heater to its lowest setting, and then put insulation on the accessible basement piping. The insulation looks like black foam tubing and slips around the pipes quite easily. These toilet and shower projects only took a couple of hours and will save both energy and water for years to come.

The old single-pane aluminum windows in the house were a huge area of thermal gain and loss. We could not afford to replace them right away, but I greatly improved their efficiency by making heavy, lined drapes for all the windows. The attic only had 3 inches of insulation, so we increased it to R-60. (The higher the R-value, the more effective the insulation is in keeping a house warm in winter and cool in summer.) Matthew and Clark put soffit and ridge vents in to allow adequate airflow in the attic.

For the past six months, our electric bill has ranged from a high of $18 to a low of $13. The gas and water bills are similarly modest, thanks to these types of small changes throughout the house.

The kids and I planted apple, pear, peach, and cherry trees in our yard and started a vegetable garden on the south side of the house. The garden is prospering, thanks to a load of old manure from a neighbor's organic farm.

We fit a bicycle with a carrier made from an old milk crate, which makes it safe and convenient for us to cart groceries without using the car. But the most important energy-saving decision we made this year was the choice of our home's location. It is two blocks from our children's college, which has eliminated the need to fly them home for school breaks. We also chose a home that allows us to walk to the store, the bank, and work, which means far less time commuting and more time for family and ministry.

In our three decades together, one of the things Matthew and I have learned is that our home is about a whole lot more than Matthew and me. It is about our children, our calling, the example we set, and the legacy we leave.

IN THE LAUNDRY ROOM

Washing machine

Energy-efficient washing machines use about one-third less electricity than conventional washers. We have an energy-efficient front-load washer, which not only saves electricity and water, but also spins out most of the moisture, so clothes dry much more quickly. I use the coldest water setting that gets the job done, and I only run full loads. Be frugal with detergent (use no more than the recommended amount), and don't wash items such as pants, skirts, dresses, and sweaters every time you wear them—they'll last longer and you'll save time, water, and energy.

> **GO GREEN**
>
> About 80 to 85 percent of the energy used to wash clothes goes toward heating the water.

Dryer

When we first went green, I resisted hanging our clothes on the line. We were living in a postcard-picture-perfect town on the coast of Maine, and no one in my upscale neighborhood used a clothesline. Besides, I didn't want the towels or my jeans to feel stiff. Spoiled me—as if Jesus (or my grandmother) had needed a clothes dryer. Talk about confusing a want with a need!

Matthew led by example, stringing a line in the backyard despite my objections. It didn't take long for me to start feeling bad about my already hardworking husband doing all the laundry—so I joined

Ten Great Investments in Your Children's Future

When Joseph was asked to interpret the pharaoh's dream about seven fat cows devouring seven lean cows, and seven plump stalks of grain consuming seven scrawny stalks, he explained that a severe drought was coming. He urged the pharaoh to assess a 20 percent tithe to prepare for the seven lean years ahead.

Today, many financial, spiritual, and political forecasters are warning of some pretty dire times ahead if we continue business as usual. We still have time and the infrastructure to invest in long-term energy-saving technologies before energy costs ramp up (just take a look at your recent heating and electric bills) and the social disruption that will result from increasingly severe resource scarcities. Here are ten suggestions for long-term investments you can make today to prepare for the future, in approximate order of cost from low to high:

- Green power from your public utility

- Efficient home electronics—laptops instead of desktops, Energy Star printers, TVs, DVD players

- Energy-saving appliances—dishwasher, refrigerator, front-load washer, efficient dryer with moisture sensor

- Insulation in the attic, exterior walls, basement, and crawl spaces

- High-efficiency furnace, air conditioner, or heat pump

- Solar water heater

- Double-pane windows with low-e (low-emissivity) coatings

- Geothermal heating and cooling

- Hybrid car

- Solar panels

What's the best way to be prepared for energy shortages? Move to a smaller, Energy Star home (townhouses and condos are most efficient) within walking or biking distance of work, school, and shopping.

in. And then the kids started helping. And we realized it's not such a hardship after all to go outside a few times a week and listen to the birds while hanging clothes on the line. Now I look forward to hanging clothes, a welcome break away from my desk and a time to enjoy the beauty of God's creation in my own backyard.

Dryers are one of the most energy-intensive appliances. We've intentionally lived without one for more than six years now. In summer, we dry our clothes outside on the line. In winter, we use a line strung in the basement—it saves us from using a humidifier, too, because the damp clothes add moisture to the dry air.

If you do use a clothes dryer, make sure you purchase one with a moisture sensor, which allows the dryer to automatically turn itself off when the clothes reach a specified level of dryness. Always run full loads and keep the lint filter clean. Switch your dryer off when the load is finished since the dryer still uses power while on standby.

Dry cleaning

I try to avoid purchasing any clothes that must be dry-cleaned. Dry cleaning with perchloroethylene, or "perc," is associated with environmental and health risks. I've found that many clothes can be

Laundry Hints

INSTEAD OF	DO THIS
Putting stained clothes in the hamper	Wash out spills right away. Never iron stained clothes—heat sets the stains.
Washing clothes to remove lint	Use a lint brush.
Washing lightly worn clothes	Hang them up immediately and let them air out for a day before returning them to the closet.
Pressing suits	Hang in the bathroom while you shower to remove wrinkles.
Dry cleaning	Wash gently by hand and then dry flat. (Use discretion! Delicate fabrics and most suits still need to be dry-cleaned.)

hand washed, even when the labels say dry-clean only. And alternative professional cleaners are becoming available, including wet cleaning, liquid carbon dioxide, and Green Earth methods. The only item I recall dry cleaning in the last five years is Matthew's sports jacket (once!), which he wears constantly for business trips.

Ironing

I don't do nearly as much ironing as I used to—hanging clothes on the line takes care of most of the wrinkles. When I do iron, I begin by ironing fabrics that require the least high temperature— so I can use the iron before it reaches peak heat. Then I turn the iron off shortly before finishing and iron the last couple of items on residual heat.

GO GREEN

Every American creates 4.5 pounds of trash per person, per day. Over the course of a lifetime, that adds up to 90,000 pounds of garbage for every one of us.

TRASH AND RECYCLING

Reducing

The best way to cut down on trash is to get everyone in the family to reduce what they bring into the home. When comparing products, consider how much packaging the item comes in. I try to avoid individually wrapped items. Instead, I buy in bulk, refill, and choose concentrated versions. I also avoid anything with "disposable" or "single use" on the packaging. Emma and I pre-cycle at the grocery store by checking to see if a certain container can be recycled before we bring it home. Matthew has taught us to look for quality, take care of what we buy, and repair what we have. And Clark is the least materialistic person I know—almost Spartan in his commitment to not owning more than he needs.

Here's one of the best money, time, and energy-saving tips in the whole book: Try going on a spending fast one week out of every month. Only buy food and bare essentials, such as medicines—*nothing* else. You'll save money and time, and you'll greatly reduce the waste you produce.

Reusing

My family gets a kick out of seeing how many times we can reuse items before throwing them away. Shipping boxes, padded envelopes, birthday candles, gift bags, and cards all can be reused several times. Worn-out clothing can be turned into quilts and pillows. Magazines and catalogs make great wrapping paper or even origami paper—our daughter, Emma, folded one thousand paper cranes from discarded catalogs with the help of a few friends and a paper cutter.

Because Emma loves to create art projects, my mother always kept a box of "treasures" for Emma's visits—scraps of material, ribbon, buttons, broken jewelry, pretty cards, and unusual stamps—more hours of fun than any trip to the toy store could have provided.

One of the reasons Americans throw so much stuff away is that very few of us live in true community with our neighbors. Talk to your neighbors, and find out what people around you need. Yard sales, http://www.craigslist.org, http://www.eBay.com, and

The Art of Receiving

Our son, Clark, was getting ready to set up his first apartment, so I put the word out to our neighbors that he would welcome basic kitchen supplies. A few days later, we found several boxes in our carport filled with plates, glasses, cooking utensils, pots, and pans—everything needed to set up a medical student's kitchen, including the exact model of toaster oven we bought when he was a baby (and still use). Most of the items came from a friend whose elderly mother recently had passed away. How grateful we are to save not only the expense of setting up Clark's kitchen but also the cost to the planet of manufacturing, shipping, and marketing new goods.

http://www.freecycle.org are great ways to make sure your stuff gets a second life.

Recycling

Learn about the recycling program in your area, and recycle everything possible. Check the bottom of plastic bottles and food containers for the little recycling symbol. Inside that triangle, you will find a number 1–7, which tells what type of plastic the container is. Some recycling centers accept plastics 1–7; others only accept numbers 1 and 2.

If you live somewhere that only accepts plastics 1 and 2, pay attention to those numbers in the store, and try not to purchase items labeled with a higher number. Seek out items made from recycled materials—visit http://www.amazingrecycled.com for inspiration.

Peer Pressure

What man is wise enough to understand this? Who has been instructed by the Lord and can explain it? Why has the land been ruined and laid waste like a desert that no one can cross?
—JEREMIAH 9:12

Wednesday is recycling day. We only have curbside pickup every other week, so getting our blue barrel out before the truck comes at 8 a.m. is a big deal.

This morning Matthew and I walked across town. (Don't be impressed. It's a small town.) Block upon block, we saw nary a bin. And then we'd pass a cul-de-sac where every household had their recyclables ready for pickup—hallelujah! And then a wasteland again, and then a block chock-full of the blue bins.

I asked Matthew what he thought caused this phenomenon—some blocks unanimously recycling, some blocks not at all. His answer was simple: peer pressure.

My husband is a pretty smart guy, and I think his assessment is right on. Peer pressure can be a force for good or for bad. In this case, it is clearly a force for good.

A friend once told me that Matthew and I had "revolution-ized" our neighborhood, simply by remembering to put our recyclables out the night before. When people went out to walk the dog or leave for work, they were reminded it was *the* day to roll out the cart. And once three or four families started regu-larly recycling, the rest joined in.

I remember one Tuesday evening when we came home from a speaking tour. It was late—about 11 p.m. Was tomorrow the day the town picked up recycling? I walked down the street to inves-tigate. No blue bins. Then I walked around the corner. No blue bins. Then I made another right—and saw one bin! One bin in the moonlight was enough to motivate me to gather the cardboard and cans and plastics and glass and haul them out to our curb.

The next morning I slept in a little later than usual. But when I looked outside a few minutes before eight, the whole street was lined with blue bins. The moral of the story: even one blue bin can start a revolution! Be the first to put in a vegeta-ble garden or hang a clothesline. Carry a bag and pick up trash whenever you go on a walk. In time, others will join in. A little peer pressure can be a very good thing.

Plastic

There are two main problems with plastic. First, most plastics are made from a nonrenewable (petroleum) source, and second, they take a very, very long time to break down. It's hard to elimi-nate plastic from your life, but you can cut back by refusing plas-tic bags, buying items packaged in glass, avoiding bottled water, and steering away from anything that comes in a lot of plastic packaging.

Is it worth recycling plastic? Yes! The energy saved from recy-cling just one plastic bottle can run a 60-watt lightbulb for six hours. As petroleum grows scarcer and economic times grow harder, more and more new goods are being made from recycled plastics. Other good news: some grocery items are now packaged in plastics made from cornstarch and other plant materials that are biodegradable.

About 80 percent of our plastic waste ends up in landfills—including 60 million plastic water bottles a day.

Glass

Recycling one glass bottle can conserve enough energy to run a 100-watt lightbulb for four hours. Some municipalities require that you sort glass by color. Remember to remove the lids—they can go in with steel cans.

Americans are by far the biggest paper users in the world, consuming more than 400 pounds of paper per person, per year.

Paper

Matthew was the one who got me in the habit of using cloth napkins and handkerchiefs, but it wasn't until a few years ago that I realized I didn't need to fold all the handkerchiefs. What a liberating "Aha" moment! Now we just toss our clean handkerchiefs in a drawer.

When we do buy paper products, we make sure they are made from recycled paper. We try to use both sides of office paper, or we cut up paper used on just one side for scrap paper. Other paper-saving hints: Only print pages that you really need. Use newspaper to wrap presents—better yet, share a newspaper with your neighbor, read it at the library, or catch the headlines electronically. Used paper towels and coffee filters can be added to your compost.

A Not-So-Dirty Secret

When our children were born, Matthew insisted on using cloth diapers. I fussed at first—none of my friends were using cloth diapers—but once we got a system going, rinsing them out in the toilet and washing them was really no big deal.

Here's how we made using cloth diapers simple and convenient. We borrowed and purchased an ample supply of diaper covers in several sizes with adjustable Velcro. When diapering, we folded a cloth diaper in thirds vertically and put it in the diaper cover. Then we placed a thin disposable diaper liner on top of the cloth diaper, so it would be next to the baby's skin. Finally, we laid the baby on the prepared diaper, fastened the Velcro on the sides, and off we'd go.

When it came time to change the diapers, solids were deposited in the toilet along with the diaper liner, cloth diapers went in a drywall bucket filled with water next to the toilet, and covers went into the laundry basket. Every couple of days, we did a load of diapers.

The average family spends about $1,000 per year on disposable diapers or about $3,000 per baby. We invested $1,000 total for two kids, including laundry costs. The diapers themselves made great dusting rags for many years, and we were able to give away our diaper covers to new families when we were done.

Bonus: earlier toilet training. Let's face it—a wet cloth diaper is more cumbersome to a toddler than a paper diaper. Emma was out of diapers by eighteen months—before she could even talk. At first we had to rush after her when we heard her little feet pitter-patter toward the bathroom—afraid that she would climb up on the toilet and fall in! In the end, cloth diapers saved us both time and money—as well as hundreds of God's beloved trees.

Metal

Most towns collect aluminum and steel metals. Aluminum (soda cans) is one of the most efficient and energy-saving forms of recycling; it takes only 4 percent of the energy to make a can from recycled aluminum as it would from virgin aluminum. If you want to hold a fundraiser, collect aluminum cans—recyclers will pay about a penny a can. Today, aluminum recycling saves about 11.5 *billion* kWh of energy—enough electricity to light a city the size of Cincinnati for six years. Many towns will recycle aluminum foil as well as cans. One little-known benefit of recycling aluminum is that it reduces the need for bauxite mining. Obtaining this aluminum ore causes extensive pollution, often in poor tropical countries that can ill afford to clean it up.

At home you should recycle all of your soup, dog food, coffee, and whipping cream cans—nearly all metal food containers except beverage cans are made of steel.

Garbage In, Garbage Out

It was a life-changing revelation for me when I realized there is no "away." Everything we use goes somewhere; everything we manufacture has a by-product. In the end, we (and all of God's creatures) ingest the 4 billion pounds of industry toxins produced each year, either through the air we breathe or the food we eat. How can you help?

INSTEAD OF	DO THIS
Individually packaged items	Buy in bulk
One-time use or disposable products	Purchase refillable and reusable items
Buying new	Take care of the old and repair when broken
Buying stuff you don't really need	Go on a spending fast
Throwing away usable items	Donate on http://www.freecycle.org or sell on http://www.craigslist.org
Buying craft paper or scrapbook supplies	Cut up catalogs and magazines
Going to the toy store	Visit yard sales and keep a treasure box
Accepting plastic bags at the store	Bring fabric bags
Buying bottled water	Drink tap water
Purchasing paper plates	Use washable dishes
Buying paper napkins, paper towels, and tissue	Invest in cloth napkins, cloth towels, and handkerchiefs
Tossing plastic and glass bottles in the trash	Remove lids, and then recycle
Throwing food scraps in the trash	Compost
Purchasing your own newspaper and magazines	Share with a neighbor, read at the library, or catch headlines electronically

IN THE BASEMENT AND ATTIC
Furnace

If your furnace or boiler is more than twenty years old, replacing it with a high-efficiency model will prove a good investment. Old models have an efficiency rating of about 65 percent; new models can be more than 90 percent efficient.

Replace your furnace filter every three months; if the filter is clogged with dust, your air-conditioning or heating system can't "breathe" and won't run as efficiently. When you buy a new filter, select a pleated model that will filter the smallest particles—dust mites and allergens. It may cost a little more, but it will help keep both you and your furnace healthier in the long run. To save trips, Matthew writes down the size of the filter before he heads to the hardware store and buys about half a dozen filters at a time. Some filters can even be washed and reused.

Getting Real: Heating System Maintenance

Regular maintenance can have a big effect on fuel bills!

- Clean all registers.

- Replace your furnace filters every three months.

- Keep baseboards and radiators clean and unrestricted by furniture, carpets, or drapes.

- Tune up your system. Oil-fired systems should be tuned up and cleaned every year, gas-fired systems every two years, and heat pumps every two or three years. Regular tune-ups not only cut heating costs, but they also increase the lifetime of the system, reduce breakdowns and repair costs, and cut the amount of carbon monoxide, smoke, and other pollutants pumped into the atmosphere by fossil-fueled systems.

- Seal your ducts. In homes heated with forced-air heating, ducts should be inspected and sealed to ensure adequate airflow. Ducts can leak as much as 15 to 20 percent of the air passing through them. Insulating ducts can save as much as 20 percent on heating and cooling bills.

Water heater

Many water heaters are set around 160 to 180°F. Especially in milder weather, you don't need to keep the water that hot. We set our water heater manually to 120°F, reducing fuel consumption significantly. The thermostat control is usually located in a metal box connected to the water heater. Check your owners' manual if you can't locate yours.

> **GO GREEN**
>
> Heating and cooling (including water) account for about 56 percent of the energy used in a typical household.

If your water heater is hot to the touch or over ten years old, consider a water heater blanket or jacket. A water heater jacket costs about $20 and saves $34 per year for gas heaters and $54 per year for electric. Choose one that is at least three inches thick. You might also want to consider alternatives like tankless, solar, and on-demand heaters. Tax credits can help defray initial costs.

Also be sure to insulate your hot water pipes. The insulation only took us minutes to install at our house—it just clips on—and is inexpensive.

> **GO GREEN**
>
> If your water heater is not insulated, about three-quarters of the energy used is wasted. Not sure if your water heater needs to be insulated? If it's hot to the touch, you need a water heater jacket.

Insulation

Attic insulation is one of the easiest and most effective ways to reduce your energy usage. Most energy guides recommend at least 10 inches of insulation in the attic. The house we bought had only 3 inches so we upped that to 18 inches with a 3.5 R-value per inch.

If you are adding insulation yourself, be sure to wear protective clothing and a face mask. Or let the pros do it—a tax credit can offset some of the cost.

If your walls are hollow, consider having insulation blown in. Ask the insulator what size hole he will be making and discuss which method will involve the least noticeable repairs.

Air-conditioning

Matthew can't tolerate the heat, but we try doing without air-conditioning as long as possible in the summer, and we shut it down a few weeks early in the fall. We also keep heat out of the home by minimizing use of the stove and oven and by closing curtains during the day. Painting the outside masonry of the house a light color last year also has kept the house significantly cooler.

A house is built by wisdom and becomes strong through good sense. Through knowledge its rooms are filled with all sorts of precious riches and valuables.

PROVERBS 24:3-4, NLT

One of the simplest, no-cost energy savers is to set the thermostat three to five degrees higher than you usually keep it. If you have a basement, try using the fan-only option of your central air conditioner to bring up the cooler basement air. Change the thermostat gradually, and then stick with the new temperature for a week or two, even if it seems uncomfortable at first. It's amazing how quickly your body will adjust.

For those who live in a dry area, such as out West, consider a swamp (evaporative) cooler. These can only be used in areas with low natural humidity, but require much less energy than air conditioners.

Attic fans

A whole-house fan draws cool air into your home through the windows while forcing hot air out through your attic vents. Use after sundown when the outside temperature drops below eighty degrees and in the early morning to cool your house and help reduce your air-conditioning use. Be sure you have proper ventilation in your attic by installing soffits (air vents).

Dehumidifiers and humidifiers

Much of the summer, we can get by with little air-conditioning as long as we use our much-less-energy-consuming dehumidifier. To limit your dehumidifier's energy consumption, remember to turn it off when it's not needed.

In cold months, we use some old-fashioned methods to increase the humidity, like hanging wet clothes on a clothes rack to dry. Try placing a pan of water on a radiator or woodstove. Leave the plug in while you shower and don't drain the tub for a few hours.

Stuff

Do you have things in your attic or basement that you haven't used for years? Could someone else put them to better use? Jesus tells us not to store up treasures here on earth, and yet the majority of most Americans' lives are spent accumulating, paying for, organizing, and caring for things. Schedule a yard sale, sell items on eBay, give furniture to young couples just starting out or refugees arriving from other countries, or donate things to charities—you are sure to feel lighter. We got rid of about half of our possessions, and still we are looking for new ways to lighten the load. The more we give away, the less that stuff keeps us from answering God's call.

Lighten the Load

The average person on eBay sells $210 worth of stuff (http://www.eBay .com). You can also sell your wares locally at http://www.craigslist.com, which also saves on the energy costs of shipping and transport. For tips on making yard sales more profitable, visit http://www.yardsalequeen.com. Rather give away? I am a big fan of http://www.freecycle.com, which keeps 300 tons of materials out of landfills each day. Or you can clean out the attic by donating to your church's next yard sale or local charity thrift store.

IN THE GARAGE
Toys

Nearly all my children's toys were purchased at yard sales. The major exception is a wooden train set, which was a gift from grandparents that is now being used by another family in our church. Once upon a time, we had fleets of toy trucks and drawers of art supplies and beads, all bought for pennies on the dollar at local rummage sales. When our children outgrew them, we passed them along.

Even at yard sale prices, we tried to avoid flimsy toys that end up in landfills. When children outgrew items like sports equipment, we exchanged with neighbors.

Recreational items

Does everyone on your block need a canoe, or can you share one? What about other little-used items, like tents, backpacks, croquet sets, badminton nets, and bocce balls? At one time or another, we

The $100 Green Shopping List That Keeps On Saving

- Ten fabric grocery bags (some stores offer four cents back per bag every time you shop)

- One water filter pitcher (so you drink more tap water)

- Two spray bottles for homemade cleaning solution

- Five CFL bulbs

- Two low-flow showerheads

- Ten handkerchiefs

- Two power strips with on/off switches

- One furnace filter

have borrowed or lent all of these items. Make sure your neighbors feel welcome to borrow from you, and when you borrow, return items in good shape.

Cars idling

Simple fact: an idling car gets zero miles to the gallon. Even when we lived in northern New England, we almost never needed to warm our car—the rare exception being when it was too encased in ice to clear the windshield and drive safely.

If every one of the 65 million garage owners in the United States let their cars idle five fewer minutes per day, the total savings would be enough for 10 million people to drive across the country—a savings of 845 million gallons of gas a year. With gas prices at an all-time high, maybe it's time to reconsider the need to warm up the car before work.

Security lighting

Instead of leaving security lights on all night, consider motion sensors. In our carport, we installed an inexpensive movement sensor so the light is only on when we need it. If you do need to leave a light on for security reasons, invest in an LED bulb. LED lights can be ordered online or purchased in some home improvement stores. They cost more, but use far less energy—much less than CFL bulbs. Try solar lights for walkways.

How to Save Money This Year

(Estimated savings are *beyond* any initial investment; actual savings will vary from family to family and region to region.)

Wash laundry in cold water	$60
Adjust thermostat by three degrees	$200
Turn lights and electronics off when leaving room	$40
Purchase smart power strips for computers, TV, and audio	$100
Install energy monitor	$100
Stop refrigerator gazing; turn to warmest setting	$50
Unplug second refrigerator	$100
Install two low-flow showerheads	$130
Don't run water while brushing teeth or shaving	$70
Stop buying disposable plates, cups, utensils	$50
Purchase recycled toilet paper in bulk	$30
Purchase used clothes instead of new	$250
Purchase yard sale toys instead of new	$150
Don't buy carryout coffee	$250
Drink tap water instead of bottled water	$260
Share newspaper with neighbor	$260
Close fireplace damper when not in use	$100
Recycle electronics, printer cartridges, etc.	$25
Insulate water heater	$120
Seal ducts	$50
Caulk windows and doors	$100
Wash by hand instead of dry cleaning	$150
Make some of your own nontoxic cleaning products	$100
Go on a spending fast one week/month	$600

TOTAL   **$3,345***

*Suggested ways to steward your savings: Put one-third of it toward debt reduction, one-third toward charity, and one-third toward investments in additional energy savings.

. . . And Share It with Those in Need

What could you do with $3,345 in savings?

- Plant 33,450 seedlings (great birthday and Christmas presents!) in environmentally devastated parts of Ethiopia, Kenya, Madagascar, and the Sudan. Visit http://www.edenprojects.org.

- Sponsor nine villages for a year in the Dominican Republic, Haiti, Mexico, or Tanzania. Village sponsorship helps people become self-sufficient, teaches families to overcome hunger, and replants degraded watersheds, allowing streams to flow anew. Visit http://www.floresta.org/sav.htm.

- Give fifty-five Earth Baskets through Heifer International. The Heifer Earth Basket is full of good things like seedlings and honey from bees that offer families a source of income, help replenish eroded land, and enhance the quality of the environment. Visit http://www.heifer.org/site/apps/ka/ec/product.asp.

- Provide 111 families with two weeks of emergency food, clean water, and supplies through Compassion International's disaster fund. Many of these disasters are caused or exacerbated by human deterioration of God's natural ecosystems. Visit https://www.compassion.com/contribution/giving/disasterrelief.htm.

- Give your church a green-up kit: purchase recycling containers, a compost bin, reusable dishes and mugs, a year's supply of 100 percent postconsumer recycled paper for bulletins, multiple copies of faith-based environmental books for the church library and small group study, a stock of fair-trade coffee, and trees for planting on church grounds or in the neighborhood. Or arrange for an energy audit with your facility manager and local utility, and offer to pay for weather stripping, energy-saving lightbulbs, a water heater blanket, and other energy-saving recommendations. Visit http://www.theregenerationproject.org for more ideas.

Putting Your Faith into Action

Dear heavenly Father, Creator, and Sustainer, give me the knowledge and will to honor you by using resources wisely in my home. Help me to preserve rather than destroy; teach me to conserve rather than waste. Remind me that everything I possess is on loan from you. Help me to create a God-centered home that I share freely with others. Strengthen my desire to become a better steward of your abundant blessings.

Lord, help me *today* to:

- forgo using one electronic device
- reduce my shower time by two minutes
- turn off the faucet while brushing my teeth and shaving
- turn my water heater down to 120 degrees
- turn my thermostat up three degrees (in summer) or down three degrees (in winter)
- turn off the lights, TV, radio, and stereo when I leave the room
- use cold water if I use the garbage disposal
- turn my refrigerator and freezer to the warmest setting
- run only full loads in the dishwasher
- flush one less time

Lord, help me *this week* to:

- read Psalms 23, 24, 104, 147, and 148
- find out if my public utility company offers a green power option, and sign up
- avoid using aluminum foil and plastic wrap
- change at least five lightbulbs in my home to CFL bulbs
- wash my clothes in the coolest water possible, and only run full loads
- donate a box of books to the library
- buy only "tree free" toilet paper, paper towels, and tissues made from recycled paper

- air-dry my laundry—if I use the dryer, use the moisture sensor option
- hand wash clothes instead of taking them to the dry cleaner
- pre-cycle by buying minimally packaged goods and choosing reusable over disposable
- cut back on the amount of junk mail I receive by registering at https://www.dmachoice.org

Lord, help me *this month* to:

- stock up on handkerchiefs, cloth shopping bags, and cloth napkins so I can kick the paper habit
- clean out my closets and donate clothes I have not worn in the past year
- install low-flow showerheads
- switch to green cleaning products
- clean or replace air filters throughout my house
- wrap my water heater in an insulating jacket if it is hot to the touch or more than ten years old
- caulk and weather-strip around my windows and doors to plug air leaks
- disconnect the ice maker in my freezer
- unplug the TV and stereo when not in use, or put them on a switch-controlled power strip

Lord, help me *this year* to:

- donate my old cell phone, computer, or printer to a good cause
- make or purchase insulated window treatments
- purchase only the most efficient Energy Star items when appliances and lighting fixtures need to be replaced
- ask my utility company to conduct an energy audit on my home, and follow up on their advice
- insulate my walls and ceilings to save up to 25 percent on my energy bill
- use the money I save to advance your Kingdom

Summing It Up

Getting Started

I have:

- ○ conducted an energy audit
- ○ replaced at least three lightbulbs
- ○ turned off lights when leaving the room
- ○ implemented at least one water-saving strategy
- ○ adjusted my thermostat at least two degrees
- ○ started recycling

On the Journey

I have:

- ○ conducted an energy audit and made at least five energy-saving changes
- ○ replaced at least seven lightbulbs
- ○ put electronic devices on smart power strips
- ○ implemented at least three water-saving strategies
- ○ adjusted my thermostat at least four degrees or installed a programmable thermostat
- ○ reduced my heating bill and electricity bill by 20 percent
- ○ reduced my weekly trash production by 20 percent or more

Green Superstar

I have:

- ○ conducted an energy audit and made at least ten changes
- ○ replaced all my lightbulbs
- ○ replaced at least one major appliance or made one long-term energy investment
- ○ implemented at least five water-saving strategies
- ○ reduced my heating bill and electricity bill by 40 percent
- ○ reduced my weekly trash production by 40 percent or more

Late in the day we sat together to weed the strawberry patch. A feeling of joy and peace overcame me. I felt close to God. I experienced "the peace that passes all understanding." I was in communion with the saints and with Nancy. Do you know why?

God created a man and a woman to work together in a garden. We were doing what our Maker designed us to do, and we were reaping the spiritual blessings.

—*Serve God, Save the Planet*

I believe we need to get our facts right, to take small steps, and to cooperate with others working toward the same goal. But I also think we need something else, something bigger, in order to save the planet. We need God.

—*It's Easy Being Green*

2

Lawn and Garden

Restoring Eden in Your Own Backyard

The Lord God took the man and put him in the
Garden of Eden to work it and take care of it.

GENESIS 2:15

IF I CAN LEARN TO GARDEN, ANYONE CAN.

I grew up in the suburbs. Every spring, I helped my mom plant annuals—petunias in our sunny beds, impatiens in the shade, and a few geraniums in planters. One of my chores was to deadhead the flowers—especially the petunias. Pinching back the dead blooms and leggy stems always left a sticky residue on the tips of my fingers, and the smell of summer under my fingernails.

In early summer, my dad had a load of steaming mulch dumped in our driveway. It was the children's job to shovel the mulch into the wheelbarrow and spread it evenly around the trees and bushes. I know that everything looks bigger to a youngster's eyes, but that pile of mulch seemed endless. When we finally scraped up the last shovelful, our yard looked beautiful, but gardening had sunk to the bottom of my list of desired vocations.

By the time I was twelve or thirteen, I discovered a way to avoid most outdoor work. Mom would rather weed in the sunshine than be tied to the kitchen. So I traded outside chores for fixing dinner. I wish I could say that my motives were altruistic, but the truth is that I enjoyed cooking infinitely more than mowing and raking.

I was twenty years old when Matthew and I married—by then skillful in the kitchen, but still with no desire to be a gardener. For the first seven years of our marriage, we mostly lived in apartments where gardening was not an option anyway.

> Even if you are old, you must plant. Just as you found trees planted by others, you must plant them for your children.
> —Midrash Tanchuma, Kodashim 8 (4th to 5th centuries)

My attitude adjustment occurred during Matthew's residency, when each family was provided with a modest house to live in for three years. Our next-door neighbors had been raised in a Mennonite farming community. Thinking it would be fun to grow some of our own food with our young children, we decided to start a garden together—they would share their knowledge, and I would weed and water.

The house we were assigned already had a small garden plot adjacent to the garage. I planted easy-to-grow carrots, tomatoes, radishes, and peas—not enough to feed a family, but the look on Clark's face when he pulled up his first carrot was payment enough for my meager effort. Later we added corn and squash in my neighbor's plot. Growing food fit my frugal nature, and it got me out of the house. I was hooked.

After Matthew finished his residency, we moved to northern New England. Although the growing season there is short, people plant magnificent perennial gardens. Thanks to generous neighbors who offered to give me divisions from their plants, I was able to plant a spring-to-fall succession of blooms—bluets, violets, and bleeding hearts in spring, followed by hostas, daisies, lilies, bee balm, peonies, and black-eyed Susans, culminating in our annual first-day-of-school photograph in front of the lavishly blooming rose of Sharon.

Learning to work with perennials saved me money—most were

free clippings from my neighbors, or inexpensive divisions from the yearly school fund-raiser plant sales—and kept many dozens of throwaway plastic plant containers out of the landfill. Next to my vegetable garden, I planted blueberry bushes and a small orchard of apple and pear trees. Our next-door neighbor told Emma that eating a lot of blueberries helped keep her eyes blue. Emma believed him, so we always saved blueberries to harvest on her August birthday.

The biggest shift in my gardening practices, however, came when we built our house in New Hampshire. I went totally native. Instead of planting grass, I sowed two-thirds of an acre with wildflower seed. The field thrived and attracted wildlife—birds, fox, deer, wild turkeys . . . and tourists. Strangers stopped to ask if they could photograph and paint the field. Neighbors were invited to pick bouquets. Churches used our wildflowers for special occasions.

As a housewarming present, two friends helped us construct raised beds for my vegetable garden. The vegetable garden was so successful the first summer that we decided to double it in size the next, and double it again the next. By the third year, we were growing enough potatoes, carrots, onions, and tomatoes to last year-round. Clark and Emma often weeded with me in the cool stillness of early morning. Matthew used our pressure cooker to can our bounty. It was a family enterprise.

The Lord will surely comfort Zion and will look with compassion on all her ruins; he will make her deserts like Eden, her wastelands like the garden of the Lord. Joy and gladness will be found in her, thanksgiving and the sound of singing.

Isaiah 51:3

In late winter, I started most of my plants indoors along the south windows of the house. Several neighbors and I bartered our successful seedlings; one summer I was on the receiving end of luscious and prolific yellow pear tomatoes. We were also fortunate to have a family-run organic nursery just up the road, so I could always grab a few plants to fill any gaps.

When we moved to Kentucky, one of my first priorities was preparing a small organic garden on the south side of our house. A friend of a friend donated a truckload of well-aged organic manure. We've used the garden for teaching college students basic gardening skills: how to prepare the earth with compost, rake out the beds, plant the seeds, water and weed, and—finally—harvest, cook, preserve, and feast. When I work with the students, sometimes I get the feeling that I'm an impostor—I still feel very much like an amateur gardener, with so much yet to learn.

Matthew's family grew the majority of their vegetables, fruit, eggs, chicken, and milk for economic reasons. For a long while, gardening brought back not-so-fond memories for him—of picking potato bugs off plants and endless weeding wars. But recently, Matthew has happily joined me in the garden.

Come evening, when we work in comfortable silence among the rows, it feels like Paradise restored: just as God intended, husband and wife together, tending and caring for the Lord's earthly garden.

GETTING STARTED

Using more environmentally sound practices in the garden is a gradual journey. If you can put 10 percent of your lawn into native plants, or use 10 percent less water for irrigation, then you are definitely on the right path. Below are six simple principles to get you started:

1. **Grow some fruit and vegetables.** Start simple. Squash, peppers, and tomatoes are nutritious, delicious, and easy to grow. Add a few fruit trees that do well in your area.

2. **Compost your vegetable peelings and weeds.** Composting doesn't have to be complicated. Place a pitcher or covered container by the kitchen sink to collect your food scraps. Then start a compost pile outside. Turn it over every now and then, and watch it turn into free fertilizer.

3. **Water your lawn less.** When you do water, do so at night or early in the morning to reduce evaporation loss. Gradually reduce the size of your lawn and mow high. Learn more at http://www.lesslawn.com.

4. **Stay sharp.** Keep your mower well serviced and the blades sharp. If you can reduce the size of your lawn to a third of an acre or less, you'll be able to comfortably switch to a manual push mower or a solar-powered electric mower.

5. **Embrace the natives.** Research plants that are native to your state, and share divisions with neighbors. Buy perennials over annuals.

6. **Skip the chemicals.** Fertilizers and pesticides filter into our watersheds and are ingested by people and animals. Replace lawn chemicals with natural fertilizers, weed killers, and pest control.

LANDSCAPING
Native plants

Work with God's plan, not against it. Selecting native plants when landscaping ultimately means less time, money, and energy spent on lawn care. Plants that are native to your habitat were designed to withstand extreme weather conditions, will not need to be replaced after most frosts or drought, and require half the amount of water of nonnative plants—saving significantly on your water bill. They also contribute to a balanced ecosystem. Filled with native plants, your yard will quickly become a haven to local birds and butterflies.

Not sure which plants are native? Contact your local cooperative extension program, or visit http://www.plantnative.org to find recommended plants for your area.

Prairie grass

Who says a beautiful yard must be covered in 2-inch-high, monoculture green grass? Plant a mixture of native tall grasses or plants around your yard that require minimal maintenance. Prairie grasses and flowers grow taller than standard lawn grass and will provide areas of interest throughout the year. Planting the right grass substitute can eliminate the need to mow and fertilize altogether. Visit http://www.prairiefrontier.com for more on native grasses.

> **GO GREEN**
> Growing indigenous plants with low water requirements could save you up to 550 gallons of water per year.

Perennials

Annuals like petunias and impatiens are popular among landscapers in the United States. Although annuals are especially great for container planting, perennials offer a better long-term value and provide a more eco-friendly garden. They come back year after year, and they spread. After a few years, you'll be able to divide your plants and share them with friends and neighbors. The more you fill your beds with perennials, the less you'll have to weed. Perennials like bee balm, black-eyed Susans, speedwell, daylilies, hibiscus, daisies, and hollyhocks are beautiful and easy to grow. And many of them attract butterflies and other helpful insects. They also attract fewer pests and require less water than annuals.

> **SAVE GREEN**
> Landscaping doesn't have to cost a fortune. In spring and fall, start a plant exchange board at your church. Ask if your town offers free mulch and compost, and check out demolition sites that may want to get rid of bricks and stones.

Trees and shrubs

Trees help cleanse the air and provide habitats for wildlife. But did you know they can also help lower your home energy costs? Consider these planting tips to cut energy costs:

- *West side*—Plant trees with high canopies on the west side of your house to provide shade from steamy afternoon sun.
- *East and west side*—Position shrubs that allow filtered light and breezes outside east- and west-facing windows.
- *South side*—Plant deciduous trees and vines, which provide shade-giving foliage during the summer and allow light and warmth during the winter.
- *North side*—Plant evergreen trees in your yard as a wind barrier, preventing cold winds from reaching your house.

Whenever possible, install window air-conditioning units in a shaded spot on your home's north or east side. Direct sunshine on the outdoor heat exchanger decreases efficiency by as much as 10 percent.

Tree Hugger

And the Lord God made all kinds of trees grow out of the ground—trees that were pleasing to the eye and good for food.
—GENESIS 2:9

Matthew recently received a call from a minister. At the close of the conversation, Matthew mentioned that our next speaking engagement was with an environmental group headquartered in California. There was a pause, and then the pastor said, "I wouldn't go within 6,000 miles of that bunch of tree huggers."

The pastor's call got me thinking about trees and tree huggers. When Matthew was a medical resident, we lived in a place we jokingly called "the treeless town." We asked our neighbors if we could plant trees along our street, and now those trees are big enough for kids to climb.

After residency, Matthew and I planted maples in front of our house, pines along the northern border, and fruit trees in the backyard. In honor of Father's Day, the kids and I planted a large maple to shade our deck. The row of arborvitae ("tree of life") that we planted along the street is now twice my height.

We are told that in the beginning, in the Garden of Eden, God planted the tree of life. Genesis 2:15 is explicit about caring for trees and for all of God's creation. We're to protect and serve it. That's our job; it's not optional.

A good man or woman who meditates on the Word of God is described as a tree planted by a stream. The tree yields delicious fruit—and its leaves never wither. In addition to being useful, trees have another, perhaps even greater, value: they're pleasing to God. When we stand under an aspen or pine and hear the wind, the trees are singing their praises to the Lord.

Revelation 22—the last chapter of the Bible—gives us a description of heaven. In front of God's throne stands a tree of life, with leaves that will heal the nations, watered by an unpolluted river.

It's easy to look around us and point a finger at neighbors using chemicals on their lawns, or agribusiness that's genetically modifying seeds. Jesus tells us not to worry about the speck of sawdust in our neighbor's eye. First, we should work on removing the plank blocking our own vision.

We are all part of the problem. America makes up only 6 percent of the world's population, but we consume half of the world's paper. That's a lot of God's trees going to junk mail and meaningless memos. None of us is doing such a great job of protecting this big, beautiful garden called earth. We're consuming it.

The Bible begins and ends with a tree of life. But the most wonderful reference occurs when Jesus spread out his big, strong, calloused carpenter's hands—hands that had worked with wood all his life—and died on a cross made from a tree to save us.

So when someone speaks disparagingly about tree huggers, I think about Jesus, my Lord and Savior, hugging the cross.

Call me a tree hugger: I like the company.

Dear Lord, help me to become a protector of trees, not a destroyer. Teach me to love trees, not only for the way they clean our air and provide homes, furniture, and paper, but also because they are pleasing to you. Help me to plant trees wherever I live, and to encourage others to do the same.

Bird feeders

Hang bird feeders in trees near the house. Birds not only are colorful and fun to watch, but also can pollinate flowers and scatter plant seeds. Each day, they consume as much as half their weight in weed seeds, insects, rodents, and other pests.

LAWN MAINTENANCE

Chemicals

Look closely at a natural field, and you'll see many grasses and tremendous diversity. Diversity shields nature from blights and ensures the health of an ecosystem. Perfectly manicured monoculture lawns are not in God's plan.

Using weed killers and other chemicals on your lawn has long-term health consequences for you, your children, your pets, and your neighbors. Instead, pull weeds by hand. If you have children, make weeding a regular part of their chores.

Wearing golf shoes while you mow can help aerate your lawn. And growing native plants and grasses will significantly reduce the need for chemical fertilizers and irrigation.

> How can a person of flesh and blood follow God? . . . God, from the very beginning of creation, was occupied before all else with planting, as it is written, "And first of all, the Eternal God planted a Garden in Eden." Therefore . . . occupy yourselves first and foremost with planting.
> —*Leviticus Rabbah 25:3*
> *(between 5th and 7th centuries)*

If you still think your lawn needs help, consider organic fertilizers, which are available at most lawn and garden centers. For more

ideas on natural alternatives, visit http://www.extremelygreen.com/
fertilizerguide.cfm, http://www.basic-info-4-organic-fertilizers.com,
or http://www.cfspecial.com.

Mowers

If you're not ready to abandon mowing completely, consider a manual reel mower. This option will allow you to keep your yard looking neat without burning gas or using electricity. Reel mowers work
best for mowing yards that are a third of an acre or smaller. And
although using a reel mower will take more work, you will enjoy
the benefits of exercise while emitting no pollutants.

To learn more about manual push reels, visit http://www.reel
mowerguide.com.

Power tools

Before you spend a chunk of your hard-earned paycheck on a
leaf blower or electric shrub trimmer, ask yourself if there is a

way you can accomplish the task without the machine. More than likely, the answer will be yes, and you'll have a chance to get some exercise in the process. Avoiding the purchase of unnecessary power equipment saves money, cuts consumption of fossil fuels, avoids clutter, and reduces both air and noise pollution.

> **SAVE GREEN**
>
> If you do decide to purchase a piece of lawn equipment, consider going in with a neighbor. Sharing tools means fewer raw resources are used to manufacture, ship, and market the item. The more stuff we own, the more sheds and garage space we need to house those items. Sharing also builds community and saves money.

Mulch

Mulching refers to spreading organic material—like grass clippings, leaves, or wood chips—on the ground's surface where it will decompose naturally. Leaving your grass clippings on the lawn after mowing is the most common mulching technique, saving you time (and blisters) from raking while providing organic material for your yard and retaining water in the soil. It also can reduce the amount of fertilizer needed by 25 percent, or about 3 pounds per year. Work less; save more!

Leaves

Don't let the rich organic matter in your leaves go to waste. Instead of bagging leaves and sending them off to the landfill, rake piles around tree trunks, leaving a few inches of open space around the bases for air circulation. Chopping them into smaller pieces using your push mower and watering them will speed up the decomposition process and make them less likely to be blown away by the wind.

Leaf compost

If you have space in your yard, pile deciduous leaves together, soak them with water, and let them decay. For a neater look, place leaves in a wire compost bin or wooden box. In a couple of years, you will find a pile of rich humus to use in the garden—God's great fertilizer, absolutely free.

Rainwater

Most of the rain runoff in your area probably flows along gutters and pipes, then eventually ends up in the storm drains. Why waste that valuable resource when you could make it work for you? Consider setting up a barrel or tank to collect rain. The water you salvage could be used for watering your garden or washing the car. For more tips on harvesting rainwater, visit http://www.harvesth2o.com.

> **GO GREEN**
>
> A 2,000-square-foot home can collect as much as 36,000 gallons of rainwater in one year by using rain barrels to capture water from downspouts—more than enough to meet the average American family's water needs. In many regions, only an inch of water per week is necessary to maintain a healthy lawn. Keep a cat-food-size can outside to monitor rainfall. If rain fills it to the brim each week, you don't need to water at all.

Soaker hose

Sprinklers waste water because of overspray, runoff, and evaporation. Instead, use a soaker hose. Soaker hoses are placed in your garden, then attached to a regular hose. Water seeps out of millions of pores along the entire length and circumference of the soaker hose, drip by drip. A soaker hose will save:

- time—no more standing and feeding mosquitoes while you water
- money—efficient watering means lower water bills

- plants—avoiding water spray can reduce leaf diseases
- the environment—soaker hoses save water and are usually made from recycled tires

Because a soaker hose only works correctly if the pressure is 10 pounds per square inch—and most faucets run at 50 psi—be sure you attach a pressure gauge to the faucet. No single soaker hose should exceed 100 feet. You'll get better results if you bury the soaker hose under 2 inches of mulch, but be sure to expose the hose before doing your spring planting; it's very easy to slice through a hose with your shovel. To determine how long to run the hose, bury a tuna can

Reducing Water Waste

1. **Use drip irrigation.** Instead of using regular sprinklers, water your flower bed and garden using drip irrigation or a soaker hose. This method saves water by minimizing evaporation and watering only the base of your plants. *Water savings: up to 70 percent of the water typically used.*

2. **Use a shut-off nozzle.** To prevent waste when the water is turned on and your hose is not being used, fit your garden hose with a shut-off nozzle. *Water savings: up to 6.5 gallons per minute.*

3. **Plant a native garden.** Conserve water by replacing little-used grass areas like your front yard with a native garden. A native garden can reduce street noise and offer more privacy for you and your family. *Water savings: up to 75 percent of the water typically used.*

4. **Use mulch.** Mulching your plants reduces the amount of water lost through evaporation, limits weed growth, and improves soil conditions. *Water savings: 70 percent of water typically lost through evaporation.*

5. **Reclaim your water.** Collect water that has been used for bathing, washing dishes, and other household duties, and use it to water your plants. *Water savings: up to 300 gallons per month.*

6. **Cover your pool.** When you're not going for a swim, cover your pool to reduce water lost to evaporation. *Water savings: 90 percent of water typically lost through evaporation.*

by a plant and run the hose. When the can fills (about one inch), you know how long to set the timer. For more ideas, visit http://www .savingwater.org/docs/SuccesswithSoakerHoses.pdf.

Xeriscaping

In dry regions of the United States, like the South and Southwest, many homeowners have abandoned high-maintenance, water-guzzling yards for xeriscape landscaping. Xeriscaping involves planting grasses, bushes, and shrubs that can thrive with very little water, allowing you to significantly reduce your household water consumption. One example is planting clover in your lawn instead of grass. Clover is drought-resistant, tolerant of weeds and insects, requires little mowing, and provides a soft cushion for walking. A well-executed xeriscape can reduce your outdoor water consumption by as much as 75 percent.

The Well

How great is God—beyond our understanding! . ... He draws up the drops of water, which distill as rain to the streams; the clouds pour down their moisture and abundant showers fall on mankind. —JOB 36:26-28

Last summer, we visited a friend on his family land in eastern Tennessee. The stone cabin under construction at the top of the hill seemed like a metaphor for the young couple's marriage—strong yet fledgling, promising yet new. The view from the hilltop must have been spectacular one hundred years ago; it was still quite pleasant. But now the skyline was obscured by a persistent haze. The nearby mountains, it was explained, act like a catcher's mitt, keeping a close hold on the ball of smog that collects in this region.

But it wasn't only the pollution that detracted from the view. We were standing on the only large tract of land that had resisted a highly destructive invasive species—suburban sprawl.

After our picnic, I dipped a 5-gallon bucket into the barrel that connects to a rainspout on the roof and started to carry water to their newly planted saplings. After the first round, I realized that 5 gallons was too heavy for me to carry any significant distance, so I started filling the bucket halfway full. Despite the drought, they had enough water collected in the makeshift rain barrel to bring several gallons to each young tree.

Driving home, I confessed to Matthew that I had never really thought about how much water weighs and how much energy it must take to pump it up from the river and to our home. It takes about 5 gallons to flush a traditional toilet, and about 2 gallons to flush a low-flow toilet. Imagine if we had to carry that water from several miles away, like the people Matthew met when practicing medicine in Honduras. I think I would be much more careful about the water I pour down the drain.

The Bible is full of references to women drawing water from wells—women like Rebekah, who was kind to God's creatures and remembered to water the camels, and the Samaritan woman with five husbands, who met Jesus and found eternal life. These women were reminded daily that water is a gift from God, not something to take for granted when we turn on the tap.

Carrying those pails of water to the saplings reminded me that it's not just water we conserve when we take shorter showers; it's also the energy it takes to transport that water. It requires loving and grateful hearts, in relationships of marriage and in relationships with God, to appreciate the gifts right before us.

Dear God, the Creator, thank you for the water that sustains every living creature on earth. Help me to become a more conscious steward of this precious resource. Fill my heart with gratitude each time I water the garden or turn on the tap, and remind me to say a prayer of thanks.

GARDENS
Fruits and vegetables
Growing your own produce is a great way to save money and enjoy nutritious, organic food. When you grow your own fruits and vegetables, you know exactly what went into their production and don't have to worry about ingesting hazardous chemicals. Having fresh

produce readily available also encourages your family to make healthy eating decisions—what could make a more fresh and delicious snack than cherry tomatoes still warm from the afternoon sun? You'll also have access to a tremendous range of produce—not just a few varieties bred for mass production and long-distance travel. Plus, you will eliminate the huge amount of fuel required to haul your produce from the far-off location where it was grown.

Learn more about starting a vegetable garden at http://www.backyardgardener.com/veg.

GO GREEN

Each item of food in a typical American meal has traveled an average of 1,500 miles. Energy calories consumed by production, packaging, and shipping outweigh the energy calories we receive from the food by a ratio of ten to one. Growing your own vegetables, supporting farmers' markets, joining a CSA (Community Supported Agriculture), and buying products like apples, potatoes, and honey from the closest possible source will greatly reduce the number of energy calories required to get food from the farm to your plate.

Miracles

Last week at a women's spiritual group meeting, we decided to each write down a question for all of us to answer, as a way of getting to know each other better. The most creative question came from the woman on my left, author of more than twenty Christian women's novels: if you had to give up either your hair (no wigs or scarves allowed) or your car (no mopeds or motorcycles), which would it be and why? Our small group was equally divided in our answers, with those of us who dislike traffic holding on to the vanity of our hair, and those with young children who are more difficult to transport by bike or public transportation holding on to the convenience of their cars.

But the slip of paper that produced the most interesting response was deceptively simple: describe a miracle in your life.

I had been holding a foster baby named "Miracle" throughout the meeting, yet as I listened to the woman seated to my right, I knew her story was no less miraculous than the sleeping infant in my arms sucking contentedly on my upturned pinky finger.

The Lord will guide you always; he will satisfy your needs in a sun-scorched land and will strengthen your frame. You will be like a well-watered garden, like a spring whose waters never fail.

Isaiah 58:11

This young woman had been raised in an affluent community where she took for granted that fresh pineapple appeared year-round in the produce section of her grocery store, neatly cored and diced. Everyone in her neighborhood had gardens, but no one she knew grew food.

Just out of college and equipped with a degree in finance to enter the lucrative banking world, something (or Someone) led her to purchase a 5-inch tomato plant. Moving the plant to her patio, she wondered how that weak little stem could ever support a full-grown tomato. Every day after work, she sat on the patio for an hour or more and stared at that plant. She continued to watch in amazement as the plant grew and developed flowers. Her wonder only increased when those flowers turned into small green balls. The green balls grew as large as her fist, and then slowly blushed crimson.

That tomato plant changed her life. No longer desiring the career she had prepared for in banking, she started learning about a totally different form of currency. In a series of conversations, her pastor discussed ways she could live out her faith not just on Sundays, but in her everyday life. These two revolutionary ideas—that people could grow their own food *and* could grow their own faith—merged.

She learned as much as she could about sustainable agriculture, quit her job, and interned with an organic farmer. She had never realized that fruit comes from flowers. She had never realized that pineapples don't grow on trees, but from plants on the ground, or that potatoes sprout green foliage and white flowers above the soil while the tubers grow underground.

Today, nearly five years later, she works for an environmental nonprofit and volunteers in several community gardens. She's now excited about starting an urban orchard, where children can learn to grow fruit and nuts in the city.

As I extracted my wrinkled pinky and handed the baby back to her foster mother, I thought, *Who says that God is no longer in the miracle business?*

Using one tomato plant to change a life—now that's what I call miraculous.

Preserving

To enjoy the fruits of your labor year-round, give canning a try. Whether you use the boiling-water-bath method or invest in a pressure cooker, you can fill your pantry with jars that require no refrigeration. You'll save money and eliminate unnecessary trips to the grocery store. Sun drying tomatoes, blueberries, strawberries, apple slices, peaches, and herbs is another healthy, low-cost option for preserving produce. Freezing fresh produce—yours or from the farmers' market—is an easy way to ensure a local, chemical-free supply year-round.

Church Supported Agriculture

For as the soil makes the sprout come up and a garden causes seeds to grow, so the Sovereign Lord will make righteousness and praise spring up before all nations. —Isaiah 61:11

I received an e-mail from a pastor friend, sharing a link to a congregation-CSA program. CSA stands for Community Supported Agriculture, but my hope is that someday soon it will also stand for *Church* Supported Agriculture.

Here's how CSAs work: Individuals buy shares in a garden. The CSA farmer does all the hoeing, planting, watering, weeding, and harvesting, and you—for a small fee—get to do the eating. Not only is the food locally grown and good for you, but also you are guaranteeing a market for a rapidly disappearing species—the small, local farmer—and keeping agricultural land in productive use. As an added bonus, most CSAs limit the use of petrochemicals, both for fertilizers and transportation.

CSAs either deliver or provide a central place to pick up your share of the week's produce. In addition to the familiar sweet peas, string beans, tomatoes, potatoes, carrots, onions, and melons, you will most likely get some vegetables in your weekly basket (especially early and late in the season) that are new to you—perhaps leeks or beet greens or winter squash or fresh brussels sprouts. Look at these less familiar vegetables as opportunities to try a new recipe and to encourage a wider palate for your family.

At one church in Dayton, I was told how gardeners bring in produce every Sunday morning. After church, people can purchase a wide variety of items ranging from tomatoes, peppers, squash, and beans to basil, Swiss chard, and even catnip! Money raised from the vegetable donations is forwarded to the local hunger fund. Last year approximately $1,000 was raised from the garden surplus table to help combat hunger in the Dayton area.

Another church in Kentucky has 6 acres of land. Last fall, they plowed about 2 acres and planted clover to increase the nitrogen content. In the spring the church offered 10-foot by

10-foot plots to people in the congregation and those living in nearby low-income apartments. The group also tended plots of vegetables to share with neighbors in need.

As we travel around the country, my heart gladdens whenever I hear of churches adopting CSA farmers or offering space on church, school, municipal, or private property for a community garden—a small piece of Eden where all generations can till the soil together.

Lord, help me to be conscious of where my food comes from. Though it may cost a little more to support a neighboring farmer, help me to seek out local produce. If I have the space, give me the will to start or expand my own vegetable patch and to use organic gardening practices whenever possible.

GO GREEN

If you don't know of any CSAs in your area, call the local extension office or 4-H club. Gather some like-minded friends and buy shares. Know people with green thumbs who would like to expand their gardens? Ask if they would be interested in starting a church-based CSA next spring. Or turn over some sod this fall in a sunny spot for your very own vegetable patch. Start small, and expand as your knowledge and skill grow.

Compost

Composting is a great way to nourish your plants and reduce the amount of trash you place by the curb each week. Combine organic materials like food scraps, yard trimmings, coffee filters, and even ashes from your fireplace in a bin. Don't include meat, oil and grease, or pet droppings because they tend to attract disease-infested rodents that can kill the beneficial organisms.

A wide variety of composting options are available, ranging from a bucket with holes to a dual chamber barrel on a tubular

GO GREEN

Composting can reduce household waste by as much as 70 percent.

steel stand. One simple method involves drilling small drainage holes in a galvanized trash can and burying the bottom about a foot below ground. Fill it with scraps, stir the contents now and then for about ten months, and return to find a fresh batch of nutrient-rich fertilizer.

The resulting dark brown, earthy material can be used to improve soil texture, prevent weed growth, increase air and water absorption in the soil, and mulch the lawn and garden. Check with your local extension or utility offices to see if they offer compost bins.

To learn more about composting options, visit http://www.composters.com or http://www.compostguide.com.

Get Wormy with Vermicomposting

If you're already a seasoned composter, consider advancing to the next level by composting with worms. After some initial setup work, indoor worm bins will start converting your table scraps into the richest food-based compost—vermicompost. Plus they make great educational tools for kids.

Once your bin is ready, soak dead leaves, shredded paper, and fine wood shavings in water. (Avoid using glossy paper from magazines and junk mail because they often contain toxins, which are harmful to the composting system.) Fill the bin with this mixture for a moist bedding to mimic the worms' natural habitat. Then dump in red wigglers or red earthworms. Start off slowly, feeding the worms about one-half their body weight daily until the population grows enough to handle all your food scraps.

Visit the following links to learn more about vermicomposting and where to order worms:

- http://www.journeytoforever.org/compost_worm.html
- http://www.earth911.org/composting

Helpful insects and animals

Form an alliance with beneficial insects and animals to get rid of pests in your garden. To attract them, offer shelter and nectar by adding bordering flowers around your garden. Plants like carrots, parsley, Queen Anne's lace, daisies, goldenrod, black-eyed

Controlling Pests the Natural Way

Every year, Americans spray millions of tons of artificial pesticides and fertilizers into their gardens. These toxic chemicals seep into our groundwater and eventually make it to our waterways, causing cancer and harming our nervous and reproductive systems. How can you keep your garden pest free and your lawn beautiful without wreaking havoc on the planet and your health, while saving money? Try these natural alternatives for controlling unwanted insects and fungi:

- **Basic insect spray**—*Repels insects; kills fungi and mites.* Mix two tablespoons of dishwashing liquid soap into one gallon of water. To target fungi, add one to two tablespoons of baking soda. Add sulfur to kill mites.

- **Peppermint tea**—*All-purpose insect spray; ant repellent.* Brew peppermint leaf tea. Cool and place in a properly labeled spray bottle.

- **Garlic spray**—*Repels insects.* Mix two teaspoons of garlic juice, one teaspoon of cayenne pepper, and one teaspoon of liquid soap in one quart of water.

- **Banana peel repellent**—*Repels aphids.* Place banana peels around roses and other plants.

- **Lemon spray**—*Repels white flies and soft-bodied insects. Also gets rid of fleas.* Boil three lemon peels in one quart of water. Let cool, remove peels, and put solution in a properly labeled spray bottle.

- **Lemongrass wasp repellent**—Place lemongrass in a vase on your picnic table to keep wasps away.

- **Vinegar spray**—*Combats fungal disease and black spots on roses.* Combine three tablespoons of apple cider vinegar with one gallon of water.

Susans, and asters can help attract beneficial bugs. Insects such as hoverflies, ladybugs, and praying mantis feed on pests like cinch bugs and weevils. Birds, frogs, and lizards love caterpillars and grubs. Not only will they eliminate pests, your new insect friends will help pollinate flowers, fruits, and vegetables. Share your lawn with beneficial creatures and watch your pest population decrease naturally.

GO GREEN

According to the *American Journal of Public Health*, children who live in homes that use chemical weed and insect killers are four times more likely to develop cancer than those who do not. Skip expensive and harmful chemicals, and get rid of pests the natural way. Adding French marigolds, borage, dill, nasturtium, garlic, parsley, thyme, onion, sage, and fennel to your garden will help repel insects without harming the watershed.

Bat houses

How's this for a romantic gift idea? For Matthew's birthday this year, I bought him a bat house. Working in the garden, we've both been bothered by mosquito and other pesky bug bites. Each bat can eat up to one thousand insects per hour. Bat houses encourage these helpful mammals to take up residence in your backyard and make outdoor living much less itchy.

Not Your Ordinary Garden Club

I made gardens and parks and planted all kinds of fruit trees in them. I made reservoirs to water groves of flourishing trees.
—ECCLESIASTES 2:5-6

Solomon, the wisest man who ever lived, planted gardens and parks and all kinds of trees, as did God, the Creator. The Lord also commanded us to care for our neighbors, particularly the least among us. My husband and I have a particular heart for finding places where these two mandates—to care for and tend the Garden, and care for our poorest neighbors—intersect. So I was absolutely delighted, after leading a workshop at a megachurch, when a woman came over to share an idea that I had never heard before.

She belongs to a garden club. Immediately, the stereotype of an upper-middle-class woman with a penchant for peonies and antique roses—a woman much like me before Matthew quit being a doctor—came to mind. But this woman shattered my preconceptions.

A friend of hers is involved with an inner-city ministry for women. They run a home for about twelve recovering addicts. These women are separated from children and family, without hope—exactly where so many of us finally find Jesus. The director of the recovery center had a dream to transform the patch of ground out back, enclosed by a dilapidated metal fence, into a place for rest, restoration, and renewal—a peace garden—but she did not have the knowledge or resources to make her vision a reality.

> *For as the soil makes the sprout come up and a garden causes seeds to grow, so the Sovereign Lord will make righteousness and praise spring up before all nations.*
>
> ISAIAH 61:11

That's where my new friend came in. Recognizing a need and a chance to serve, this woman approached her garden club. The garden club, which had never done anything like this before, embraced the idea with enthusiasm. And now, as they prepare to design, plant, and tend a beautiful garden space, her hope is that this project will serve as a model for garden clubs throughout the country.

Imagine if we all found ways to use our God-given passions to care for the earth while caring for the poor? A minister friend just told me that his congregation is planning a community garden right on the church grounds to serve two neighboring low-income projects. They also want to build a nature path around the perimeter of the property for the community to use. A church in California is asking people with handyman (and handywoman) skills to help insulate low-income homes. And a friend in Texas is helping schools in her low-income neighborhood xeriscape their grounds with indigenous plants and natural landscaping.

It's time to stop hiding our talents under a basket—with a little creativity, we can all find ways to serve.

GO GREEN

Is there a home for battered women, an addiction center, a halfway house, a teen center, a Head Start program, or a prison near you that could benefit from a garden? Investigate. Make some inquiries. Listen to their needs, and then join forces with friends and dig in.

SAVE

How to Save Money This Year

Grow summer vegetables	$300
Preserve fruits and vegetables for winter use	$400
Harvest rainwater and use bath and dishwater for garden irrigation	$120
Share a piece of power equipment instead of buying new	$150
Nourish your plants with compost instead of fertilizer	$70
Use a manual reel mower instead of a gas-powered one	$80
Gather leaves using a rake instead of purchasing a leaf blower	$100
Shade your air-conditioning unit and the south side of your home	$65
Plant perennials instead of annuals, and divide them among neighbors	$60
TOTAL	**$1, 345**

SHARE

. . . And Share It with Those in Need

What could you do with your lawn and garden savings to help someone in need?

- Transform urban roofs in inner-city America into green space and gardens that improve air and water quality and save energy. (http://www.earth pledge.org/ep/your-financial-support)

- Work with a neighborhood association to line the streets with trees. Donate money to purchase the trees.

- Protect birds in sixteen countries throughout the Americas, ranging from species found only at one remaining site to birds that migrate to Latin America and the United States each year. (http://www.abcbirds.org)

- Help create, fund, improve, and maintain gardens in urban and rural places of need in four states. (http://www.gardensforhumanity.org)

- Fund a garden for your school system, or jump-start a garden through a local church or Christian organization that uses the produce to supply fruits and vegetables to needy people in your community. Purchase the necessary seeds and equipment, and volunteer to help.

Putting Your Faith into Action

Dear heavenly Father, thank you for being the giver of all life and for the privilege of caring for your creation. Help me to see the miracle of new life through your eyes. Teach me to appreciate the beauty right before me—in my yard, in my garden, and in my community. Give me wisdom as I learn to become a better steward of your creation, so that I can leave the world a healthier and more beautiful place for my children and generations to come.

Lord, help me *today* to:

- worry less about what others think about my yard and more about what you think
- water my plants during the coolest part of the day to minimize evaporation
- spend at least five minutes in my yard enjoying your creation
- pray for people around the world who do not have access to clean water

Lord, help me *this week* to:

- reclaim water from bathing and washing dishes and use it for irrigation
- read and memorize John 15:1-8, where Jesus speaks about the vine and branches
- find out what plants and grasses are native to my region at http://www.plantnative.org
- use a broom instead of a hose to clean my driveway and sidewalks
- attach a shut-off nozzle to my hose

Lord, help me *this month* to:

- make and use my own natural insect repellent for the garden
- start a compost pile
- leave grass clippings on the lawn after mowing
- resist buying a power tool when I could complete a task manually
- avoid watering my lawn unless absolutely necessary
- start a plant-exchange board at my church

Lord, help me *this year* to:

- harvest my rainwater and use it for watering my lawn and garden
- trade in my gas lawn mower for a manual reel mower or solar-powered mower
- mulch leaves instead of sending them off to the landfill
- use native plants and prairie grass for my yard in place of traditional grass
- provide food for my family by raising a garden and canning vegetables
- plant flowers that attract helpful insects
- avoid the use of pesticides
- use the money I save to help beautify the earth or provide fresh fruits and vegetables to those in need
- hang a bird feeder in my yard
- garden with perennials instead of annuals
- select and plant fruit or nut trees that grow well in my climate
- site trees and shrubs where they will provide shade, act as a wind barrier, and reduce energy costs

Summing It Up

Getting Started

I have:

○ planted a vegetable garden

○ only watered the lawn and garden in the morning or evening

○ begun composting lawn waste

○ mowed my lawn higher and less frequently

On the Journey

I have:

○ canned, frozen, or dried some fruits and vegetables for winter

○ used reclaimed water from my house to water plants in my yard

○ begun composting food waste

○ reduced my lawn size by at least one-tenth

○ integrated native plants into my landscaping

Green Superstar

I have:

○ grown at least half of the vegetables my family consumes

○ stopped using chemicals in my lawn and garden entirely

○ composted all lawn and food waste

○ replaced a significant portion of my lawn with native plants or natural landscaping

○ traded in my gas-powered lawn mower for a manual reel or solar-powered mower

○ used the money I've saved to help beautify the earth or support a worthy cause

Physical work gives us health and meaning. While the disciples sailed, Jesus walked across the Sea of Galilee to meet them. He picked grain. He washed his disciples' feet. Work was not beneath him. He thought no physical labor was undignified. The washing of feet is a sign that God is willing to stoop low and to work to save us. For millennia, men and women have used simple manual labor as a way to connect with the divine qualities of Jesus.

—*Serve God, Save the Planet*

I have a hard time believing God ever intended for us to be judged by what we wear or to judge others by how they look. Yes, God invented clothes. But he didn't invent fashion.

—*It's Easy Being Green*

Work

The Triple Bottom Line

*Do not work for food that spoils, but for food that
endures to eternal life.*

JOHN 6:27

FOR BETTER—OR FOR WORSE—your work habits can affect your
health, the planet, and even your pocketbook.

My first real job after college was as a technical writer at a
Department of Energy research facility. My office was in a trailer
that had been salvaged from the 1977 Johnstown, Pennsylvania,
flood. The orange carpet was perpetually damp and the air had a
distinctive, old-mold smell.

Six months later I was promoted to the administrative offices—
a bunch of newly manufactured trailers linked together to create
one large maze of cubicles. If you've ever gotten a whiff of a "new
car smell," multiply that tenfold and you'll have a sense of the air
we inhaled eight hours a day.

My officemate's husband worked as a coal miner. Compared to
his long shifts underground breathing in coal dust in hazardous tun-
nels, our working conditions were nirvana. At twenty-one, I wasn't
particularly concerned about the long-term health consequences of

indoor air pollution or the number of trees we destroyed editing multiple drafts of long bureaucratic reports—I was just grateful to have a job that paid the bills.

My colleagues were mostly engineers. They were trying to find ways of burning fossil fuels, particularly coal, more cleanly and efficiently. Three decades later, scientists and engineers are still spending millions searching for the holy grail of "clean coal," a term many now consider an oxymoron. Despite good intentions, my work at the research facility probably did more environmental harm than good—using lots of resources with little or no benefit to the planet.

When I switched from technical writing to teaching English, the results of my work seemed more straightforward—though the work conditions were not always ideal. Over the next couple of decades, I found myself teaching in a variety of environments: in a night school where I was told to carry mace for protection between classes, at a workplace literacy program where the factory workers wore all sorts of protective gear, in a stacked cubes, 1960s-style modern office where none of the windows opened; in a primary school that had once been a restaurant, and at a New England boarding school.

His master replied, "Well done, good and faithful servant! You have been faithful with a few things; I will put you in charge of many things. Come and share your master's happiness!"

MATTHEW 25:21

It wasn't until I taught at the boarding school, however, that my advocacy for health, environmental, and money-saving changes went into high gear. By then, Matthew had left medicine, and we had significantly downscaled our lifestyle. After successfully implementing so many changes at home, I now felt it was time to help lighten the footprint of my workplace.

During my first contract meeting with my boss, I explained that taking care of the planet was my passion. He politely told me that it was not his.

It took a few years, but—despite some initial resistance—the workplace gradually became greener. We began to use recycled paper in all copiers and offices; set double-sided printing as the default in printers, installed LED bulbs in exit signs; added motion detectors for interior lighting; installed dimmers in rooms with natural light; added Dumpster-sized recycling receptacles for paper, glass, plastics, and metal; greatly reduced the use of Styrofoam in the cafeteria; and began composting food waste.

> " The great and firm foundation of the spiritual life is the offering of ourselves to God and being subject to his will in all things. We must completely forget ourselves, so that we regard ourselves as an object which has been sold and over which we no longer have any rights. We find all our joy in fulfilling God's pleasure—his happiness, his glory and the fact that he is our great and only delight. Once we have this foundation, all we need to do is spend our lives rejoicing that God is God and being so wholly abandoned to his will that we are quite indifferent as to what we do and equally indifferent as to what use he makes of our activities.
> —*Jean-Pierre de Caussade (1675–1751)*,
> Abandonment to Divine Providence "

The key to success was working *with* the system—and forming a green team—to make the workplace a healthier, more environmentally responsible, and more cost-effective place to learn and work.

The school's colors? Green and white. My former boss? He's now the king of green!

GETTING STARTED

Saving energy at home is absolutely the first step—we need to change ourselves before we can hope to influence others. Once we've lightened our own footprints, we can extend our influence much further by going green at work.

With a little imagination, any field can be made more green: office workers can arrange a rideshare board, hairdressers can compost hair clippings, landscapers can use native plants and natural fertilizers, house cleaners can switch to green cleaning products, restaurants can purchase local, sustainably grown ingredients. Starting a green team that recommends ways to save the company money while saving the earth and creating a healthier work environment will result in a win-win-win bottom line.

Can it be challenging to initiate changes at work? Yes. Will you face obstacles? Definitely. The great thing about changes in the workplace is that they have the potential to make a big difference. Not only can you reduce the environmental impact of the entire company, but your example can also influence coworkers' behavior at home.

When colleagues ask *why* you are going green, don't hesitate to say that your faith is a primary motivation. By adopting good stewardship practices, you are sharing your love of the Creator—a testimony of how the Bible can influence our behavior throughout the week. Think of creation care as a 24-7 mission field—an opportunity for us to grow ever closer to the nonconsumerist example set by Jesus, and a tangible way to share his perfect love with those who have fewer resources than we do.

> **GO GREEN**
>
> The typical office worker uses a quarter of a ton of materials in a year, including ten thousand pieces of copy paper.

IN THE OFFICE
Supplies

Little things *do* make a difference, even the items inside your desk drawer. Try a water-based correction pen instead of bottled correction liquid. You'll use less, and it won't dry out as quickly. Choose refillable pens and pencils. Disposable plastic pens are neither recyclable nor biodegradable. Send one to the landfill, and it will still be

Low-Hanging Fruit

Make changes in your own habits first, then work within the system to recommend changes that will create a healthier, more environmentally sound, and more cost-effective workplace. It's often easier to make changes at work when you are cooperating with others, so start a green team at work. Encourage your team to go after the low-hanging fruit first—changes that cost little or nothing and save money are usually no-brainers for higher-ups to approve. Here are nine actions your green team can recommend immediately that can save your company money or are at least cost neutral.

- Contact your local utility provider, and find out if the company offers energy audits for businesses—usually the cost is nominal. Then implement the changes that help the bottom line. Or hire a performance contractor. Most charge nothing up front, earning their fees from the savings you garner.

- Recommend that the thermostat be adjusted three or more degrees company wide. Turning the thermostat up in the summer or down in the winter can save about 3 percent in energy costs for each degree. Install programmable thermostats to adjust even further at night.

- Suggest that all lightbulbs in exit signs be changed to LED bulbs—the payback is usually earned in a couple of months, and after that, the company is saving money.

- Post reminders next to all light switches to turn off the lights when leaving the room.

- Cut paper costs in half. Ask that the default on printers be set to double-sided printing. (Employees can still print single-sided when needed.)

- Encourage signs to be posted by all copiers, asking that employees print double-sided pages. And switch to 30 percent postconsumer recycled paper in all copiers.

- Suggest a simple way that all computers can be completely powered down at night—usually with a power strip or hard off switch. The last one out or the nightly cleanup crew can be asked to assure that all computers are completely turned off.

- Reset computers so that they go into sleep mode after five minutes of inactivity.

- Start a rideshare board. Ask that people who carpool be given special parking privileges.

there in sixty thousand years. If possible, stop using rubber bands—or at least reuse them until they break. Three-fourths of rubber bands are synthetic, made of crude oil. When they reach the incinerator at the dump, they can release toxic fumes into the air.

Consider purchasing an eco-stapler or another staple-free stapler for your office. It works for tasks that require binding five pages or less and does not use metal staples. Not only will you save metal, but you also won't have to waste time removing staples before shredding confidential documents. Purchase one online at http://www.inkdiscovery.com.

The Mechanical Pencil

Matthew produces a lot of writing—articles, reviews, books, sermons—and he does it all by hand. For several years, he's written on old-style computer paper I scavenged from a Dumpster. When his supply finally started to get low, I posted a request on http://www.freecycle.org and received enough paper (free!) to last a few more years.

To write, Matthew uses a mechanical pencil. When he was a child, Matthew had his right thumb cut off in an accident; thanks to some skillful doctors, it was successfully reattached, but it still aches with repetitive movements. It took a while for Matthew to find a mechanical pencil that is comfortable. He used the same brass pencil for four years, until it gave out. The company stopped manufacturing that particular model, but fortunately we found one—and a backup—on eBay. Much cheaper than a computer, and the software never needs to be updated!

Computers

To keep energy costs down, choose the lowest energy settings for all electronic devices. Little differences add up: if ten employees activate the power management function on their computers, they would save almost $500 in energy costs in one year.

Set your computer to its energy-saving mode and shut it down completely when you leave at the end of the day. Don't settle for standby mode; your computer will continue to draw power. Avoid screen savers, which are big energy wasters.

To completely shut down your computer, plug it into a power strip with an on/off switch and turn off your entire desktop setup in one easy step. Giving your computer a complete rest will reduce heat and mechanical stress. Make it a practice to leave printers, scanners, and other infrequently used devices unplugged or switched entirely off until needed.

For even greater savings, switch to a laptop. Laptops use as much as 90 percent less energy than desktops. Set your laptop to go into sleep mode after five minutes of inactivity.

If you have a desktop with an old cathode-ray tube (CRT) monitor, consider replacing it with a liquid crystal display (LCD)—which can use up to 75 percent less electricity.

> **GO GREEN**
> Monitors use up to 60 percent of the energy consumed by your computer system. Turn off the monitor when you leave your office for more than two minutes.

Working and Saving at Home

My laptop is on for much of the day every day, except on the Sabbath. It's probably considered clunky and out of date (it has no internal wireless connection and the DVD player broke years ago), but it gets the job done. Even though we run our nonprofit from home and host frequent guests, our typical non-summer electricity bill is around $15.

Working from home has many bonuses (zero commute, no makeup, lunch with my husband), but I do get interrupted—a lot. Often I think that I'm stepping away from my computer for two minutes, and suddenly find that two hours have passed. My son changed the settings so that my computer goes into sleep mode after five minutes of inactivity—which happens quite a bit with phone calls, visitors, and across-the-hall consultations with Matthew.

Of course, the most reliable no-cost, nonelectric commu-
nication technology is face-to-face communications. With
our offices just 3 feet apart, Matthew and I communicate frequently—the old-fashioned way!

Faxes

Want to eliminate paper on your end of the fax? Consider purchasing GFI FAXmaker, a fax server software for your computer that
saves time, money, and paper. No more waiting for the fax to go
through, paper printouts, or physically walking to the fax machine
because GFI FAXmaker allows users to receive and send faxes
directly from their e-mail. Learn more at http://www.winfax.com.

If you need paper copies of faxes, consider using a bond-paper
fax machine, which uses regular, recyclable paper that doesn't fade
and can be filed easily. Bond paper costs much less than traditional
thermal fax paper. Thermal paper is coated in clay, making it difficult to recycle.

Envelopes

Buy envelopes with postconsumer recycled content. Make it company policy to reuse envelopes that are still in good condition to
circulate interoffice memos, and reuse mailers by applying sticker
labels.

A business contact took note when I returned a signed contract
in the same mailer that I had received it in. The contact was also
pleased when I turned over the cover letter and handwrote my return note. This has been Sleeth standard practice for years, and
we've only had favorable responses.

Packaging

Reuse boxes you receive in the mail to ship other products, and use
shredded waste paper for packing material. When packing items,
less is more. Unless shipping fragile items, don't put a box inside
another shipping box or an envelope inside a letter pack.

E-Waste Recycling

According to the Environmental Protection Agency, more than 2 million tons of e-waste end up in landfills each year. When burned or dumped, cell phones, computers, and other gadgets release toxins—including lead, mercury, and cadmium—into the air and water.

What should you do with your old electronic devices at work?

- If your computer is in working order, consider donating it to a local school or nonprofit organization. For school donations call your local school district or visit http://www.pcsforschools.org. Learn how to donate used computer technology to nonprofits and public agencies at http://www.cristina.org.

- Donate your old cell phone to http://www.eco-cell.org, an organization that provides refurbished phones for first-time users abroad or hospital patients for emergency 911 calls.

- Your business can earn money by selling used equipment. Web sites such as http://www.BuyMyTronics.com purchase iPhones, cell phones, BlackBerrys, and other technology.

- Check out large electronics and office supply stores with recycling programs:

  Best Buy has kiosks inside U.S. stores where you can drop off unwanted electronics at no cost. If your electronics still have some life left in them, you can trade them in and get some money back (http://www.bestbuy.com).

  Staples' recycling program covers everything from desktops, laptops, and printers to keyboards, mice, and speakers. Take your electronic device to the store's customer service desk and have it sent to a recycler for $10 per large item (http://www.staples.com).

- GreenDisk sells collection boxes for discarded laptops, CDs, DVDs, ink cartridges, and cell phones. For $29.95, you can purchase a standard-sized Technotrash can, which holds up to 35 pounds of e-waste. Cost includes postage, processing, and an audit report with a Certificate of Destruction (http://www.greendisk.com).

For a directory of local, responsible electronics recyclers, visit http://www.computertakeback.com. For hard-to-recycle items, http://www.Earth911.org or http://www.mygreenelectronics.org will direct you to a recycling center or hazardous waste disposal facility near you.

In our home office, I keep a drawer of used mailers, a plastic tub of used bubble wrap and packing materials, and a shelf containing boxes that I am likely to reuse. If I gather too many boxes, they get cut down and go out with the recycling—but the supply usually balances nicely with demand. Even though our nonprofit ships things out regularly, I cannot remember the last time I needed to buy a new box or packing material.

Mailing lists and catalogs

Keep mailing lists current to avoid (costly!) duplicates.

On the receiving end, share magazine subscriptions at work by attaching a routing list and highlighting important articles for others to read. Ask suppliers to send only one catalog to your office. Be vigilant about getting off junk mail lists. Register at https://www.dmachoice.org/dma/member/regist.action. If companies continue to send unwanted catalogs, call their toll-free numbers and ask to unsubscribe. Recycle junk mail you do receive, including envelopes with plastic windows.

For more ways to reduce junk mail, visit http://www.newdream.org.

IN THE COPY ROOM

Before printing

The best kind of paper is no paper at all. Only print when you must, and keep all other documents digital whenever possible. Reducing waste at the source will mean less need for recycling and reusing. Cutting down on the amount of paper you purchase will save trees and cash.

Save time and paper by keeping files on computers instead of in file cabinets. Edit documents onscreen rather than on a hard copy, and review them carefully before printing. Decreasing your margins in your word processing program from the standard 1-inch to ¼-inch allows more text to fit on one page, saving you pages in the end. Choose e-mails over paper letters.

Set the default on all computers and copy machines in your office to double-sided printing. Producing only double-sided documents will cut paper consumption by 50 percent. Individuals can always change the printer settings if a particular job requires single-sided printing.

Post memos and company publications online or on an office bulletin board instead of distributing paper copies to each employee.

> **GO GREEN**
>
> For more efficient printing, consider investing in software like Greenprint, a program that eliminates wasted pages. Learn more about this program at http://www.printgreener.com.

Think ink

Refilled and remanufactured ink cartridges will save you money, while helping the planet at the same time. The cheapest option is to buy a kit and refill cartridges yourself—though for some printers this can be time-consuming and messy. Many offices find it more convenient to take empty cartridges to a store that refills cartridges, such as Walgreens, Cartridge World, Caboodle Cartridge, Island Ink-Jet, or Rapid Refill Ink. Another cost-effective option is to purchase remanufactured cartridges online. Remanufactured cartridges, also called recycled cartridges, have been refilled with ink and given new printer heads. They can cost up to 85 percent less than new cartridges. To compare prices, visit http://www.ink-cartridge.nettop20.com.

> **GO GREEN**
>
> Use the draft mode when printing documents that aren't final. Your printer's draft mode uses about half the ink it would for a normal print job.

Did you know that you can earn big bucks by recycling your ink cartridges? Go to http://www.myinkrecycling.com to review a database of over one hundred cartridge recyclers, complete with the prices that each recycler pays. Prices in the database are updated weekly. It pays to research—for one brand I looked at, the payment offers ranged from $1.30/cartridge to $5.00/cartridge.

Paper

Recycling paper has two components—purchasing paper with recycled content and recycling the paper you use. In most cases, paper with 30 percent postconsumer recycled content will cost about the same as regular paper. Paper with 100 percent postconsumer recycled content (the higher the percent, the better) will cost more, but that cost is easily outweighed by making double-sided printing the default.

When printing drafts or sending faxes, reuse discarded paper that is printed only on one side. To avoid confusion, strike out the previously used, irrelevant side. Shred sensitive papers and use for packing.

Each year 188 *million* trees are cut down to make office paper in the United States—that's 8 million tons of copy paper.

Copy machines

Want to lighten the energy load on your copier? Using the standby button will decrease energy consumption by 70 percent. To reduce paper waste, make sure everyone in your office knows how to use the copy machines properly. Consider posting a sign near the copier with instructions on how to perform the most common tasks and who to call for troubleshooting help.

EATING

Lunch

If you want to save money, reduce packaging waste, and stay healthier, bring your lunch from home in reusable containers. Skip the plastic wrap and aluminum foil, and opt for more durable glass or

Recycling at Work

If your office doesn't recycle, take the lead and help establish a program. First, make a list of the most common items in your office that are accepted by your local recycling facility. Below are some possibilities:

- computer paper

- aluminum cans

- plastic bottles

- batteries

- lightbulbs

- computers and peripherals

- glass bottles

- telephone books

Before starting a program, get approval from your boss, and decide how you will collect, store, and haul away your recyclables. If you anticipate a small volume of materials, consider taking them yourself to a drop-off recycling location. Visit http://www.Earth911.com to locate one near your work site. If the volume is large, you'll need the cooperation of your facilities manager or custodial crew.

You'll also need to decide how to separate the collected items, and set up clearly labeled bins in strategic places. Place a paper recycling bin in the copy room and next to the trash at each employee's desk. The kitchen/break room is the ideal place for aluminum, glass, and plastic recycling bins. You also should establish a convenient location to collect empty ink cartridges. In the storage room, designate a bin for electronics that no longer work.

If you anticipate obstacles, estimate how paid recycling (ink cartridges, cardboard, electronics) will offset costs. And don't forget that trash removal costs will decrease in proportion to the amount your recycling increases.

ceramic containers. Keep a couple of cloth napkins in your desk—take used napkins home on Fridays to be washed and bring a fresh supply on Mondays.

When you do go out for lunch, choose restaurants that are nearby so you can bike or walk. If you are eating out and think you might have leftovers, bring a reusable food container and skip the Styrofoam take-out box. When you order food to go, ask them to not include plastic utensils, individually wrapped condiments, or paper napkins. If you eat in the company's cafeteria, choose silverware and plates over plasticware whenever possible. A single office worker could use up to 250 plastic forks in a year!

GO GREEN

A disposable, fast food–style lunch creates between 4 and 8 ounces of waste. One office worker who eats out regularly could be responsible for creating as much as 100 pounds of trash per year.

The Lunch Whistle

When I worked in an office, I nearly always brought my lunch from home. I was given an hour for lunch, so most of the time I ate my meal at my desk, then used the remaining time to go on a walk. The fresh air and time away from the office cleared my mind and helped me work more productively in the afternoon.

When Matthew was in medical school, I packed him a lunch. Later, in residency and when he worked in the ER, he ate cafeteria food. Fortunately, these hospitals still used real plates, glasses, and silverware, so waste was minimal.

Now we usually eat lunch at our dining room table, except when Matthew is on the road. Matthew has been very good about blowing the metaphorical lunch whistle and emphasizing the importance of sharing our meals. Taking time to break bread and talk provides a welcome oasis in the midst of our workday.

Coffee breaks

Bothered by the half pot of coffee you dump out at work at the end of each day? Here's a startling statistic: one-third of the tap water used for drinking in North America is used for brewing coffee. If each of us avoided wasting just one cup of coffee a day at work, we could save enough water over the course of a year to provide 2 gallons to the more than 1.1 billion people who don't have access to fresh water at all. In addition, it takes *37 additional gallons* of water to grow the coffee used to brew each cup. With as many as 5 million people dying unnecessarily each year because of lack of water and water-related illnesses—one-third under age five—we all should be more careful about our coffee-drinking habits.

Would cutting back on coffee drinking really make that water accessible to those who need it? In a literal, legalistic sense, no—not any more than the food left on your plate can be shipped to starving children in India. The mind-set of being careful stewards of resources, however, *does* collectively make more available to those in need, especially if we use some of the money we save to support drilling new wells in Africa. Moreover, reports of droughts right here in the United States are becoming increasingly common. Just as Joseph wisely ordered the Egyptians to conserve resources in the seven fat years, we need to alter wasteful habits and learn to conserve in small ways before water shortages become rampant.

Therefore, my dear brothers, stand firm. Let nothing move you. Always give yourselves fully to the work of the Lord, because you know that your labor in the Lord is not in vain.

1 CORINTHIANS 15:58

How can you cut back on the environmental impact of your coffee break? Cut back on the amount of coffee you drink (tap water is cheaper and healthier), and only brew what you need at work. Stop stocking the break room with paper and Styrofoam cups; instead, ask coworkers to bring mugs from home for coffee and tea drinking. Avoid disposable coffee stirrers and use a nonplastic spoon, or pour in sweetener and cream before adding coffee. For sweeteners, choose loose containers over individual packets. Try to buy and use fewer paper napkins. Each American uses just over six paper napkins a day, amounting to twenty-two hundred per year. Use a biodegradable detergent to clean the dishes.

Ask your office manager to switch to fair-trade, shade-grown coffee and replace standard coffee filters with a reusable one. Shade-grown coffee protects biodiversity in coffee-growing countries, and a reusable coffee filter will reduce trash. If you do use a disposable coffee filter, remember that it can be composted along with the coffee grounds—volunteer to bring the compost home, or rotate the responsibility.

I'm not a coffee drinker, but some people claim that a second pot of coffee can be made by adding half the usual amount of new coffee grounds to the old, without a significant difference in taste.

Ditch the Disposables

Instead of this	Use this
Disposable cup	Ceramic coffee mug
Disposable stirrer	Nonplastic spoon
Individual packets of sugar and cream	Loose or bulk packaging
Paper napkins	Cloth napkins or handkerchiefs from home
Regular coffee	Fair-trade, shade-grown coffee
Disposable coffee filter	Reusable coffee filter

> **GO GREEN**
>
> Employees use twice as much energy commuting to work as they do occupying their offices.

PURCHASING

One of the most significant ways that workplaces can help the planet is by leveraging their purchasing power. When the federal government mandated that all offices purchase 30 percent post-consumer recycled paper, the price plummeted. What you buy at work can affect both the price and availability of green products for all of us.

Green Purchasing Power

Instead of this	Use this
Single-use items	Reusable/durable supplies, like rechargeable batteries and mechanical pencils
Regular paper and envelopes	Products with the maximum postconsumer recycled content available, including envelopes, copy paper, business cards, forms, and stationery. Also look for unbleached paper products.
Standard fax machine	Bond-paper fax machines
Desktop computers	Laptops—they can use up to 90 percent less energy than the standard desktop
Laser printers	Ink-jet printers; they require almost 90 percent less energy than laser printers
Single-sided printers	Printers with double-sided capabilities
Single-sided copiers	Photocopiers with automatic double-sided capabilities so that double-sided copies can be made quickly and easily. Also be sure to select photocopiers with an automatic energy-saving standby feature.
Standard electronic equipment	Equipment that carries the Energy Star label (http://www.energystar.gov)
Single-use packaging	Bulk items with minimal packaging

GETTING THERE: GREENING YOUR COMMUTE

Ridesharing

Share a ride to save money, reduce toxic fumes, and lower your stress level. For a 40-mile round-trip commute, you could save $2,726 in one year by ridesharing. Advertise at work, on community bulletin boards, or on http://www.craigslist.org.

> **GO GREEN**
>
> If every commuter in America carpooled with one other person to work, we would save 600,000 gallons of gas every day.

Car maintenance and driving habits

Getting oil and air filters changed regularly and having your tires properly inflated can increase your miles per gallon by 20 percent or more. Improve mileage even further by accelerating gently, avoiding sudden stops and starts, and using cruise control on the highway while commuting to work.

> **SAVE GREEN**
>
> The average American could save about $64 a year by maintaining proper tire pressure. Invest in a $2 tire gauge and check tires every month.

Public transportation

Only 4 percent of Americans use public transportation regularly to get to work. If public transportation is available in your area, try taking a bus, train, or subway once a week or more. Let someone else deal with the stress of traffic while you catch up on reading, work, or even sleep. A full-size transit bus seats forty people, meaning there are forty fewer cars on the road.

Talk to your employer about providing a tax-advantage spending account to cover the cost of riding the bus, train, or subway. With this account, employees can pay for mass transit with pretax dollars.

Biking

Commuting by bike is the cheapest way to get around town on wheels. Consider combining your workout with your commute by riding your bicycle to work. Not only will you trim your body, but you'll also save money and contribute less to air pollution.

Allow plenty of time for the commute, and keep extra clothes, deodorant, and a washcloth handy at the office. If facilities are available, consider showering when you arrive at work instead of at home.

Working from home

More companies now offer employees the option of working from home, a practice often referred to as telecommuting. Instant messaging, videoconferencing, and other innovative technologies make telecommuting a viable option in many fields. Studies have shown that telecommuting actually improves productivity.

If your company doesn't already offer this option, talk to your employer about the possibility of telecommuting one or more days each week.

Four-day workweek

If telecommuting isn't an option, consider a consolidated work-week—working four 10-hour days instead of five 8-hour days. Readjusting your work schedule could cut the energy and time spent on commuting by 20 percent. Many employees relish three-day weekends, which allow for more time with family.

GREENING YOUR WORK WARDROBE

Want to achieve a professional look for work without draining natural resources—or your wallet? Shop thrift stores. Some people donate never-worn items with tags still attached. Look for classic pieces that can be accessorized and that won't go out of style. If you buy new, look for clothes made with organic or recycled fibers. Avoid "dry clean only" pieces.

Dress for the weather

Pay attention to the weather report and dress accordingly. Ask employers to relax the dress code on Fridays in summer so men don't have to wear ties or jackets. When the weather turns cool, keep extra layers at work.

Cost Benefits of Telecommuting

- Less wear and tear on your car, which means fewer trips to the mechanic

- Lower gasoline bill and fewer $50 fill-ups

- Less need for fancy clothes since you can work in your sweats.

- Less dry cleaning means you save money and avoid nasty chemicals

- No need to blow-dry your hair, which saves time *and* electricity

- Less need for makeup so you keep chemicals off your skin and out of the water stream

- No tempting restaurants, which allows you to eat healthier and save money

Spot cleaning and airing out

Does your entire outfit need to be washed every time you wear it? Many clothes can be spot-cleaned and aired out before returning to the closet. Save water, energy, and time by only washing clothes when they really need it.

Sometimes Dreams Come True

For the first seven years I was married, I worked in an office. The minute I got home, I changed out of my suit and into jeans. My dream was to work someplace I didn't have to wear panty hose.

That dream has come true. I now work at home, where I no longer need a separate work wardrobe. Dress clothes are reserved for special occasions.

Matthew was a student during my office years, studying to become a doctor. Medicine is one of the few jobs where people can wear pajamas (scrubs) to work. When Matthew left the ER, he thought he'd never be able to work in pj's again.

Fortunately, Matthew's work wardrobe has remained pretty uncomplicated. About half the time Matthew is on the road, where he wears one of his two professional outfits. The other half of the time, he writes at home—often in his scrubs!

Not only is our lack of fashion-consciousness frugal and green, but it's also biblically based. The world says that "clothes make the man," but Jesus shares a very different message in Luke 12:27, one our whole family has adopted. None of us can ever be as beautifully clothed as the lilies of the field, so why toil in vain pursuits?

My idea of wardrobe heaven? Well-worn jeans, a comfy T-shirt, and clogs with good arch support!

THE OFFICE BUILDING

Temperature

In many offices, the heating and cooling is centrally controlled. If this is true where you work, suggest that the temperature be turned up three degrees in summer and down three degrees in winter. Your employer will save money while helping the planet.

If you do have some control over the temperature, use a fan rather than air-conditioning in warm months. Air-conditioning is the second largest energy user in commercial buildings, accounting for about 15 percent of total consumption. If possible, close blinds and drapes to block out the sun and keep your area cool.

In the cold months, leave an extra sweater at work and keep blinds open to allow the sun to heat the room; if it's not sunny outside, close the blinds to trap the heat.

Lighting

Make the most of natural lighting in your workspace. Not only is it free, but also natural light has been shown to boost worker productivity and improve moods. You're also less likely to suffer from eye fatigue due to glare.

To use less electricity when the lights must be on, replace incandescent bulbs in your office with compact fluorescents. Consider purchasing LED desk lamps that use even less energy, and limit your use of overhead lighting.

Always turn off the lights when you step out of your office, even

Alternative Work

Alternative work means that employees can work anywhere (their kitchen table, the back porch) and anytime (after the kids go to bed), as long as the work gets done. Most employees see this option as a net benefit, helping them to juggle their personal and professional lives. For employers, it means less investment in real estate, lower utility and water bills, higher productivity, and a lot of money saved. And we *all* benefit from fewer cars on the road— less rush-hour congestion and less smog—and less building construction.

Some companies are setting up satellite work sites closer to where employees live. Another option is to use public places such as local libraries, cafes, and coffee shops to conduct meetings and get work done so you don't have to commute long distances.

when you think you'll be back in a couple of minutes. Contrary to popular belief, it does not take more energy to turn the lights back on. When you leave the restroom, turn off the lights. Take initiative and flip the switch when passing by empty rooms where lights have been left on.

Encourage your employer to replace exit-sign lightbulbs with LEDs. Because exit signs are on 24-7, the payback is very quick—usually just a couple of months.

> **GO GREEN** Lighting an average-sized empty office overnight wastes enough electricity to make one thousand hot drinks or print eight hundred sheets of paper.

Smart cleaning

According to the U.S. Environmental Protection Agency, the air inside a typical building is two to five times more polluted than the air outside. Many cleaning products contribute to indoor air pollution and contain toxic chemicals. They also can contribute to skin irritation, respiratory problems, and cancer in workers regularly exposed to their fumes.

Fortunately, it's getting easier than ever to clean with nontoxic products. Companies like Nature Clean, Ecover, Shaklee, Seventh Generation, and Clorox make biodegradable cleaners without toxic ingredients. Talk to your office manager or someone on the janitorial staff about choosing cleaning supplies with the following descriptions on their packaging:

- Nontoxic
- Renewable
- Plant-based ingredients
- Chlorine- and ammonia-free
- Nonaerosol
- Biodegradable

- Phosphate-free
- No animal ingredients
- Cruelty free
- Hypoallergenic
- Recycled or recyclable packaging

When cleaning your own office, avoid using paper towels and choose reusable cloths instead. For necessary paper products like bathroom tissue, look for postconsumer recycled content and non-chlorine bleaching or unbleached products.

Coming Clean

Would Jesus have reached out to the cleaning staff and had compassion for them? One way to thank your cleaning crew is to encourage the use of safe cleaning products in your workplace.

While at a speaking engagement, Matthew had the pleasure of meeting Stephen Ashkin, a man whose entire ministry is devoted to helping the often overlooked population of janitors and custodians. Many are exposed to toxic cleaning products, all day, every day. Steve, considered the "father of green cleaning," literally wrote the book on the subject.

Visit http://www.greencleaningnetwork.org to learn more about how you can keep your workplace clean without polluting the planet—or harming those responsible for cleaning up after you.

The High Cost of Indoor Air Pollution

- Allergies
- Asthma
- Sinusitis
- Autoimmune responses
- Increased absenteeism
- Low productivity and poor performance

Air quality: Getting real with plants

Replacing silk plants with real ones adds natural beauty to your office while improving the quality of indoor air. Keep this in mind especially if you work in a newer building that is tightly sealed to conserve energy. Live indoor plants also provide a natural defense against harmful pollutants from synthetic carpeting and fabrics, wallpaper coated in plastic, or laminated countertops, often found in older buildings.

LEED certification

In the 1990s, the federal government began constructing Leadership in Energy and Environmental Design (LEED) certified buildings, and the private sector soon followed. The average LEED-certified building uses 30 percent less energy, 30 to 50 percent less water, and diverts up to 97 percent of its waste from the landfill compared with a conventional building.

If you are building a new office, consider LEED certification. This move sets an example for other businesses and sends a message to your clients and the community that your organization cares about the environment. Find out more from the U.S. Green Building Council at http://www.usgbc.org.

ON THE ROAD AGAIN: WORK TRAVEL

Teleconferencing

Could your business be conducted without the high economic and environmental costs of business trips? Traveling less is one of the simplest, most effective ways to significantly lower your company's carbon footprint *and* save money. You can save travel costs, conserve employee time, and reduce pollution by using teleconferencing or videoconferencing.

Traveling smart

If work obligations make travel absolutely necessary, take a bus or train, carpool, or choose direct flights whenever possible.

Nonstop flights use less energy than multisegment flights because a tremendous amount of energy is consumed by taking off and landing repeatedly, and because flying to hubs can add hundreds of extra miles to your trip.

Stay at hotels that make caring for the environment a priority. If staying in a hotel more than one night, do not have your sheets or towels washed until you check out. You can view an index of green hotels at http://www.istaygreen.org.

Get a Green Job

If all this talk about environmental stewardship around the office has gotten you excited, now is a great time to consider an environmental job. Conservation organizations and sustainable energy companies need qualified, dependable individuals to work in a wide array of capacities. View the environmental jobs directory online at http://www.ecobusinesslinks.com/environmental_jobs.htm.

How to Save Money This Year

(Actual savings will vary according to distance from work, family situation, etc.)

Bring lunch from home instead of eating out	$400
Purchase half of your work wardrobe from thrift stores	$250
Cut back on dry cleaning	$100
Share a ride to work	$1,400
Work alternative schedule to reduce childcare costs	$3,600
TOTAL	**$5,750**

. . . And Share It with Those in Need

What could you do with $5,750 in savings?

- Help eleven entrepreneurs in third-world countries launch small businesses to support their families and meet basic needs through http://www.kiva.org. Kiva is a micro-lending organization that allows individuals to lend directly to entrepreneurs in developing countries. Loans are generally repaid within six months to a year. When you get your money back, you can relend to someone else in need.

- Provide disadvantaged women with suitable professional attire, a support network, and career development tools to help them achieve economic independence through http://www.dressforsuccess.org.

- Support a job skills program such as http://www.yearup.org, where urban youth from the ages of eighteen to twenty-four receive mentorship, training, and apprenticeships, or donate directly to your local Goodwill job training program.

- Support a prison ministry that provides job skills for reentry. To find a prison ministry near you, visit http://www.prisonministry.net, or call area churches and ask about their prison outreach programs.

↗ Putting Your Faith into Action

Dear heavenly Father, help me today to honor you in my work and to exercise wisdom and discernment when using the resources you put into my care. Fill my heart with gratitude for your daily provisions and help me take personal action to become a better steward at my workplace. Teach me to become a servant leader of environmental stewardship through the way I live and work. Give me courage and perseverance as I learn to care for your creation. Strengthen my desire to make you Lord over every area of my life.

Lord, help me *today* to:

- turn off the lights when I leave my workspace, and choose natural light if possible
- switch off my computer, printer, and peripherals when I leave work for the day
- turn off the water while washing my hands
- turn the thermostat up three or more degrees in warm months and down three or more degrees in cold months
- activate my computer's standby mode setting
- set my printer to double-sided default
- bring my own coffee mug to work and skip the paper or Styrofoam cups
- set up a recycling box and bring home the recyclables myself if there is no recycling program at work
- pray that my work habits would reflect Christ's love for people and creation

Lord, help me *this week* to:

- carpool with someone who lives and works near me
- print documents only when necessary; think before I print
- reuse envelopes and packaging products in the office
- take the stairs instead of the elevator
- use draft mode for printing when documents aren't yet final
- give up two restaurant lunches; bring a healthy lunch from home in reusable containers instead
- investigate ink cartridge and e-waste recycling opportunities

Lord, help me *this month* to:

- talk to my employer about the possibility of telecommuting one day a week or working a four-day week
- set up a recycling program at work, or help support one already in place
- post reminders next to light switches to turn off lights when leaving the room
- switch to refillable pens, pencils, ink cartridges
- shop at a thrift store when I need to purchase work clothes
- dress for the weather in my office to minimize heat or AC use
- set up a rideshare board to encourage others to carpool

Lord, help me *this year* to:

- encourage my employer to recycle electronics
- bring live plants to work to improve indoor air quality
- carpool, use public transportation, walk, or bike to work
- start or participate in a green team
- facilitate an energy audit
- encourage my employer to switch to nontoxic cleaning supplies

Summing It Up

Getting Started
I have:

- ○ turned off lights when leaving the room
- ○ activated my computer's energy-saving function
- ○ adjusted my office's thermostat at least three degrees
- ○ used the draft function to print documents that are not final
- ○ only printed out documents when a hard copy is absolutely necessary
- ○ used paper with at least 30 percent postconsumer content

On the Journey
I have:

- ○ started a recycling program at my workplace
- ○ brought live plants to work
- ○ walked, biked, used public transportation, or carpooled to work at least twice a week
- ○ worked from home one day a week, or negotiated a four-day workweek
- ○ advocated for nontoxic cleaning supplies
- ○ replaced incandescent bulbs with energy-saving bulbs

Green Superstar
I have:

- ○ stopped using disposable tableware for meals
- ○ walked, biked, carpooled, or taken public transportation to work the majority of the time
- ○ purchased at least half of my work clothes at a thrift shop or secondhand store
- ○ brought lunch from home in reusable containers
- ○ started or participated in a green team at work
- ○ donated money saved to a worthy cause

Energy—electricity, wood, coal, gasoline, propane, and oil—is like food. It is a blessing, and it sustains us. Our relationship to God's gifts can be one of entitlement, ignorance, and gluttony or one of praise, thanks, and temperance.

When was the last time you bowed your head in thanks when filling your car with gasoline? If you haven't done so, is it because you don't think it's a blessing?

—*Serve God, Save the Planet*

Our generation has a choice. On the one hand, we can keep flying too high and continue thoughtlessly harming God's creation with unrestrained plane travel and the pollution that goes with it. Or . . . we can break the "rules" and choose to travel less frequently and less far. You don't have to step onto that plane. It might just save the world.

—*It's Easy Being Green*

Transportation

Save Gas, Save Money, Save Lives

*As he rode along, the crowds spread out their garments on
the road ahead of him. When he reached the place where the
road started down the Mount of Olives, all of his followers
began to shout and sing as they walked along, praising God
for all the wonderful miracles they had seen.*

LUKE 19:36-37, NLT

I HAVE BEEN CAR-LESS FOR FOUR DAYS . . . and loving it.

Yesterday morning, I decided to go for a swim, but first I got a
bit of extra exercise by biking the half mile to the pool. Midday, I
needed to ship three packages, so I put them in my backpack and
pedaled to the post office. Toward the end of the day, I biked to
the bank—and picked up a couple of items at the grocery store.
Tomorrow I will be taking a Greyhound bus to meet Matthew, so
I walked to campus this evening to say good-bye to our daughter,
Emma, and shared some mother-daughter time before my trip.

When we moved to Kentucky, we intentionally chose a house
where we could walk or bike pretty much everywhere. We only have
one car (a Toyota Prius hybrid). Matthew has to travel for work, but
I've learned that being car-less can be a blessing, not a burden. With
no temptation to hop in the car, I am more deliberate about my day.
I tend to get more work done, spend more time with family and
friends, and visit the gas station only once every few weeks.

If I *need* to get somewhere, I have plenty of neighbors who will share a ride or lend me a vehicle. One generous pastor friend gave us an extra key to his pickup truck. He keeps the truck parked outside his home a few blocks from us, and we are welcome to use it at any time. When his truck lost the muffler, we were only too happy to cover the repairs—a small thanks for two years of carte blanche use of his truck—and he was grateful for the much quieter exhaust system.

Unlike most teenagers, our kids did not rush to get their licenses when they turned sixteen. Clark got his permit at age fifteen, but did not take his driver's test until the summer after he turned nineteen—when he needed a car for medical school. We helped him purchase an economical and environmentally responsible Geo Metro that gets 45 mpg. It is ten years old and has 50,000 miles on it. The paint job isn't pretty, but the purchase price was beautiful: $3,000.

Emma, eighteen, is a junior in college. She's about to take the test for her Kentucky driver's permit so she can get plenty of practice before she graduates. As parents, Matthew and I want to encourage responsibility and independence, not a mall-centered lifestyle. Our children know that driving is not a right—it's a privilege that must be earned.

The Lord directs the steps of the godly.
PSALM 37:23, NLT

We have good reason for not hurrying to get our kids behind the wheel. For more than a decade, my husband worked as an emergency room doctor. Telling parents that their child had been maimed or killed in a crash was one of the most difficult parts of Matthew's job.

Motor vehicle accidents are by far the most common way for teenagers to lose their lives. Mile for mile, teens wreck their cars four times as often as older drivers. Nearly half of the car fatalities involving sixteen-year-olds are single car accidents. Delaying a license by a few years has kept our teens safer, saved on insurance, left the planet cleaner, and encouraged employment and fellowship close to home.

As far as we know, Jesus only rode one time, and that was on a borrowed colt. Much of the world today still cannot afford one personal vehicle, much less two or three cars per household. If the world were a village of one hundred people, only seven would own an automobile.

In our vehicle-based American culture, I treasure the times when Matthew has the car. If nothing else, these short respites give my body a bit of extra exercise, my soul some peace away from traffic, and my heart a chance to beat in time with our Lord, who accomplished all of his great works on foot.

Heavenly Father, thank you for reprieves from the car, from traffic, and from the constant running around that pulls me away from you. Thank you for the rabbit that crossed my path on my walk this evening, and for the cows that stopped munching in the field while I passed, and for the purple and orange sunset that graced us all—but which we seldom pause to see. Help me to conserve our finite resources and share them with those around the world who are less fortunate, as well as with future generations. Remind me to travel on foot, even when a car is available, so that I can walk more closely in your path.

GETTING STARTED

People get behind the wheel for an astounding 1.1 billion trips every day in the United States. With many of us commuting an hour or more each day, it is little wonder that our choice of vehicles has the greatest environmental impact of any decision we make. Driving a sports utility vehicle that gets 13 mpg for one year wastes more energy than leaving the refrigerator door open for six years, the light on in the bathroom for thirty years, or the TV turned on for twenty-eight years.

One of the first ways you can cut back on transportation costs is to pay attention to the things that are within walking or biking distance of your home—the convenience store, video shop, school, soccer field, playground. Make it a point to walk to these places at least once a week. Most children will consider it an adventure to travel someplace without a car, and will appreciate the time spent alone with Mom or Dad.

Wherever you're going, keep in mind that less is more—less driving and distance means more time for family, friends, and fellowship. Bikes, buses, and other forms of mass transit can transform your rush-hour stress into a time to exercise, read, or listen to music. Staying close to home on your next family vacation means less time traveling and more time having fun. Combining trips, walking to nearby destinations, and carpooling result in big savings at the gas pump and more money in your pocket.

Serving others while serving our Creator—now *that's* a journey worth taking.

DAY-TO-DAY TRANSPORTATION

Everything about our lives seems to be geared toward instant gratification, getting what we want quickly and easily. Yet there is nothing quick or easy about sitting in rush-hour traffic, filling our tanks at the gas station, or working an extra job so we can cover car payments, repairs, and insurance costs. So often we jump in our cars for short trips to the grocery store or post office, when walking or biking would be better for our bodies and for the environment.

Each summer, elevated levels of smog pollution send 159,000 people to the emergency room, cause 53,000 people to be admitted to the hospital, and induce 6 million asthma attacks.

Walking

Exhaust from our vehicles contributes to smog; every year 30,000 Americans die from smog-related symptoms—more than the number killed in traffic accidents. One way we can show our love for our neighbors is by reducing our personal contribution to air pollution.

The next time your destination is within walking distance, leave the car in the driveway and get your 10,000 recommended daily steps while lessening your impact on the environment. Giving your car a rest will keep you fit, save gas, and leave more money in your wallet.

Biking

Bike riding isn't just for kids. Research shows that trips less than 3 miles (half of all trips!) can be covered just as quickly on a bike. Biking tones muscles, improves heart rates, and gives a mind-clearing break.

If your job situation allows, consider biking to work. You could save more than $75 per week by biking 30 miles round-trip each workday.

Healthy biking

Wondering about the impact of traffic fumes on bikers? Now you can breathe easy. Riding a bike is at least as safe for your lungs as driving, if not more so. Harmful particles from car, bus, and taxi engines are most intense in the middle of the traffic zone and less dangerous around the edges where bikers remain. Studies show

Creating a Bike Route

- **Be safe.** If you have never seen a cyclist on your normal route to work, look for a bike route with bike lanes and wide shoulders.

- **Use a map.** Check to see if your city or local bike club offers maps of safe biking routes in your area.

- **Get a second opinion.** After choosing a potential route, ask other cyclists if they consider your route safe.

- **Take action.** Visit the League of American Bicyclists' Web site at http://www.bikeleague.org to find out how to bring better bicycling to your community.

that car passengers are affected the most by harmful particles—including carbon monoxide and benzene.

Community bike programs

Community bike programs (also called yellow bike, white bike, or shared bike programs) are becoming increasingly popular in the United States. These programs provide free (or nearly free) access to bicycles for inner-city transport, with the goal of reducing the use of automobiles for short trips inside the city and diminishing traffic congestion, noise, and air pollution.

In many cities, the fleets are painted yellow or white so they can be easily distinguished, and stations are set up all over the city. Patrons can ride the bikes one way and return them to the most convenient station. As many as fifteen different users can ride the same bike in one day.

If your city does not have a community bike program, get one

Car Pool Savings

As of 2008, the American Automobile Association estimates that it costs an average of $0.541 per mile to drive a car. This figure includes gasoline, oil, maintenance, tires, and depreciation. However, tolls and parking—plus insurance and registration—are additional. See the chart below to determine how much you could be saving by sharing a ride to work with someone.

COMMUTING COSTS

Daily cost (30-mile round-trip commute)	$16.23
Monthly cost (30-mile round-trip commute)	$373.29
Annual cost (30-mile round-trip commute)	$4,479.48

POTENTIAL SAVINGS

Ridesharing annual savings (two-person car pool, 30-mile round-trip)	$2,239.74
Ridesharing annual savings (two-person car pool, 60-mile round-trip)	$4,479.48
Ridesharing annual savings (four-person car pool, 60-mile round-trip)	$6,719.22

started. To learn how, visit http://www.ibike.org/encouragement/freebike.

Sharing the ride

Tired of your daily drive to work? The average commuter in America travels 30 miles each day to and from work. By carpooling with someone, you could save 7,500 miles in one year—and about 300 gallons of gas! Talk to a friend or neighbor whose destination is near yours about sharing rides. Or find a ride online at sites like http://www.craigslist.org (under "community," click on "rideshare") or on http://www.erideshare.com.

Telecommuting

Talk to your employer about the possibility of a four-day workweek, or telecommuting (working from home) at least one day a week. Telecommuting makes economic sense, saving on office space and parking. Less commuting means happier, more productive employees, and fewer people on the road results in less traffic and smog.

Public transportation

Six out of ten Americans have access to public transportation, but only 10 percent use it with some frequency; only 4 percent use it regularly to get to work.

If public transportation is available in your area, consider taking the bus or train instead of riding in your car. Be thankful that someone else is at the wheel, and take advantage of the extra time to read, pray, or meditate. You will save gas money, lessen the wear and tear on your car, and reduce your stress level.

SAVE GREEN

The average annual cost of driving a single-occupant car is between $4,826 and $9,685. Compare that to the average cost of a year's worth of public transportation: $200 to $2,000.

BUSED   .

You whom I have upheld since you were conceived, and have carried since your birth. Even to your old age and gray hairs I am he, I am he who will sustain you. I have made you and I will carry you. —Isaiah 46:3-4

A recent journey to Knoxville marked my first bus trip in years. When I was young, my mother used to put me and my sister on a Greyhound bus to visit our grandparents, our names and phone numbers securely pinned on our jackets. We always sat directly behind the bus driver, who let us know when we reached our destination.

Once, my grandfather forgot to pick us up—what an adventure! I still remember the people we saw at the station while waiting—young people sleeping on knapsacks, bleary parents rocking babies, people speaking foreign languages and dressed in exotic clothes—all so different from the suburban neighborhood we had left behind.

Things have not changed much; taking the bus is still an adventure. When I arrived at the station, the clerk retrieved my online reservation and handed me a ticket. A group in one corner spoke softly in Spanish, frequently interrupted by the universal language—laughter. In another corner, a young couple looked teary eyed as they got ready to part. The man and woman sitting nearest me were sporting matching cowboy boots and Western-cut shirts. A little boy wrapped in a blanket slept peacefully in his father's lap.

When my bus was called, I found a seat near the front, and for two hours, I enjoyed the peace of letting someone else drive. I wrote and read for most of the journey. When we stopped at a fast-food restaurant, which doubled as a station, I got out to stretch my legs. Some passengers took a cigarette break; others grabbed a bite to eat.

Just before we reached Knoxville, a man asked to borrow my pencil, then thanked me profusely. I also felt grateful—for this space to write, to read, to look out the window without interruption. Everyone, from the driver to my fellow passengers, was courteous and thoughtful.

My husband was waiting for me at the station in Knoxville.

I thanked the driver, gave my husband a hug, then said a prayer of gratitude for the safe journey.

Dear Lord, thank you for bus drivers and bus station attendants and the energy that fuels our travel. Thank you for getting millions of people safely to their destinations every day. Just as the father carried the baby in his arms, please carry us in your arms, dear Father, and help us to become messengers of your love. Help us to choose forms of travel that best use the resources that you have so graciously put in our care.

GO GREEN

Buses are often the least expensive and most energy-efficient form of transportation. A motor coach bus gets an average of 184.4 passenger miles per gallon—compared to 101.1 mpg for a van pool, 85.8 for a commuter rail, and 27.7 for the average car. Pack a lunch, enjoy the scenery, and let someone else drive.

Scooters and electric bikes

Instead of purchasing or replacing a second car for your household, consider a small scooter or electric bicycle. Three out of every four times we hop in the car, we travel alone. Purchase a 49cc scooter engine and you can get up to 100 mpg; in most states, you will not need a special license to drive scooters under 50cc. Because scooters have automatic transmissions, they are much easier to drive than motorcycles.

One student we know who attends a very large state university bought a slightly used 49cc scooter for $700. She can travel nearly 100 miles on one gallon of gasoline; the scooter can't go over 40 mph, but that's fast enough to get her everywhere she needs to go, with much less impact on the environment and her wallet than even the most energy-efficient car.

Some good friends in Lexington also bought a 49cc scooter. Lisa is about my age and has three children. She runs errands and takes her preteen/teen kids to after-school activities on the bright yellow scooter—she's the coolest mom in town. Her scooter tops out at 35 mph, which is as fast as she needs to go in town, and their gasoline bill has dropped dramatically.

Visit http://www.electric-scooter-world.com to learn about scooters and compare different types, and http://www.motorcycle.com/categories/scooter.html to read reviews.

CARS

Cars are a major drain on our budgets and the environment. If you want to know the real cost of car ownership, check out the Edmunds.com True Cost to Own calculator at http://www.edmunds.com/

The Hidden Cost of Driving

From insurance to road maintenance, the true cost of driving is more than what you pay at the car dealership or at the pump. The government subsidizes car travel by $32 *billion* per year! The real cost always trickles down to us, the taxpayer, through:

- insurance

- wear and tear/depreciation

- road construction

- traffic lights and road signage

- snow removal and mowing

- road repairs

- police enforcement

- "free" municipal parking

- medical costs of treating asthma and respiratory illnesses

- missed days of work due to air pollution

- water runoff abatement

apps/cto/CTOintroController. Just plug in the make, model, and year of your car, or the one you are considering, and see how much car ownership really costs.

As an example of how a new car can bite into a family's budget, I plugged the information for a 2009 Camry SE sedan into Edmunds.com True Cost to Own calculator:

	YEAR 1	YEAR 2	YEAR 3	YEAR 4	YEAR 5	TOTAL
Depreciation	$3,009	$2,513	$2,212	$1,961	$1,759	$11,454
Financing	$1,357	$1,094	$812	$510	$185	$3,958
Insurance	$1,339	$1,386	$1,434	$1,485	$1,507	$7,151
Taxes and Fees	$1,354	$15	$15	$15	$15	$1,414
Fuel	$2,272	$2,340	$2,410	$2,482	$2,556	$12,060
Maintenance	$390	$633	$535	$844	$1,471	$3,873
Repairs	$0	$0	$97	$234	$340	$671
YEARLY TOTALS	**$9,721**	**$7,981**	**$7,515**	**$7,531**	**$7,833**	**$40,581**

Now that's encouraging: by owning only one car, Matthew and I save more than $8,000 per year!

Hybrids

If you're in the market for a new car, consider a hybrid. With gas prices skyrocketing, you'll quickly notice a difference at the pump; hybrids like the Toyota Prius can get double the miles per gallon of similarly sized cars. In addition, a hybrid's engine burns fuel more cleanly and gives off about half the emissions. To save even more, check to see if you are eligible to receive a federal tax credit for purchasing a hybrid vehicle.

SAVE GREEN

Still not convinced that a hybrid is for you? Check out the savings you can reap in fuel costs: A conventional car will cost you about $43 in fuel per week, or $11,180 over five years' time. A hybrid is less than half that: $22 per week, or $5,720 over five years.

Our Love Affair with the (Hybrid) Automobile

At the turn of the last millennium, when it came time to replace our Camry, we decided to investigate the new hybrids.

We had exactly two hybrid models to choose from: the early Toyota Prius and the Honda Insight. At the time, Matthew was still a practicing ER physician with a sixty-minute commute. We test-drove the Prius sedan and the two-seater Insight. The Prius was nice, but it "only" got 41 mpg. The Insight was rated at more than 60 mpg. At first I thought that the Insight would be impractical for a family of four, until we realized that 90 percent of the miles we drove were with two or fewer people.

No one wanted to be the guinea pig for this new technology, so the two Insights just sat on the showroom lot of our local Honda dealer. We watched the price fall month after month. By the time it hit $15,000 with the federal tax credit—still a lot of money, but not bad for a new car—we decided to make the leap.

My daughter christened our 2001 Insight the "Jelly Bean Car," saying it looked like a jelly bean on steroids; Matthew called it the "George Jetson Car." For the first few years, nearly every time I stopped in a parking lot, someone would come up to ask about the car. It was a great conversation starter and allowed us to share our gospel of green living.

In 2005, we replaced our second car with the reengineered and vastly improved Prius, which now gets about 50 mpg and holds up to five passengers. Both cars proved to be incredibly reliable—no major repairs—and we only had to fuel up every few weeks.

When we moved to Kentucky and chose a house within walking distance of everything, we decided it was time to let one of our hybrids go. Because we need to seat at least four adults, we kept the Prius and sold our beloved Insight.

Honda discontinued the Insight in 2006, but is reintroducing an economical and roomier five-seater model in 2009. The Prius is in higher demand than ever. In many regions, people have to get on a waiting list to purchase a Prius, and a used Prius demands a premium price.

Sometimes people who are purchasing a new car tell me that they can't afford to buy a hybrid. I agree—they are expensive, but no more than other new cars. The average price of a new automobile in 2008 was $28,715. The sticker price of the standard model 2008 Prius is only $20,950, though in reality, most Prius hybrids sell for more—the cheapest one I could find in my area was $24,300. But even so, that's still $4,500 *less* than the average new car.

Used cars

Yes, new cars may look shiny and sleek, but they can depreciate in value as much as 35 percent in the first year. The manufacturing process accounts for 9 percent of the energy used by a car over its lifetime, and buying a used vehicle saves over 2,150 pounds of steel. By not creating demand for another new car, you are helping reduce your impact on the planet.

Small cars

If you aren't ready for a hybrid, purchase the smallest car that will accommodate your family. A smaller car can save between $300 and $700 a year in fuel costs and more than 2 tons of greenhouse gases. Look for cars that get at least 30 mpg. Visit http://www.fuel economy.gov/feg to compare car models, read tips on improving gas mileage, and evaluate the energy efficiency of your current car.

Smaller vehicles also emit less CO_2 into the air. In this case, less is definitely more. Consider the following:

CAR	FUEL EFFICIENCY	ANNUAL CO_2 EMISSIONS
Large SUV	12 mpg	13.0 tons
Six-cylinder family wagon	20 mpg	8.0 tons
Four-seat sedan	25 mpg	6.5 tons
Hybrid (Prius)	47 mpg	4.0 tons

Cheap Wheels

When our son, Clark, recently moved to his own apartment and needed to purchase a car for medical school, he considered fuel economy, safety, and price. The top cars on his wish list were a low-mileage Geo Metro, Toyota Corolla, Chevy Prism (essentially the same as a Toyota Corolla, but less expensive), and Honda Civic. When a ten-year-old Geo Metro showed up on Craigslist with only 50,000 miles and a $3,000 price tag, he grabbed it. Clark is getting 45 mpg and doesn't have to worry about his car being stolen—it's clean and serviceable, but not exactly a showstopper.

With Clark now the primary driver of the Metro, our total premium actually fell a couple hundred dollars when we insured two cars instead of the Prius alone.

Shop with Your Conscience

When it comes to the automobile industry, all companies are not created equal. In *The Better World Shopping Guide*, Ellis Jones ranks car companies according to socially responsible criteria, including the environment, human rights, community involvement, animal protection, corporate crime, discrimination, employee treatment, and philanthropy. Using these criteria, the guide lists Toyota as the most ethical car manufacturer, with Lexus, Scion, Honda, and Acura also receiving high marks. The lowest ratings go to Mitsubishi, Buick, Cadillac, Saturn, Chevrolet, GMC, SAAB, Hummer, and Pontiac.

> Our conscious relationship with God is enhanced if we treat all the things He has made in the same way as He treats them. —*Francis Schaeffer (1912–1984), Pollution and the Death of Man*

To see how your car rates, visit http://www.betterworldshopper.com/r-cars.html.

Car Share

If you drive less than 7,500 miles per year and you don't use a car for work every day, car sharing can save you thousands of dollars a year, give you greater mobility, and reduce pollution.

About 75 percent of Americans live in cities. Many people don't drive enough to justify the expense and hassle of owning a car, yet they don't want to give up the freedom of driving a car when they want to. Car sharing provides instant access to a network of cars throughout the city, twenty-four hours a day. You can select the kind of vehicle you need—car, van, or truck—and pay per trip. No need to worry about repairs, insurance, or monthly parking. And because you are paying per use—and see the hidden cost of cars up front—you have more incentive to walk, bike, or use public transportation when possible. Visit http://www.carsharing.net to see if there is a car sharing program in your city.

At the Pump

When driving a car is the only viable mode of transportation, our choice of fuel can affect how we impact the planet. Try to purchase

More than Just Smog

- The manufacture and use of automobiles makes up 20 to 25 percent of carbon dioxide emissions. In the United States, the typical car also emits 3.4 grams of carbon monoxide *per mile*. Emissions from cars leave an ugly and unhealthy dome of smog hanging over most cities.

- Automobile traffic contributes significantly to noise pollution.

- Increased road building negatively affects wildlife by breaking up their habitats and altering surface runoff. New roads built through sensitive habitats can damage ecosystems.

- The materials required for roads come from large-scale rock quarrying and gravel extraction, which can harm sensitive ecological areas.

- Road construction also alters the water table, increases surface runoff, and raises the risk of flooding.

gasoline from companies that are at the high end of the socially responsible list:

- Sunoco, BP, Amoco, and ARCO all earn A ratings from Ellis Jones's *The Better World Shopping Guide*
- Marathon, Ashland, Citgo, Valero, and Beacon earned B ratings
- Total, Hess, Cosco, and Shell earned C ratings
- Conoco, Phillips, 76, Jet, Coastal, Chevron, and Texaco earned D ratings
- Exxon and Mobil earned F ratings

Oil Addiction

In righteousness you will be established: Tyranny will be far from you; you will have nothing to fear. Terror will be far removed; it will not come near you. —ISAIAH 54:14

We all remember where we were when we first heard the news on September 11, 2001. I had walked to the post office, and Vince, the postmaster, told me that some "crazy lunatics had flown a couple airplanes smack into the Twin Towers." I immediately went back home and turned on the radio. It was true. America had been attacked.

Matthew resolved to do something to keep this act of senseless violence from happening again: he wrote an editorial about our addiction to oil. The editorial said that this was a pivotal moment for our nation. The most patriotic thing we could do was not to donate blood, but to end our dependence on foreign oil. Blood donations made people feel like they were doing *something*, but Matthew reminded us that conserving energy would allow us to help not just today or tomorrow—but for decades to come.

Only one paper published the editorial. Though prescient and true, his was not a message that our leaders were ready to convey, or that the American public was prepared to hear. Instead, we were encouraged to go out and spend money. I remember one neighbor who said she was buying a new minivan the week after 9/11 because "it was the patriotic thing to do."

This is not the first time America has given up the moral high ground for the sake of cheap, plentiful energy from foreign soils. Remember the lessons of slavery? Slavery, like oil, is the importation of cheap energy with no regard for its moral cost. States such as Georgia that initially banned slave energy envied the wealth of their neighbors and eventually sanctioned slavery. Our generation, like the antebellum South, has allowed itself to be blinded by a lifestyle built on energy derived from foreign countries that hold very different values.

God does not ask us to take the easy road; he asks us to take the high road. Jesus gave us a new commandment, that we "love each other in the same way I have loved you." Just as there is a right side and a wrong side to the slavery question, there is a high road and a low road on creation care issues. The high road involves stewarding resources carefully and sharing them with our brothers and sisters around the world, as well as with future generations. It means that we may need to sacrifice a little comfort or convenience so that those least able to defend themselves will have clean air to breathe. It means that we may need to vacation closer to home so that petroleum can be used for agriculture—to feed the one billion people who go to bed hungry each night—instead of our cross-country flight.

God instructed us in Genesis 2:15 to tend and protect the Garden. One way I can serve God, and our country, on a daily basis is to conserve precious resources.

Dear God, teach me to pray for the men and women who inflict terror in this country and around the world. Let me not be complacent, but actively seek to question the cause of such acts, including my own hubris, materialism, and dependence on oil over God. Lord, I cannot understand what goes on in the minds of those who kill, but I can no longer pretend that I am blameless. I pray for all of our global neighbors who have lost loved ones through acts of terror. May we remember to ask you to heal our wounds and look to your living Word and the love of Jesus for answers.

Nine Great Things about the High Cost of Gas

- Less traffic—People start combining trips and using public transportation when driving to the mall costs $15 or more!

- More demand for public transportation—Increased demand will result in better service and more convenient public transportation.

- Four-day workweeks and telecommuting—More employers see the wisdom of flexible schedules and allowing employees to work from home.

- More frugality—With gasoline taking a bigger bite out of our budgets, people are turning to old-fashioned frugality. The result? Fewer impulsive purchases, less eating out, and more time for family, neighbors, and God.

- Cheaper insurance—Insurance premiums are determined, in part, by how much people drive. If you telecommute or work a shorter workweek, call your car insurance provider. It could save you 10 to 15 percent on your insurance bill.

- Fewer traffic deaths—Most people know that driving slower consumes less gasoline. Statistically, driving slower also results in fewer traffic deaths and less accidents—another way to love our neighbors.

- Less air pollution–related deaths—Driving slower, and less driving in general, results in less air pollution. J. Paul Leigh, a health economics professor at the University of California in Davis, estimates that at least two thousand lives per year have been saved due to reduced air pollution since gas prices went up.

- Less suburban sprawl—Cities are being revitalized as 30-plus-mile commutes become impractical. Living closer to work means less stress and more time with family.

- Less obesity—The less people drive, the more they will walk or ride their bikes, which results in better overall health. The last time I was in New York City, I was struck by how few people are overweight. One of the biggest reasons is that people walk—a lot! Instead of the rubber hitting the road, let your sneakers hit the sidewalk.

Think you're not driving a gas guzzler? The average U.S. family car travels about 15,000 miles each year. This adds up to 5.8 tons of greenhouse gas pollution and $2,222 in gasoline. If you have two family cars, that's $4,444 in gasoline alone.

High-octane fuel

Unless your owner's manual gives specific instructions, don't buy the more expensive high-octane fuel. If your vehicle was designed to run on 87 octane, filling the tank with 92 octane will not improve your engine power, fuel efficiency, speed, or performance. It will, however, increase your bill by the price of an extra gallon per fill-up.

Biodiesel

Drive a vehicle with a diesel engine? Consider converting to biodiesel. This vegetable oil is made from soy, rapeseed, palm oil, or even leftover restaurant grease, and is compatible with diesel engines. Biodiesel is more energy efficient than other fuels and doesn't contain sulfur pollutants like traditional petrodiesel. Visit http://www .biodiesel.org to learn more about biodiesel engine conversions, making biodiesel from restaurant grease, and the availability of commercial biodiesel in your area. Because biodiesel is not yet widely distributed, most people arrange to pick up a supply of grease from a local restaurant and make their own.

> *Each of you should look not only to your own interests, but also to the interests of others.*
> PHILIPPIANS 2:4

Speed

To save gas and money when you drive, slow down, accelerate gently, avoid sudden starts and stops, and use cruise control on the highway. Driving 55 mph on the highway results in better gas mileage. Higher speeds increase aerodynamic resistance, or drag. When you cruise at speeds above 60 mph, you get 23 percent less gas mileage, or the equivalent of paying 67 cents per gallon more than you would at 55 mph. Race to 75 mph, and your car will use 15 percent more fuel than it would at 65 mph.

Tire Pressure

Want to save 12 cents per gallon? Improve your gas mileage by 3.3 percent by keeping your tires inflated to the proper pressure. Under-inflated tires lower gas mileage by 0.4 percent for every one psi drop in pressure of all four tires. Properly inflated tires also are safer and last longer. The recommended tire pressure for your vehicle should be listed inside the driver's door and in your owner's manual.

Hurry! Hurry!

I have a bad habit of trying to squeeze too many activities into too little time. For years, nearly every week I was the last one in our family to be ready for church. Speeding to church is not the best way to start the Sabbath.

One New Year's, I had the epiphany that this habit was self-ish, since both my husband and my children feel stressed when they don't get places early. I also tend to drive too fast and get tense when I'm running late.

So I changed. Am I always on time now? Of course not. It's so easy to fall back into bad habits, but setting my watch and car clock five minutes ahead has worked wonders. I also have learned that allowing plenty of time to get to my destination makes for better family relations while saving money and stew-arding resources. Better to arrive at church early so I can hug friends, pray, and peacefully enjoy Sabbath time.

Car Maintenance

Getting regular oil changes and air-filter changes and replacing your spark plugs when recommended can increase your miles per gallon by 20 percent.

You might want to consider asking about re-refined motor oil next time your car gets a change. Producing 5 quarts of high-quality re-refined lubricating oil requires only 2 gallons of used oil; 2 barrels of crude oil are needed to produce the same amount of virgin oil. The two most readily available brands are America's Choice and Nature's Choice. For a state-by-state listing of shops that offer re-refined oil, visit http://www.ofee.gov/recycled/refined.asp.

VACATIONS: GETTING AWAY

If you're like most Americans, vacation time is something you dream of fifty weeks out of the year. Ninety-one percent of all adults spend thirteen days each year on vacation, escaping the responsibilities of home and work to relax and reenergize. Vacations can be a great way for families to reconnect and enjoy time together in different surroundings. However, where we go, how we get there, and what we do once we reach our destinations can be detrimental to the planet and our pocketbooks.

At the Car Wash

Which is better—washing your car at home or taking it to a commercial car wash? Ask your local car-wash manager if they recycle the water; if they do, it's more efficient to use a commercial car wash—provided you don't make a special trip to get there.

If you decide to wash your car at home:

- Park the car on your lawn instead of the driveway. It will act as a natural filter for the soap, dirt, and oil that would otherwise flow into storm drains, eventually causing damage to rivers, streams, and other wetlands.

- Use less water. Buy a nozzle for your hose that controls the water flow or use a bucket.

- Use a biodegradable soap like Simple Green Car Wash or Gliptone Wash 'n Glow. Or make your own eco-friendly car wash by using a few squirts of biodegradable liquid dishwashing detergent or laundry detergent mixed with a bucket of water.

GO GREEN

To get to their vacation destinations, 82 percent of Americans drive, 15 percent fly, and only 3 percent take a bus, train, or boat. Only 5 percent of the world's population has ever flown in an airplane.

Air travel

One of the worst things you can do for the environment is to fly. Even if you follow all of the other suggestions in this book, the toxins your travel releases into the air will quickly outweigh other conservation actions.

Why is air travel so bad? For one thing, it is rapidly becoming the largest contributor of greenhouse gas emissions. These toxins can be more damaging to the air and ozone layer because they are released at higher altitudes than ground-level emissions. In fact, their impact is three times greater than road vehicle emissions.

Imagine your family lives in Morehead City, North Carolina, and decides to take a cross-country road trip to San Francisco,

Flying Tips

Can't avoid an occasional flight?

- Use e-tickets. Printing your boarding pass at home allows you to use recycled paper and bypass the check-in counter. Cardboard boarding passes are often difficult to recycle because of the ink used and the magnetic strips placed on the back.

- Bring your own luggage tag. Using a permanent tag saves time at the ticket counter and eliminates waste from flimsy paper tags.

- If possible, only take a carry-on and skip the checked luggage. On average, an airline passenger will wait twenty-five minutes at the carousel to pick up luggage. Also, the electric motors that operate carousels are energy hogs. If you must check a bag, keep it as light as possible. The more weight on the plane, the more energy it uses.

California. If you drove a carbon-producing SUV from coast to coast, it would release only half the emissions of a single, one-way flight of the same distance.

When planning your next getaway, choose a destination closer to home that doesn't require an environmentally damaging flight. Staying closer to home also means less stressful travel and more time for fun.

Ecotourism

Wherever you travel, try to make as little impact on the local ecosystems as possible. Visit sites like http://www.ecotourism.org for hundreds of environmentally sensitive tours, hotels, and destinations and http://www.rainforest-alliance.org/tourism for information on

Simple Steps for Green Travel

1. More and more hotels are becoming eco-friendly because it saves them money. Wherever you stay, use the same linens and towels during your visit. Washing fewer sheets and towels can save up to 40 percent of a hotel's water use.

2. Use online maps instead of paper ones. They're free, and you can print on the blank side of used paper, and then recycle after you're finished. Try http://www.randmcnally.com or http://www.mapquest.com. If you have a GPS navigation system in your car, you can eliminate paper waste altogether. If you have an old map, use it as gift wrap instead of throwing it away.

3. Take public transportation once you reach your destination. In major cities, try http://www.hopstop.com to plan your bus and subway routes. Stay close to the attractions you want to see to cut down on travel costs.

4. Use and refill a nonplastic water bottle, canteen, or thermos during your trip.

5. Skip the souvenirs. Most trinkets end up on a closet shelf—or in the trash. Use a travel journal and digital photographs to capture memories, then only print the photos you like. If you must buy souvenirs, purchase from local manufacturers to help support the local economy.

sustainable travel. Consider traveling during the off-season. By traveling during a less popular time, you can save 40 percent of costs while avoiding crowds and putting less stress on sensitive ecosystems.

Parks

For your next vacation, consider visiting a nearby state park. They offer spectacular scenery, serene settings, and great outdoor activities—an affordable, close-to-home vacation is often the least stressful one. Many parks also offer discounts for state employees and teachers.

Parking It

When we first married, we were high on love and low on earnings. Matthew was in school, and I had just landed my first job as a technical writer, earning $15,000 per year. When it came time for my annual vacation, we decided to visit a local state park. It was everything we needed: cheap, clean, and full of docile deer that would eat right out of our hands.

One morning, we woke up early and decided to rent a fishing boat on the lake. The boatman had a difficult time starting the small motor, but we had the whole lake to ourselves and happily made our way toward the opposite shore. Matthew stayed in the boat while I went for a swim. When it came time to restart the engine, it wouldn't turn over. Finally, it engaged—in gear!—sending my husband over the side of the boat, fully clothed, with no life preserver.

Did I mention that Matthew does not know how to swim?

The boat headed straight for the rocky shore, with me up front, the motor in back, and Matthew desperately trying to keep his head above water. Somehow I got the boat turned around just before it would have crashed, threw Matthew a life jacket and missed him by a mile (it's harder than it looks!), and eventually got close enough to pull him on board.

It was a long time before I would go out on a lake again.

Fortunately, that has been our *only* bad experience at a state park. When we lived in Maine, every summer I took the kids camping with friends at a favorite state park. In Vermont and

New Hampshire, we often went hiking in the majestic local parks and state forests. Here in Kentucky, as recently as two weeks ago, Matthew and I took a last-minute getaway to a state park. We made the reservation late Friday night, packed a lunch Saturday morning, hiked and swam all weekend, ate a lovely dinner in the lodge, and returned Sunday afternoon refreshed and renewed. We used less than 2 gallons of gasoline for the entire trip. Total cost: about the same as the cost of transportation *taxes* on a pair of airline tickets.

Volunteer vacations/mission trips

Want to serve with your family while having fun at the same time? Consider taking a volunteer vacation. Organizations like http://www.globalvolunteers.org coordinate one-, two-, or three-week work trips. You can also try contacting a church, the Salvation Army, or other local mission organizations in the area where

National Park vs. Theme Park Vacation

Trying to decide on your next vacation destination? Consider visiting a national park near where you live. Below is a projection of how much money a family of four would save on a five-day vacation to a national park instead of a theme park. This hypothetical family from Ocean City, New Jersey, decided to visit Acadia National Park in Maine instead of Walt Disney World. They camped in tents instead of staying in hotels and replaced two meals a day from a restaurant with grocery purchases. Their car got 30 mpg and gas cost $4.05 per gallon.

EXPENSE	NATIONAL PARK (MAINE)	THEME PARK (FLORIDA)
Gas (round-trip)	$167	$284
Park entrance fees (four days)	$20	$807
Food	$158	$375
Lodging	$70	$545
TOTAL COST	**$415**	**$2,011**
TOTAL SAVINGS	**$1,596**	

you'd like to serve. Most large churches in the United States organize short-term mission trips and welcome new volunteers. You can also visit http://www.christianvolunteering.org or http://www.missionfinder.org. Instead of hopping on an international flight, give priority to stateside mission trips.

Stranger in a Strange Land

Our son feels called to be a missionary doctor, but when it came time to go on a mission trip this summer, he decided to stay close to home, for both environmental and financial reasons.

Instead of flying to Central America or Africa, Clark spent three weeks working at a church-sponsored clinic in eastern Kentucky, just a couple of hours from our home. The poverty in this region is legendary—and tragic. For the first time in his life, Clark encountered people who could neither read nor write. He met healthy men in their thirties who had no jobs. He received unsolicited parenting advice that shocked him: "Every once in a while, you need to beat your kids so bad that they know you can still kill them." He paid house calls to elderly people living in near-primitive conditions.

But he also met some of the kindest, most Christlike people he has ever encountered: A husband and wife doctor team who served in Africa for a couple of decades and now care for the Appalachian poor. A nurse who grew up in extreme poverty, received an education, and returned to spend the next four decades healing her neighbors. An uneducated but big-hearted woman who cares for the housebound in isolated valleys.

Our son saw firsthand what so many of us close our eyes to: there are plenty of poor people in our own backyards. I doubt Clark would have received a more eye-opening cultural experience if he had traveled halfway around the world, and he certainly saved resources by volunteering close to home.

Cruises

Cruise ships are costly, release toxic emissions into the air, and have been scrutinized for discharging their waste into the sea.

Although expensive, eco-friendly sailing cruises are another option. Organizers such as http://www.inthewild.org and http://www.adventuresmithexplorations.com work to lessen the environmental impact of their trips, and a portion of each cruise fare purchases carbon offsets to support climate-friendly projects and ocean conservation.

Cruising Idols

I once met a woman who saved all of her money and vacation time to go on several cruises every year. Those trips were what she looked forward to, lived for, and worked for.

She and her friend talked to me for more than an hour about all of the cruises they had been on, which cruise lines had the best food, and the airline hassles they had getting to port. Even though she traveled to some pretty exotic places, she rarely disembarked. Before she finished one cruise, she was already planning the next. The more she talked, the less appealing cruise vacations sounded to me. For this woman, cruises seemed like a compulsion rather than a pleasure.

Harmless, right? Not really. In addition to the environmental damage of thrice yearly long-distance travel, these cruises had become an idol—the driving force in her life.

We all have false idols in our lives. For this woman, it was travel. For others, it may be sports or work or video games or chocolate desserts. (I can definitely relate to the latter!)

False idols take us away from God. Anything that takes us away from God is ultimately harmful—for us, our families, and our futures.

Trains

Want to see the sights along the way? Leave your car at home and take a train on your next vacation. Trains emit less than one-third of the pollution per passenger mile as a car, and are more than thirteen times safer.

One of our most memorable trips as a family was taking the overnight train from New England to visit my family in

Washington, D.C. You see the world differently from the top bunk of an Amtrak car! Visit http://www.amtrak.com to view schedules or book a ticket.

Carbon offsets

Carbon offsets, which provide funds for planting trees or supporting wind and solar projects, can help reduce the impact your travel makes on the planet. When you make reservations for an airplane trip, you can usually purchase carbon credits online by simply checking a box and paying a small fee. Visit the following Web sites to find out more about purchasing carbon offsets: http://www.terrapass.com, http://www.e-BlueHorizons.net, http://www.carbonfund.org, http://www.natsource.com, and http://www.treesftf.org.

Offsetting travel is a step in the right direction, but be wary of becoming complacent. Common sense says that paying $10 may ease my conscience but will not fully compensate for the pollution caused by my cross-country flight. Although I believe that organizations such as Trees for the Future do help (for $30, this group will

Before You Leave for Vacation

- Unplug appliances (except refrigerator) to avoid using standby energy.

- Turn off the lights. Use timers on outside lights instead of letting the porch light burn constantly. Or leave the lights off and ask a neighbor to keep an eye on your house.

- Stop the newspaper to avoid waste and save money. Ask your newspaper to credit your account for the days you are going to be away.

- Close the shades. Depending on the season, drawn shades will help heat or cool your home while you're on vacation.

- Set your thermostat to fifty degrees during cold months and eighty-five degrees in the summer. Depending on the length of your trip, you could save as much as $100 in heating- and cooling-related energy costs for your home while you're on vacation.

Go Carbon Neutral

Want to get a better sense of how much carbon dioxide your travel is creating—and how much you need to offset? Use these simple formulas.

Air Travel
Flight miles per year _____ (× 0.64) = Year total _____ pounds of carbon emission

Driving
Number of gallons of gas used per month _____ (× 20) = Year total _____ pounds of carbon emission

plant 300 trees for you to offset the amount of greenhouse gases your car will produce during its lifetime), cutting back on travel is still the best—and only sustainable—answer.

SAVE GREEN

Do you want to have fun, save money, and give to charity? Auction sites such as http://www.cmarket.com/auction/Bidding ForGood.action allow you to donate tickets or travel (as well as dining, jewelry, toys, and electronics), or to bid on items donated by others. More than $46 million has been raised to date.

How to Save Money This Year

TRANSPORTATION HABIT	ANNUAL SAVINGS
Telecommute (twice a week)	$624
Share a ride to work	$780
Keep your car tuned	$150
Practice good driving techniques	$634
Substitute camping trip in park for Disney trip	$1,596
Purchase scooter instead of second car	$6,000
TOTAL ANNUAL SAVINGS	**$9,784**

$AVE

. . . And Share It with Those in Need

$HARE

- Protect 97 acres of rain forest at http://www.rainforest-alliance.org/aar/donate.cfm

- Purchase 978 mosquito nets to shelter children from deadly malaria at http://www.nothingbutnets.net

- Donate materials for 195 wood-conserving cookstoves that vent outdoors, so that women and children do not inhale the equivalent of eight packs of cigarettes per day from open fires; visit http://www.sustainableharvest.org/stoves.cfm

- Support a Christian organization working to save our mountains, such as http://www.christiansforthemountains.org; http://www.discoveret.org/tnleaf; http://www.ccappal.org

- Support the Leave No Trace Center for Outdoor Ethics, an international program that helps outdoor enthusiasts reduce their impacts when they hike, camp, picnic, snowshoe, run, bike, hunt, paddle, ride horses, fish, ski, or climb; visit http://www.LNT.org

↗ Putting Your Faith into Action

Heavenly Father, Provider and Creator, thank you for blessing me with resources to get where I need to go. As I drive, walk, or ride my bicycle, make me aware of your glorious creation. Teach me not to seek solace in costly diversions, but in your presence alone. Increase my desire to travel in your Word, to walk in your Spirit, and to live in gratitude.

Lord, help me *today* to:

- walk or ride my bike for trips less than one mile
- accelerate gently when I start out in the car, and resist the urge to drive fast
- say a prayer of gratitude when I fill up my gas tank (If I regularly say a prayer of thanks for the food God provides to fuel my body, why not add a prayer of thanks for the gas he provides to fuel my livelihood and my lifestyle?)
- shop at stores near my house
- research public transportation options in my area
- remove any unnecessary weight from my car, such as golf clubs in the trunk
- use the stairs instead of the elevator

Lord, help me *this week* to:

- combine trips
- talk with my employer about the possibility of tele-commuting
- find someone to share a ride with
- ask my city's bicycle coalition about bike routes in my area
- only buy gas from socially responsible gas companies
- slow down; for every 5 mph above 55 mph, I reduce my fuel efficiency by 10 percent
- use cruise control on the highway, and avoid sudden stops and starts in traffic

Lord, help me *this month* to:

- make sure my tires are properly inflated
- use public transportation at least once a week
- ask for re-refined motor oil when I have my car's oil changed
- research state and national parks near my house
- investigate the possibility of a four-day workweek
- set up a rideshare board at work to help others carpool

Lord, help me *this year* to:

- cancel my newspaper before I leave for vacation
- when it's time to replace my car, purchase a hybrid or small used car, scooter, moped, or one of the EPA's SmartWay certified vehicles, which save fuel, money, and the planet (see http://www.epa.gov/smartway)
- replace the usual vacation with a service trip or eco-friendly holiday for my family closer to home
- only take a flight if absolutely necessary
- ask my family to purchase carbon offsets to replace a birthday or Christmas gift
- consider getting rid of a vehicle and joining a car club for major errands or long trips
- reduce the number of after-school sports and activities my family participates in
- make changes to keep my activities and shopping as close to home as possible

Summing It Up

Getting Started

I have:

- ◯ walked or ridden my bike for trips under one mile
- ◯ bought gas from socially responsible companies
- ◯ shopped at local stores and combined trips
- ◯ improved my fuel efficiency by lowering my speed, avoiding sudden stops and starts, and using cruise control
- ◯ reduced my annual air travel by at least 25 percent

On the Journey

I have:

- ◯ telecommuted at least once a week, or switched to a four-day workweek
- ◯ shared rides whenever possible
- ◯ vacationed closer to home
- ◯ traded in my gas guzzler for a hybrid, smaller standard car, or scooter
- ◯ reduced my annual air travel by at least 50 percent

Green Superstar

I have:

- ◯ gone from a two-or-more-car household to one car
- ◯ relied on public transportation, car pools, biking, and walking for the majority of my regular transportation
- ◯ purchased carbon credits to offset my travel emissions
- ◯ reduced my annual air travel by at least 75 percent

My grandmother used to say, "You are what you eat." She was a gardener and a canner. Her garden provided a substantial number of the calories her children ate. If her saying is true, then I worry about many children today. They are an amalgam of genetically altered, fertilized, chemically sprayed, force-fed, hormone-driven tissue raised by inhumane means. I wonder whether this contributes to why many walk around with a sense of gnawing spiritual hunger—even though they eat too many calories. It is something to think about. It's food for thought.

—*Serve God, Save the Planet*

The fact that no food is inherently sinful to consume was an important concept for Jesus' followers to understand. Yet I think we always must go back to the Great Commandment to love God and others. And if we want to love our neighbors, some food choices are better than others.

—*It's Easy Being Green*

Food

Eat Simply So Others May Simply Eat

For I was hungry and you gave me something to eat,
I was thirsty and you gave me something to drink,
I was a stranger and you invited me in.

MATTHEW 25:35

WE HAD JUST MOVED TO KENTUCKY from New Hampshire a month earlier, and I could barely understand the Southern accents—much less feel settled in our new home. We moved to be closer to our children, Clark and Emma—it would have wrecked our ecological footprint to fly them back and forth halfway across the country four times a year. Besides, Emma was young for starting college—she had just turned sixteen. We bought a house two blocks from the campus so that she could attend classes and we could still be good stewards of God's resources.

At the time, I didn't feel like I was being a very good steward of anything. The house was a mess—we were in the middle of making some energy-efficient updates to our 1960s ranch, repainting, and unpacking. Church was the one constant in our life, but that, too, was different from our church back in New England. Everyone was friendly, but I didn't even know their names. I wondered if we would ever invite people over after church like we did in New Hampshire.

Early one Sunday morning, I started a big pot of vegetable barley soup while Emma fired up the bread machine. Then we picked Clark up at his dorm to go to services. The small chapel was more crowded than usual. About fourteen Asbury College students crammed into the back pews with us. While the pastor's wife played the invocation, I studied the students' faces. They looked as homesick and lost as I felt.

We stayed awhile after the service and chatted with the students. "How are your classes?" I asked. "Getting along with your roommates?" They seemed so appreciative of a little motherly attention that there was only one thing to do: I asked them to come back to our house for lunch. They all said yes—more than a dozen hungry students.

Emma looked a little panic-stricken on the way home. "How are we going to feed all these people, Mom? You know the grocery store is closed on Sundays!" I said something vague about the good Lord providing, but inside I was anxious. *Would we have enough food? And the mess! We don't even have a kitchen table.*

Then God said, "Let the land produce vegetation: seed-bearing plants and trees on the land that bear fruit with seed in it, according to their various kinds." And it was so. The land produced vegetation: plants bearing seed according to their kinds and trees bearing fruit with seed in it according to their kinds. And God saw that it was good.
GENESIS 1:11-12

As soon as we stepped inside the house, the family got to work. My husband chopped up a watermelon. Clark set out stacks of plates and silverware. Emma sliced the freshly baked bread. I added more vegetables and broth to the pot. Within fifteen minutes, we were ladling out soup and serving up hunks of honey whole wheat bread. The kids sat in a big circle on the floor, laughing and enjoying a break from cafeteria food. Somehow there was plenty for everyone.

After we finished cleaning up, Emma whispered, "You know, Mom, it's like the story of the fish and loaves. You just need to have a little faith."

Since that day two years ago, we've had a constant stream of visitors. Our house is no longer just our own, but it's more like a *home* than ever. Recently we had thirty students over for a creation-care meeting and a vegetarian cookout. With less than an hour to prepare the meal, it was still a scramble to get the food ready, but I didn't panic. And that Southern accent that gave me so much trouble? "Y'all come back soon" is now part of our family lexicon.

GETTING STARTED

Sharing a good meal with those you love not only nourishes the body but also feeds the soul. And as we try to incorporate more environmentally sound practices into our daily lives, what better place to start than the food we eat? Below are five easy ways to "green up" your dining habits.

- **Shop locally.** When you support local co-ops, farmers' markets, and Community Supported Agriculture (CSAs), you reduce the distance your food migrates and the amount of fuel and packaging it takes to feed your family.
- **Shop seasonally.** Enjoy sweet corn in the summer, apples in the fall, and citrus in the winter. Not only will the fruits and vegetables be fresher when you buy what's in season, you'll also support local economies and reduce harmful emissions.
- **Eat less meat.** More than 90 percent of meat purchased in the United States is factory farmed. Factory-farmed meat is harmful to the planet, unkind to God's creatures, and full of unhealthful antibiotics, hormones, and bacteria.
- **Pay attention to packaging.** Buy in bulk, bring your own bags, and avoid individually wrapped items.
- **Eat at home.** Cooking at home does not have to be difficult

or time consuming, and the payoff is big: fresh ingredients, less processed food, healthier eating habits, and more time together as a family.

WHAT WE EAT
Grains

When Emma was in kindergarten, her class made a book at Thanksgiving time illustrating what made them grateful. Most kids drew a picture of their dog, or their dad, or their brother. But Emma's page was like none other. She drew a big bowl of yellow-orange pasta. Underneath it said, "I am thankful for mac and cheese."

Today we are still grateful for macaroni—and for bow tie, spiral, whole wheat, angel hair, and all other pastas. Emma and I joke that we are carbohydrate-dependent life-forms. Neither of us eats much meat or fat, but we love our grains—cereals, rice, bread, and noodles form a very wide base to our food pyramid.

Both of us start our day with oatmeal. It's filling, nutritious, and fights cholesterol. About three times a week, I make a loaf of honey

GO GREEN

A GMO (genetically modified organism) involves taking genes from one species and inserting them into another to obtain a desired trait. About 70 percent of the food now found in grocery stores contains GMOs. Unfortunately, GMOs also may result in a number of undesirable health risks. For instance, milk from rBGH-treated cows contains an increased amount of the hormone IGF-1, which is one of the highest risk factors associated with breast and prostate cancer. GMO soy has been associated with an increase in soy allergies by as much as 50 percent. Antibiotic resistance, allergies, toxins, and nutritional problems have all been associated with GMO products. Children face the greatest risk from the potential dangers of GM foods because their bodies are still developing.

What can you do? Support labeling of GMO foods and purchase products that are GMO free. For a non-GMO shopping guide and information on the GM-Free Schools Campaign, visit http://www .responsibletechnology.org.

whole wheat bread. We also prepare homemade pizza throughout the cooler months. (I try not to use the oven in summertime.)

Rice or pasta makes up the bulk of my throw-together-at-the-last-minute, no-recipe-book-needed dinners: stir-fries and curries over rice, lo mein, spaghetti with home-canned sauce, pasta salads, and everything-in-the-refrigerator soups. When all else fails, there's always bread and spread—homemade bread with cheese, hummus, and cut-up fruits and vegetables can become a feast when the bread is warm and the butter soft.

Is it worth it to buy organic flour, bread, rice, and pastas? It's been difficult for me to make the transition, as I was so used to shopping by unit pricing rather than placing a dollar value on the long-term health consequences for my family or the planet. What I've come to realize is that God does not want us to think short-term; rather, the Bible calls us to focus on eternity.

Getting my pasta a buck cheaper means that petrochemicals must be used on the soil to make the land produce beyond its natural capacity. Those chemicals inevitably end up in the food we eat and in our watersheds. Is it any wonder that despite twenty-first-century prenatal care, safe deliveries, inoculations, bike helmets, seat belts, and child-labor laws, we are actually passing along shorter life spans to our children than our generation enjoyed?

For me, the compromise between cost and doing what my conscience tells me is right has been to buy a lot of grains in bulk and rely on relatively less expensive organic store brands for the remainder. When I find an organic staple on sale at a great price, I load up the cart with a year's supply and keep it stored in my pantry.

GO GREEN

If every American ate just one meal a week from locally and organically raised produce and meat, we would reduce our oil consumption by 2.5 billion gallons every year. Eating local might just become the new breakfast of (energy-independent) champions.

Fruits and vegetables

The best way to ensure that your produce is chemical-free is to grow it yourself. If you don't already have a garden, plant a few vegetables this year. It's easier than you think. By using compost to enrich your soil, watering your plants early in the morning, weeding regularly, and rotating your crops, you can have a healthy organic garden that supplies your family with fresh-from-the-vine vegetables all summer long. Visit http://www.gardeners.com to purchase Earth-friendly gardening supplies and for tips on sustainable gardening.

If your family likes fruit as much as mine does, talk to your local nursery or extension service to find out which trees and bushes grow well in your area. Fruit trees and bushes are a long-term investment, with money-saving productivity for years to come. Add a few blueberry, raspberry, or blackberry bushes if they flourish in your

Local or Organic?

My general rule of thumb: if you have to choose between organic and local, choose local. Each year, we consume about 400 gallons of oil per person for agriculture—about 17 percent of our nation's energy—nearly as much as we use for our cars. About four-fifths of that energy is consumed getting food from the farm to our plates.

If you talk to your local providers, you'll more than likely learn that they are using far fewer chemicals than agribusiness. Because they are more concerned about passing along healthy farmland to their grandchildren than squeezing out every penny from this season's crop, sustainable farming practices make long-term sense. So, going local not only saves energy and supports the local economy but also is usually chemical free, even if not "certified organic."

climate. For detailed guides on horticulture, check out the master publication list at http://www.attra.org.

If gardening is not an option, support local vegetable stands, farmers' markets, and co-ops. The United States has more than 4,500 farmers' markets, about 80 per state. Find a strawberry farm or apple orchard in your area, pack a picnic, and make your visit an annual family tradition. Canning strawberry preserves or applesauce at in-season prices allows you to reap the (delicious) rewards year-round.

Superbugs

In 1965, U.S. farmers used 335 million pounds of pesticides. By the year 2000, that amount had increased to nearly a billion pounds. The EPA has labeled 20 percent of these approved pesticides as carcinogenic in humans.

Why are we using so many chemicals? Bacteria-resistant bugs survive and come back even more resilient in the next generation, resulting in a never-ending cycle of stronger chemicals and more resistant bugs.

It's a battle we can't win. In 1948, when pesticides first went into use, farmers lost about 7 percent of their crops. Today, we lose 13 percent.

Einstein once said that the definition of insanity is doing the same thing over and over and expecting a different result. The alternative to (agri-) business-as-usual is organic.

Organic food is grown using the earth's natural growth cycle. The soil is richer and the environment safer when farmers work alongside the ecosystem instead of forcing crops to grow from bioengineered seeds and ever-stronger pesticides. Supporting farmers who follow this pattern is a practical way of tending the garden God gave us.

The most important question to ask organic food producers is "How does your garden grow?" That is precisely what makes organic food beneficial—its growth process. No pesticides, herbicides, or antibiotics are used in the making of organically grown food, and eating it keeps harmful chemicals from ending up in your family's diet.

Because the goal is to stay away from preservatives, organic food generally makes a much shorter trip from the farm to your family, which means it's fresh. Find a farmers' market and you may even get to know the face (and hands) behind your food.

For more information on certified organic standards, visit http://www.ams.usda.gov/nop.

Meat

According to the Food and Agriculture Organization, nearly a billion people go hungry annually. Even so, almost three-fourths of all grain grown in the world is used to feed livestock. Much of Central and South America's agricultural land has been converted to pastures for raising beef so people in the United States, Australia, and Europe can enjoy steak and hamburgers whenever their stomachs demand it. As a result, people suffer from hunger daily due to a lack of grain while people in the First World enjoy grain-fed beef.

What can we do to combat this injustice? Start by eating less meat. You don't have to become a vegetarian—some meat is grazed on land too rocky or steep to support agriculture. However, when you do purchase meat, make sure that it's raised locally and without antibiotics. Finding local sources takes a little research and will cost more per pound, but if you base several dinners per week around less expensive grains, your total grocery bill will actually decrease. Not only will this shift in eating habits reflect a love for our neighbors across the globe, but it will also help your budget and the environment while lowering the amount of unhealthy fats in your family's diet.

Need ideas for delicious, easy-to-prepare meat-free recipes? Visit http://www.vegweb.com.

Poultry

Concentrated animal feeding operations (CAFO) are the equivalent of concentration camps for animals. A typical CAFO houses one thousand chickens in the space the size of an average bathroom, with cages stacked floor to ceiling. These animals never see

Locating Local Food

Inspired to start supporting local food growers, but don't know where to start? Check out these sites:

- http://www.localharvest.org is a great place to find farmers' markets, CSAs, direct farm sales, and restaurants and grocery stores that support local agriculture.

- http://www.newfarm.org/farmlocator/index.php will help you locate local food sources.

- http://www.garden.org/home can teach you how to turn your balcony, back step, or backyard into a productive garden—the most local source of all.

- http://www.ams.usda.gov/farmersmarkets will help you learn about farmers' markets near you—often the easiest way to support local agriculture. Most urban farmers' markets run from spring to fall and offer everything from local fruits and vegetables to honey, eggs, meat, and flowers. Talk to the vendors; if you are looking for a product that you don't see, ask.

- http://www.csacenter.org provides information about Community Supported Agriculture as well as a CSA finder. Members of a CSA pay the farmer a fee in spring and then receive weekly shares of the produce throughout the season. Some allow members to work in the garden in exchange for reduced fees.

- http://www.communitygarden.org will teach you about the burgeoning urban-garden movement. Community gardens provide free or low-rent space to people who don't have land but want to grow some of their own food. Get to know your neighbors while ensuring an inexpensive supply of organic vegetables for your family and your community.

sunshine and live in their own excrement. Ninety-eight percent of supermarket chickens are produced by concentrated animal feeding operations.

CAFOs in America produce about six times the volume of fecal matter as the 6 billion people on the planet, in very concentrated spaces. It's no wonder that nearly three-quarters of all antibiotics in the United States are used in CAFOs; even with all these antibiotics, the Consumers Union estimates that 70 percent of standard poultry contains salmonella or campylobacter. The resulting antibiotic-resistant bacteria are posing an increasing threat to humans.

GO GREEN

The average American throws away 12 pounds of uneaten poultry per year. Encourage your family to take only what they can eat, use leftovers in soups and casseroles, and save chicken bones to make stock.

Desserts

Premade desserts are expensive, unhealthful, overpackaged, and all too easy to eat by the bag. A little discipline in the cookie aisle can save your family from becoming part of the growing epidemic of type 2 diabetes—caused by too much sugar in our diets. Parents do have some say in what their kids consume. If you don't buy it, your kids won't eat it.

Instead, focus on in-season fruit that you pick and freeze, or purchase fresh from the local farmers' market. When you do eat desserts, bake them at home. You'll save money, teach your children a valuable skill, and ingest fewer preservatives. People develop unhealthful eating habits from inhaling boxes of cream-filled chocolate cupcakes loaded with hydrogenated fats, polysorbate 60, and sweet dairy whey, not from savoring an occasional homemade cookie fresh from the oven.

Snacks

Snack foods are expensive, overpackaged, rarely locally produced, and of little nutritional value. Avoid individually wrapped snacks, like single-serving pudding, applesauce, and potato chips. When Clark and Emma would come home from school each day, I always tried to have a healthful snack ready, knowing that their hungry bellies would enjoy whatever I put on the table. I usually filled a dish with vegetables and dip or cut up fruit and cheese—which they quickly consumed—while I heated up a bowl of soup or leftovers from the previous night's dinner.

Kids (and adults) love to dip: it takes very little effort—and will save a lot of money—to serve healthy snacks like apples with peanut butter, carrots and hummus, and fruit with vanilla yogurt.

Drinks

Keep a jug of filtered water in the refrigerator instead of buying bottled water. Bottled water costs up to one thousand times more than tap water—you'll save money and cut back on the islands (literally!) of plastics that are polluting our oceans.

Recent research indicates that tap water, which is regulated, is often healthier than bottled water, which is not regulated. Plastic

The Root of Hunger

The real root of hunger is poverty and inequality, not food production. The world already produces enough food to make every one of us fat. Food sellers, however, prefer to market food to people who have a lot of money rather than to those who have little or none.

The most efficient way to feed the poor is to help them produce their own food, near where they live. Instead of handing people a bag of food, some hunger relief organizations now teach locally appropriate, sustainable farming techniques. These programs don't just feed a family for a day; they help them learn a livelihood without harming the soil.

To see how you can help, visit http://www.heifer.org, http://www.wn.org, http://www.journeytoforever.org, or http://www.sustainableharvest.org.

toxins from disposable bottles can leach into your water if reused. And to make matters worse, for every one-pint bottle of water, up to 7 pints of water are used in the manufacturing and transportation process.

The filtered pitcher we keep in the refrigerator has been one of our best investments—no more running water until it gets cold or using ice cubes—and the whole family tends to drink significantly more water now.

GROCERY SHOPPING
Buying locally

In real estate, the three most important criteria are location, location, location. In sustainable agriculture, the three most important criteria are local, local, local.

The food you bring into your kitchen has an even greater impact than the energy used by your appliances. The fewer miles from farm to table, the better. It has taken a bit of extra effort, but we have

Snacks and Desserts

INSTEAD OF	DO THIS
Microwave popcorn	Pop kernels in an air popper, on the stove using oil, or in a brown paper bag in the microwave
Ready-made cookie dough in rolls	Make cookies from scratch and freeze extra dough for next time
Individually wrapped ice cream bars	Enjoy a fruit parfait with berries, nonfat yogurt, and granola
Individually packaged peanut butter crackers	Spread peanut butter on fruit or bread
Expensive trail mix	Make your own trail mix using corn cereal, peanuts, pretzels, and a little fair-trade chocolate, purchased in bulk
Fruit roll-ups	Slice and dry in-season fresh fruit

found local sources for eggs, honey, maple syrup, beef, pork, lamb, and summer produce—all within 30 miles of our home. Bonus: locally reared meat will often be more humanely raised, and most farmers' market vegetables are grown pesticide-free, even if they aren't certified organic.

Buying in bulk

Buying in bulk saves time, money, and packaging. Find a grocery store with a bulk food and spice section, and start shopping there.

Small Is Better

Small farms can be profitable: farms of 4 acres or less have a net income of $1,400 per acre. Farms above 1,000 acres have a per-acre profit of $40 per acre.

Small farms are also more environmentally sustainable: they tend to grow diverse crops, use fewer chemicals, cause less soil erosion, and maintain more wildlife habitat.

But small farms need local markets in order to stay viable. Schools, food support programs, prisons, workplace cafeterias, caterers, restaurant owners, churches, and individuals all have a say in whether small farms can survive. If you want to preserve family-based agriculture and green space in your community, vote with your pocketbook by shopping at farmers' markets.

To learn more about farm-to-school programs, which encourage schools and colleges to purchase food from local farms, visit http://www.farmtoschool.org. To engage in food security issues, such as the USDA Farmers' Market Nutrition Program that encourages women and children receiving government support to use food coupons at farmers' markets and roadside stands, visit http://www.foodsecurity.org.

> The most sensible system for feeding people efficiently is to eat what grows nearby. If you live in Maine, buy Maine potatoes. If you live closer to Idaho, support Idaho farmers. A statistic that does *not* make sense: in America, we export 1.1 million tons of potatoes and import 1.4 million tons. Buy what grows close to home.

You can save as much as 50 percent when you purchase items in large quantities.

We set up a pantry in our basement and keep it stocked with commonly used items—flour, pastas, cereals, rice, canned goods, and other items that have a long shelf life. Our pantry averts unnecessary trips to the grocery store and provides ready meals in a pinch.

Try to cook in bulk, too. Meals that feed your family for a few days—or are shared with a neighbor—will use your appliances more efficiently and save time.

Cloth grocery bags

Each year, Americans go through 380 billion plastic bags, costing retailers $4 billion. A plastic bag may carry your groceries for only a few minutes; however, it will take up space in a landfill for hundreds of years.

Invest in a dozen sturdy reusable shopping bags (sold in many stores for only one dollar per bag), and you'll help save trees and petroleum by not wasting paper or plastic. Some stores even will give you a small discount off your purchase for bringing your own bags.

I recently spoke to a grocery store owner in North Carolina who told me that his store now offers cloth bags for economic reasons: he spends $30,000 per year on plastic bags, a cost which is ultimately passed along to us, the consumers.

Fair trade

By purchasing fair-trade coffee, nuts, oil, dried fruit, chocolate, tea, and spices, we can encourage small farmers in developing countries to use sustainable growing practices. "Fair trade" means that the farmers are paid a living wage, that the work conditions are humane, and that employers are not destroying the environment for short-term gain.

Coffee, for example, is traditionally grown under the shade of

Grocery Shopping

INSTEAD OF	DO THIS
Using the store's paper or plastic bags	Take reusable cloth bags to the store
Buying bottled water	Drink filtered tap water
Buying presliced, individually wrapped items, such as cheese	Buy items in bulk
Buying fruits and vegetables from grocery chains	Purchase at a farm stand, farmers' market, or CSA, or grow and preserve your own
Buying out-of-season fruits and vegetables	Plan menus around in-season produce
Buying apples grown in New Zealand	Purchase fruit grown as close to home as possible
Buying items with long ingredient lists	Purchase products with fewer ingredients (rolled oats instead of sugar cereals, brown rice instead of Rice-A-Roni—the fewer the ingredients, the fewer fossil fuels used in processing)
Fresh fruits	Consider dried fruits—less (heavy) water to transport
Refrigerated and frozen items	Canned and jarred items—they don't require the energy of constant refrigeration
Packaged brownies, cookies, and muffins	Bake your own—less packaging and fewer preservatives
Building every meal around meat	Choose less expensive protein options, like beans, rice, pasta, bread, and eggs

fruit, nut, and timber trees. To get our coffee a few cents cheaper, agribusiness cuts down huge forests in order to cultivate a single, large-scale crop. Though highly productive for a few years, growing coffee in fields rather than under a canopy of trees requires huge amounts of pesticides and fertilizers. In the long term, these unnatural growing practices destroy tropical biodiversity and wildlife habitats, including the nesting grounds for migratory birds. (Notice fewer birds in your backyard in recent years?) Because there are no trees to prevent soil erosion, the topsoil washes away and the land becomes unproductive, destroying already perilous local economies.

For more information, visit http://www.fairtrade.net and http://www.transfairusa.org.

> **GO GREEN**
>
> Food companies spend over $10 billion a year marketing food brands to children. We, the parents, are the advertisers' ready accomplices. Say no to expensive, overpackaged junk food and yes to a lifetime of healthy eating habits.

COOKING
Food preparation

In general, the more you can steer clear of preprepared and frozen meals, the healthier your food will be for your family and the planet. Home-cooked meals taste better too, in part because someone has taken the time and effort to prepare something especially for the people gathered around the table. (Love is the secret ingredient.)

> **SAVE GREEN**
>
> About one dollar out of every $11 spent on groceries goes toward packaging. Buy in bulk; you'll save money and reduce trash.

Sustainable Skills

While Emma and Clark were growing up, we nearly always ate dinner together. The kids learned to cook alongside me; as young adults, they now are equipped with a skill that most of their friends lack: the ability to feed themselves and others.

While I'm a competent cook, capable of consistently producing healthful meals that are economical and use little energy, my daughter is the artist. I mostly focus on results; Emma enjoys the process.

Patient and creative, Emma's the type of chef that makes her pot stickers from scratch, pounding out her own egg roll wrappers and shredding every ingredient by hand. She uses elbow grease to stir her batters—the mixer is distracting and noisy—and never sets a timer on the oven, relying on her sense of smell to determine when the cookies are the exact ratio of gooey on the inside and golden brown on top. She can also cook in quantity—one summer Emma volunteered to feed seventy campers at a Christian camp—and especially enjoys creating meals for her ever-hungry brother, an appreciative audience who always asks for seconds.

Matthew is the breakfast cook. He makes a mean omelet and was the one who introduced me to French toast made with French bread. The secret ingredient? Brown sugar in the dipping batter.

Clark, our twenty-year-old, will prep cook anything. He routinely offers to slice and dice and (most important) do dishes behind me, as long as he knows a good meal is on the way. As a newly independent adult, he's been toasting bagels for breakfast, making sandwiches with fresh lettuce and tomatoes from our garden for lunch, and cooking pasta and vegetables for dinner—a healthful, grain-based, economical diet for a busy first-year med student. When we visit, I bring some organic meat for his freezer and share a batch of chili or soup and homemade bread.

Sustainable eating is a journey—and the Sleeths still have a long way to go. The less I focus on unit pricing and the more I learn about the hidden health, environmental, and economic costs of unsustainable farming, the more naturally delicious our meals become. The appreciation I receive at the dinner table encourage me to experiment with new recipes and find more local sources, week by week.

> **GO GREEN**
>
> Unless you are cooking something delicate like a soufflé, don't bother preheating. If every U.S. household reduced oven preheating time by just sixty minutes a year, we could save enough energy to bake a pizza for every American.

Oven

Use the most energy-efficient appliance that fits the job: the toaster oven, microwave, and convection oven all use less electricity than a conventional oven. Clean the oven by hand; if you do use the self-cleaning option, do so once a month or less, and directly after cooking when the oven is already hot.

When using the oven, turn it off for the last few minutes of cooking time, and let the food continue cooking on residual heat. Do the same when cooking on the stovetop, especially when using an electric stove.

Microwave

Microwaves are 80 percent more energy efficient than traditional electric ovens.

I partially precook potatoes, carrots, onions, and other hard

> **GO GREEN**
>
> Cook in quantity and fill the oven when you bake. Yesterday when Emma prepared snacks for her campus fellowship meeting, she baked several batches of cookies and brownies together—enough to feed six dozen hungry college students. It takes a lot of energy to get your oven up to temperature, so bake a bunch at once and keep both racks of the oven full.

vegetables in the microwave before cooking them on the stove or in the oven. Use the microwave rather than the stove top when heating a cup of water or a mug of soup.

> Even now nature is lashing back at us and taking its revenge. Though we try to squeeze more and more from our lands, they produce less food. . . . An out-of-sight, out-of-mind mentality flushes toxic waste and mine tailings into our rivers and seas in the mistaken belief that they can no longer harm us. Because the living world is interconnected, the poison is absorbed by marine organisms. We in turn are being gradually poisoned when we eat seafood.
>
> —*Catholic Bishops Conference of the Philippines, "What Is Happening to Our Beautiful Land?"*

Stove

Use the stove burner that matches the size of your pan. A 6-inch pot used on an 8-inch burner wastes more than 40 percent of the burner's heat. Make sure all your pots and pans have close-fitting lids, then use them whenever possible—including when you're boiling water. Lids help reduce cooking time and keep heat in the pan where it belongs. Simmer, rather than boil, dishes. Food that has been cut into small pieces cooks faster and uses less energy. One-pot meals that use only one burner are energy efficient.

Small appliances

Small appliances, such as a slow cooker, bread maker, and pressure cooker, can be significantly more efficient than their larger counterparts. Pressure cookers reduce energy use 50 to 75 percent. Slow cookers use only as much energy as a standard lightbulb. Throwing soup ingredients in the Crock-Pot in the morning may help you avoid stopping at a fast-food restaurant on the way home from work, providing a healthful meal for pennies on the dollar with far less packaging. Add a homemade loaf of bread, and you have a feast that will satisfy the whole family.

Pots and pans

Avoid cheap utensils and Teflon-coated pots and pans that need to be replaced frequently. Purchase fewer utensils; invest in ones that will

Purchasing a new oven? Consider convection: they use 20 percent less energy than conventional ovens.

last. When you use glass and ceramic pans for baking, you can lower the oven temperature by 25 degrees.

Food storage

Avoid plastic wrap and aluminum foil; instead, store food in glass or porcelain containers. Plastic containers can leach into the food and cause health risks. Never microwave food in plastic or Styrofoam containers. If you do use aluminum foil, wipe it clean and reuse; the same goes for plastic bags. Our rolls of aluminum foil and plastic wrap have lasted two moves and more than six years—so far.

Seasonal cooking

Adjust your cooking to the seasons. Avoid baking in the oven during the summer; use the grill instead so the air conditioner doesn't have to compete against the heat you are creating. In summertime, we set up an outdoor kitchen in our carport, including a propane grill and a two-burner cooktop.

Food waste

Roughly 49 million people could have been fed by the food Americans waste each year. According to the U.S. Department of Agri-

Want to save 20 pounds of food annually? All you have to do is reduce the amount of food you waste in your household by 25 grams per day—about the weight of a slice of bread. The resulting food would be roughly enough to make sixteen meals for you and your family.

culture, about one-quarter of America's food goes to waste each year. That adds up to 130 pounds of food in the landfill per person, or $600 per household.

Use perishables before they go bad, and be creative with leftovers. Make sure your family isn't wasting God's resources while others go hungry.

Composting

Composting doesn't have to be complicated. Place a pitcher or covered container by the kitchen sink and dump in all your food scraps. Then start a compost pile outside—in a bin if you want to keep it looking neat. To hasten rotting, turn the pile every so often (ideally, once a week, but ours does fine with much less attention), and then use the composted soil in your garden. We share our outdoor compost pile with our neighbors: they provide kitchen scraps, we share the garden bounty.

Lent

For centuries, people have marked the forty days preceding Easter by abstaining from a food or habit. Although I was raised in a different faith tradition, I remember being amazed when some of my Catholic friends in elementary school gave up candy or meat each spring.

The last few years, our family has felt moved to celebrate Lent. Emma has focused on less-than-ecologically-sound food habits—last year, she gave up bananas (because they are shipped from far away) and meat (because the meat in the cafeteria is not locally raised or organic). Clark and Matthew gave up soda; the habit stuck, and now they mostly drink tap water. I'm terribly unoriginal in my addiction: I usually abstain from chocolate. The minute Lent is over, I relapse: for most of the year, I'm a nonparticipating recovering chocoholic, but it's good to know I *can* quit if I need to.

Christ went to the wilderness for forty days, forsaking comfort, food, and shelter at the beginning of his ministry. He was offered all of the things that threaten to separate us from God.

He was tempted by physical comforts, worldly status, and the abuse of religious power, yet he resisted each by invoking the authority of Scripture.

If we are to become the servants of creation, it means that we must follow in Christ's footsteps. God sent his only Son into the world to rescue everything. "All creation" groans in anticipation of this rescue and reconciliation. When Christ sets up shop in our hearts, we become the hands, feet, and voice of God on earth.

At times, it can seem like too large a task to rescue the entire planet. It might be easier to start with some small discipline and work our way up. If giving up chocolate—or coffee served in a Styrofoam cup, or fast food—for forty days instills the love and rigor that ultimately results in us becoming the servants of all, then I am for it. Ultimately, we must rely on God, for when we are faithful in the small matters, he will entrust us with greater things.

> **GO GREEN**
>
> It takes 1,500 gallons of water to produce the average (misnamed) "value meal": hamburger, French fries, and a soda. Skip the fast food and eat at home. It is healthier, costs less, and is better for the planet.

DINING OUT

Fast food

Is having it your way really worth it? Every day, one out of four Americans grabs a fast-food meal without giving its environmental, social, or health consequences much thought.

A generation ago, three-quarters of the money spent on food in the United States went toward preparing meals at home. Today, about half of the money used to buy food is spent in restaurants— mainly fast-food restaurants.

When asked "Here or to go?" always answer "Here." You will greatly reduce the packaging that comes with your order.

Just after the Depression, the Federal Farm Bill was passed to support small farmers. In recent years, three-quarters of all disbursement went to the top-grossing 10 percent of growers. As much as 70 percent of subsidies go to just two crops: corn and soybeans. Support for local foods comprises as little as one-half of one percent of recent Farm Bill budgets. Purchase food from diversified family farms to strengthen local economies, to keep excessive nitrates out of water supplies, and to promote healthier land management practices.

Locally owned restaurants

When you decide to splurge and eat out, choose locally owned, nonchain restaurants that use reusable dishes and silverware. Even better, look for restaurants that purchase ingredients locally and provide organic and fair-trade menu options.

Fast Food Nation

According to Eric Schlosser's book, *Fast Food Nation* (Houghton Mifflin, 2001):

- McDonald's is the nation's largest purchaser of beef, pork, and potatoes, and second largest of chicken (KFC is number one).

- Fifteen hundred U.S. school districts have Subway contracts, at least twenty school districts have their own Subway franchises, and nine operate Subway sandwich carts.

- Taco Bell sells products in about 4,500 U.S. school cafeterias. Pizza Hut, Domino's Pizza, and McDonald's also sell food in schools. According to the American School Food Service, about 30 percent of U.S. public high schools offer branded fast food.

- The Golden Arches are now more widely recognized than the Christian cross.

Hospitality

I used to feel like everything had to be perfect when I invited people over—but that was more about what they thought of me (was I good cook? a good housekeeper?) than about making my guests feel comfortable. People don't care if my house is spotless or decorated "Martha, Martha" style; what they hunger for is connection and fellowship.

I've learned that split pea soup and bread can make a filling meal, cut-up vegetables from the garden and dip can satisfy a bunch of neighborhood kids, and a jar of homemade spaghetti sauce can save the day when unexpected guests show up.

At dinnertime, if it looks like there may not be enough food to go around, I whisper "FHB" (family hold back) to my husband and kids, and add a couple of jars of tomatoes and beans to the chili!

FIVE FAVORITE FLEXIBLE, THRIFTY MEALS

Stir-Fry

- 1 cup brown rice
- At least 2 cups cut-up in-season vegetables (broccoli, carrots, onions, asparagus, peppers, greens, snow peas, string beans)
- 1 T minced garlic and 1 t grated ginger, or to taste
- ½ to 1 pound local poultry (optional), sliced thin and mixed with 2 T cornstarch and 3 T water (can substitute local beef, pork, or shrimp, but eliminate cornstarch coating)
- 2 T oil
- 1 cup chicken broth mixed with 2 T soy sauce and 2 T Asian hot sauce

1. Mix 1 cup brown rice with 2 cups water. Bring to boil and then simmer 25 minutes or until done.

2. Microwave hard vegetables (broccoli, carrots, onions, asparagus) with a little water until half cooked. Meanwhile, stir-fry chicken in 2 T hot oil until pink color barely disappears. Add half-cooked hard vegetables (drain first), then the fast-cooking softer vegetables (peppers, greens, snow peas, string beans). Add garlic and ginger. Stir-fry until cooked through.

3. In a separate pot, heat broth combination. Mix 2 T cornstarch with 3 T water in small bowl. Add to broth, stirring with whisk until thick. Pour sauce over vegetables, mix well, and serve with cooked rice.

Alternate: For lo mein, substitute ¾ pound cooked spaghetti or rice noodles softened in hot water for the rice, use sesame oil to stir-fry vegetables, and substitute fish sauce for Asian hot sauce. Add extra fish sauce and sesame oil to taste.

Pizza

- 1½ cups warm water
- 2 T olive oil
- 2 t salt
- 4¼ cups organic flour (white, whole wheat, or a combination)
- 2 t sugar
- 2 t yeast

1. Mix ingredients in bread machine in order listed and use dough setting. If you don't have a bread machine, mix by hand or in mixer, and allow to rise in a greased bowl covered by a damp towel, in a warm place, until double.

2. Roll out dough into desired shape, adding flour as needed. Place on pizza stone or oiled flat pan.

3. Cover dough with organic tomato sauce, plenty of grated mozzarella cheese, and desired in-season vegetable toppings (chopped onions, broccoli, mushrooms, sun-dried tomatoes, red peppers half-cooked in microwave) or local sausage that you've browned and drained. Bake at 425 degrees for 15–20 minutes.

Vegetable Barley Soup

- 2 quarts vegetable or chicken broth
- 1 cup uncooked barley
- 1 large onion, 3 carrots, 2 stalks celery, chopped
- 2 cups organic diced tomatoes, or 1 can (14.5 ounces) diced tomatoes with juice
- 1 can (15 ounces) organic dark kidney beans, rinsed and drained
- 3 bay leaves; 3 T Italian seasoning; 3 cloves minced garlic
- 2 cups fresh or frozen vegetables (peas, corn, string beans, squash)

1. Heat broth in a large pot. Add the barley, onions, carrots, celery, tomatoes, beans, and seasonings.

2. Bring to a boil, then cover and simmer over low heat for 90 minutes.

3. Add additional vegetables and continue cooking on medium heat for 10 minutes. Remove bay leaves before serving. Add salt and pepper to taste.

Mac and Cheese

- 3/4 pound of your favorite pasta, cooked al dente
- ¼ cup butter
- ¼ cup flour
- 2 cups organic low-fat milk
- 2 cups grated cheddar or other favorite cheese
- 1–2 cups in-season vegetables (peas, mushrooms, broccoli, cauliflower, onions, spinach, greens) covered with a little water and steamed in microwave until half cooked

1. Melt butter in pot. Add flour and stir over medium heat for two minutes. Add milk all at once and whisk constantly until thick and smooth.

2. Stir in grated cheese until melted. Dip in a piece of pasta and taste. Add desired amount of salt and white pepper.

3. Stir in the half-cooked vegetables (drain first) and cooked pasta. Simmer for a few minutes until well combined. Serve with sliced apples or pears and in-season green salad.

Bread and Spread

- 1½ cups warm water
- 1 T oil
- 2 T local honey, preferably local or raw
- 1 t salt
- 2 cups white flour
- 2 cups whole wheat flour
- 2 T poppy seeds
- 2 t yeast

1. Place first seven ingredients in bread-maker pan in the order given. Make an indentation in the flour and add yeast.

2. Set bread maker to whole wheat. Use light crust option when available.

   (If you don't have a bread maker, mix by hand or with a mixer. Allow to rise in greased bowl covered by a damp towel in warm place until double in size. Punch down and allow to rise again. Divide into two greased bread pans.) Bake for 35 minutes at 350 degrees or until done.

3. Serve warm bread with an assortment of spreads (hummus, cream cheese mixed with chives and smoked salmon, soft butter mixed with garlic), cheese slices, cut-up fruit, and vegetables with dip.

SAVE

How to Save Money This Year

Buy food items in bulk or purchase the largest size available	$260
Don't purchase convenience foods; make meals from scratch	$520
Replace one meat meal per week with a vegetarian option	$312
Bake your own whole wheat bread	$112
Eat fresh and canned produce from your garden	$500
Trade in one restaurant meal each week for home-cooked	$1,040
Shop with a grocery list and say no to impulse purchases	$260
Use the correct size pot on your stove burners	$36
Don't throw away edible food	$600
Earn bag credits at the grocery store by bringing your own	$20
TOTAL ANNUAL SAVINGS	**$3,660**

SHARE

. . . And Share It with Those in Need

How could you further Christ's Kingdom using the money you save on food this year?

- Partner with City Harvest to end hunger in New York City through food rescue and redistribution to more than six hundred community food programs. (http://www.cityharvest.org)

- Fight malnutrition in the Democratic Republic of the Congo and other developing countries by funding feeding centers, distribution of seeds and tools, rehabilitation of irrigation systems, and support for agricultural and fishing co-ops. (http://www.actionagainsthunger.org)

- Help end the global water crisis by providing clean water to over six hundred countries in Jesus' name. (http://www.water.cc)

- Through Bread for the World, provide food for some of the nearly one billion people around the world who go hungry, including those in the United States. (http://www.bread.org)

- Help train and send people throughout the world to deliver integrated water solutions where they are needed most. (http://www.edgeoutreach.com)

Putting Your Faith into Action

Dear heavenly Father, I thank you for the abundance of food at my table, and I ask that you plant a grateful seed in my heart. May we encourage each other to become bold servants of all creation, overcoming temptations that keep us from doing what we know to be right. May we be faithful in little things, and thus be worthy of greater things. Dear Lord, please come and dwell in the dark places of our hearts so that we may be a light to all, sharing your blessings equally with all our global neighbors.

Lord, help me *today* to:

- say a prayer before meals, not out of routine but out of genuine thankfulness
- read Matthew 15 to be reminded that Christ cares for our physical and nutritional needs
- eliminate meat from at least one meal
- replace a bottled or canned drink with tap water
- save leftovers instead of throwing them away, and eat them later
- visit http://wwwbetterworldshopper.org to educate myself about food companies that I should support

Lord, help me *this week* to:

- involve my family in planning and preparing in-season meals
- replace at least one restaurant meal with a home-cooked meal
- purchase cloth grocery bags and use them in place of paper or plastic
- shop from a grocery list and avoid impulse purchases
- increase my organic food purchases by at least 10 percent
- cook at least one meatless dinner for my family
- compost my food scraps to significantly reduce my household waste
- learn about soup kitchens and food redistribution systems in my area

Lord, help me *this month* to:

- buy produce in season
- support farmers' markets and small grocers
- purchase food in bulk
- avoid individually wrapped items
- consider how far a food item has traveled before I buy it
- share my table with others

Lord, help me *this year* to:

- stop drinking bottled water and buy a filter instead
- plant a vegetable garden and share the produce with others
- find local sources for eggs, honey, meat, and produce
- plan most meals around in-season foods
- abstain from a less-than-ecologically-sound food during Lent
- avoid fast-food restaurants
- avoid food packaged in containers that cannot be recycled
- volunteer at a soup kitchen or food redistribution center
- use the money I save to help end hunger through church or charitable organizations

Summing It Up

Getting Started

I have:

- ○ eliminated meat from at least one dinner per week
- ○ saved at least half my leftovers to eat later
- ○ lowered my monthly grocery bill at least 10 percent by shopping in bulk, avoiding precooked meals, and sticking to a grocery list
- ○ replaced at least one restaurant meal per week with a home-cooked meal
- ○ started composting
- ○ purchased reusable cloth bags for groceries

On the Journey

I have:

- ○ eliminated meat from at least two dinners each week
- ○ saved at least three-fourths of my leftovers to eat later
- ○ replaced at least two restaurant meals per week with home-cooked meals
- ○ found local sources (within 100 miles of home) for at least 25 percent of my produce, eggs, honey, and meat
- ○ Replaced bottled water with filtered tap water

Green Superstar

I have:

- ○ found local sources (within 100 miles of home) for at least half of my food consumption
- ○ eaten organic food at least 50 percent of the time
- ○ composted at least 90 percent of my food waste
- ○ gardened, or supported a CSA or farmers' market
- ○ used money saved to help a worthy cause

Most of us habitually hurry. Our schedule rules us. If it isn't our schedule, it's our children's that has us going seven days a week. Even if we say we could personally commit to a Sabbath day, our children need to be driven to this or that activity, birthday party, or sporting event. Thus we teach our children our priorities. If we are compelled to transport them seven days a week, we are teaching that sports or activities are more important than God. Our job as parents is to lead, not follow. We, who are old enough to have lived in a culture that once took and gave a weekly day off, can find answers and a model to recapture something good.

—*Serve God, Save the Planet*

God has given us a world with enough for everyone, but there are very real limits. If we continue on the path we are on, we're headed for a dangerous curve—whether we see it coming or not. We need to slow down our frantic pace, and find a new path.

—*It's Easy Being Green*

6

Sabbath

Sharing Quality Time with God

All who keep the Sabbath without desecrating it and who hold fast to my covenant—these I will bring to my holy mountain and give them joy in my house of prayer.

Isaiah 56:6-7

Before we moved to Kentucky—when we were living in the foothills of the White Mountains—I often looked forward to a Sunday prayer trek near our home. The first third of the hike was pastoral—a fairly gradual path through active dairy farms. Then came the steep incline through the forest, with a creek running alongside the trail. The final third followed a rugged and often muddy path to the overlook.

I went on these prayer walks even before I became a Christian. They were my time to talk one-on-one with God about my growing faith. Early on, I established a rule that I would praise him and express appreciation for his blessing until I reached a certain farm; once I passed the farm, I could voice my hopes, fears, and petitions.

One Sabbath, as I came down the mountain at dusk in the rain, I felt a complete and lasting assurance that Jesus was walking beside me. I could hear his steps, feel his breath, listen to his promises. It was coming down that mountain on my Sabbath prayer walk that I began a new, more personal relationship with the Lord.

I traveled up the mountain many times, mostly alone. Usually, I only climbed the first two-thirds, content to be in the woods with only God by my side. But when I felt a desire to see some spectacular evidence of his hand, I hiked all the way up the mountain to the overlook. The effort was always worth the view—20 or 30 miles up and down the Connecticut River valley—far exceeding what I deserved from the little effort it took to scale those heights.

That view is much like the forgiveness and Sabbath rest that God offers. We don't deserve it, and he asks for so little in return.

Every time I walked down that mountain—my body and soul renewed and strengthened—I found myself more in awe of the Lord, the almighty Creator of heaven and earth.

This is my Father's world. What a glorious world it is.

Dear heavenly Father, thank you for the gift of work and rest. Help me to remember the days of bondage in Egypt and Pharaoh's refusal to allow the Hebrew people time for worship and rest in you. Protect me from the self-imposed bondage of an unholy 24-7 life. Instead, teach me to honor and treasure the gift of Sabbath rest. May the Sabbath restore my soul and draw me closer to you. May it help me to resist the incessant call of the material world the remaining six days of the week. I thank you, God, for your desire to spend time with me on this holy day.

GETTING STARTED

When people ask me what they should do first to care for creation, I used to say, "Change all the lightbulbs in your home to compact fluorescents" or "Buy locally." This is still good advice, but now I offer a farther-reaching, less predictable answer: honor the Sabbath.

The Sabbath is a gift from God, a prescription for mental health.

It's not an accident that the fourth commandment begins with the word *remember*. Long ago, we were slaves in Egypt; today we are slaves to busyness. It's as if God knew we'd get so caught up in our 24-7 lives that we would forget the renewing power of a day of rest.

Yet the Sabbath is more than a day off—it is a way of life. We need to be still in order to know God. Shifting our focus from productivity to rest, from success to service, from material gain to spiritual good, from the god of money to the God of love will have a lasting impact throughout our weeks. How can we resist the nearly overwhelming messages that shout "Consume!" if we do not stop to listen to the quiet voice that reminds us to conserve?

Of all the steps our family has taken, honoring the Sabbath has given us the most joy. Until the last few decades, America still rested one day a week. A return to this custom could decrease pollution by 10 to 14 percent. Our family avoids driving on Sundays except to go to church, and we don't eat out or make purchases. Instead, we read, talk, listen to music, pray, and go for walks. When we miss a Sabbath day, we feel the negative impact throughout the week. When we honor the Sabbath, we honor our Creator with renewed faith and spirit.

PRACTICAL STRATEGIES FOR HONORING THE SABBATH

As kids, we were told to stop, look, and listen before crossing a busy road. The same advice applies to our hectic lives. Before we reenter the busy highway of work, school, and schedules, we need to stop, look, listen . . . and rest.

How can you be more intentional about your Sabbath rest? Jesus says that it's the spirit of the law, not the letter, that matters. Your Sabbath traditions can be negative—no shopping,

> Sabbath observance invites us to stop. It invites us to rest. It asks us to notice that while we rest the world continues without our help. It invites us to delight in the world's beauty and abundance. —*Wendell Berry, Foreword to* Living the Sabbath

no Internet cruising, no e-mailing, no eating out. Or they can be positive—reading aloud as a family, playing board games, going on a prayer walk.

Adapt the following suggestions to create your own Sabbath rituals. Once you start observing the Sabbath intentionally, you won't ever want to give it up. The Sabbath way of life can make every day a holy day.

STOP

The Sabbath is about ceasing. We need to cease from physical toil. We need to cease from worry and anxiety. We need to let go of the desire to be productive and successful. We need to give up control and let God in.

Jewish Traditions

I was raised in a conservative Jewish home. Every Friday night, we lit the candles, said a blessing over the bread and wine, and shared a Sabbath meal. My father and brother wore yarmulkes (head coverings), and my mother prepared a kosher-style meal. We frequently had to add a leaf to the table to make room for family friends.

In the Jewish tradition, Sabbath begins at sundown. The mother wafts the aura of the candles toward her and recites the blessing over the candles, symbolizing the putting away of daily cares. Two loaves of challah (braided bread) are placed on the dinner table and covered with a cloth to represent the double portion of manna God gave to the Israelites on the day before Sabbath when they wandered in the wilderness. A blessing is said over the wine, and the father leads special prayers and hymns, including a blessing for the children. Guests are often invited to share in this Sabbath meal. The family worships at weekly Sabbath services in the synagogue. A farewell service, called the Havdalah, is observed in a spirit of sadness that the blessed day has passed.

Although I am a Christian now, I am grateful for my heritage. It delights me to remember that Jesus, Mary, and Joseph observed similar traditions. Consider adapting some of these practices into your weekly Sabbath; they are sure to enrich your week.

Prepare

You've decided to start celebrating the Sabbath intentionally. Great! But how do you start? The first step is to discuss how you want to honor the Sabbath with members of your family. If you have teenagers, ask them what role they want to play. If you have young children, let them know a few days in advance what you plan to do and how your family will start celebrating this holiday that comes fifty-two times a year.

> *And God blessed the seventh day and made it holy, because on it he rested from all the work of creating that he had done.*
> GENESIS 2:3

Preparing for the Sabbath takes forethought. If you don't want to shop on the Sabbath, you need to make sure you have food in the house. If you don't want to clean, you need to have the house in good order. If you don't want work to interfere, you have to return phone calls and let colleagues know that you don't answer calls or e-mail on the Sabbath.

Clean

Our family cleans the house together the day before the Sabbath. We've been doing this for years; it takes about forty minutes for us to clear up clutter, dust, vacuum, scrub bathrooms, wash floors, and deep clean the kitchen. The reward is a relaxed home, with (almost) everything in its place.

Time

To step fully into Sabbath time, take off your watch. Leave it in a drawer from sundown to sundown. Notice how many times you automatically look at your wrist to check the time; instead, use that glance as a prompt to thank God for the gift of rest, so necessary for the renewal of life.

Worry

We need to cease not only working but also worrying about not working. Try putting away anything that reminds you of work.

Shut down the computer. Don't answer e-mail. Place your wallet, cell phone, PDA, and unpaid bills in a drawer. Close the door to your home office. Reminders of chores left undone, calls that need to be returned, and long to-do lists will interfere with the full rest that God wants us to enjoy.

Sabbath meal

Some families start Sabbath the night before with a special Sabbath meal. Repetition of a family favorite—perhaps something as simple as tacos or a special dessert—will add to the rhythm of Sabbath, engaging all of your senses. Consider basing Sabbath meals on local, organic foods.

Dressing in different clothes for the Sabbath meal is one tangible way of setting the day apart. Changing out of work clothes and into Sabbath clothes can add to the festive spirit. It need not be a whole outfit—perhaps just a favorite sweater or pair of earrings reserved for the Sabbath celebration.

Using your best silver and china also lets your children know that the coming day is different from the other six days of the week. We have a special set of cloth napkins and placemats that we use when welcoming guests into our home, including the Sabbath bride.

Consider setting a symbolic extra place at the table to invite all the saints who came before you to your home and all those you should welcome to God's table in the week ahead.

History of "Sabbath"

The word *Sabbath* comes from the Hebrew word *Shabbat,* which means "to cease." The Sabbath is referred to more than one hundred and fifty times in the Bible.

The ancient Babylonian calendar was based on the division of time into weeks of seven days. In these inscriptions, the Sabbath is called *Sabattu,* defined as "a day of rest for the heart."

Candles

Begin the Sabbath by lighting two candles, representing the two passages of Scripture that command the Sabbath—Exodus 20:8-10 and Deuteronomy 5:12-15. The Exodus 20 passage begins with the word *remember,* and the Deuteronomy 5 passage uses a Hebrew word for *observe.* Lighting candles helps us to remember and observe the Lord who created everything needed to sustain life, including the weekly rhythm of work and rest.

Some families light a candle for each member of the family. These candles symbolize the role each member has in God's family and in sharing the light of Christ with the world.

Others light three candles, one for each role God plays in our Christian lives: Creator, Redeemer, and Inspirer. They can also represent the Holy Trinity.

> Let every friend of Christ keep the Lord's Day as a festival, the resurrection-day, the queen and chief of all the days of the week.
>
> —*Ignatius, AD 107*

Say a candle-lighting prayer. In a traditional Jewish home, the mother circles her hands over the candles three times, welcoming the Sabbath light:

> *Blessed are thou, O Lord our God, King of the universe, who hast hallowed us by his Commandments and commanded us to kindle the Sabbath light!*

Candle lighting also can be a time to thank God, who gave us Christ to light the way. Try this simple prayer, which even children can learn:

> *May the Lord bless you with Sabbath light.*
> *May the Lord bless you with Sabbath joy.*
> *May the Lord bless you with Sabbath peace.*
> *May the Lord bless you with Sabbath holiness.*
> *Thank you, Lord, for the light of Christ!*

Fresh bread feeds lots of hungry mouths. Invite a bunch of teenagers to your Sabbath meal, and watch the challah disappear.

Sabbath bride

In Jewish literature, poetry, and music, Sabbath is described as a bride or queen, as in the Hebrew hymn *Lecha Dodi Likrat Kallah* (*Come, My Beloved, to Meet the [Sabbath] Bride*). You can welcome the Sabbath bride by opening a door and chanting the following verse or composing a similar prayer of welcome:

> *Work and labor now shall cease;*
> *Rejoice in Sabbath grace and peace,*

Challah

Another (delicious!) tradition that you may want to incorporate in your Sabbath is challah, a braided egg bread. If you have a bread machine, baking challah is incredibly simple.

Add ingredients to the bread pan in the order given:
- 1 cup warm milk
- 3 T soft butter
- 1 t salt
- 2 large eggs, beaten
- 3 ¼ cups unbleached flour (preferably local and organic)
- 2 T sugar
- 2 t active dry yeast

Set the bread maker for dough. (If you don't have a bread maker, mix and knead ingredients thoroughly by hand or with the dough hook of a stand mixer. Place the dough in a clean, greased bowl, cover it with a towel, and let it rise in a warm place for one hour.) After the first rising, divide the dough into six equal portions and roll into strands. Loosely braid three strands on a greased cookie sheet. Repeat with the second three strands. Cover dough with a towel and allow it to rise in a warm place for about an hour. Preheat oven to 350 degrees and bake for thirty minutes, or until the bread sounds hollow when tapped.

Heavenly Father, we are blessed
By the Sabbath bride of rest.

If the weather is nice, keep the door open throughout your Sabbath meal.

Blessings

Here are some blessings you can say over the wine (or grape juice) and the bread, based on Jewish traditions:

Blessed art thou, Lord our God, King of the universe, who gives us the fruit of the vine.

(Pass around the cup for all to share.)

Blessed art thou, Lord our God, King of the universe, who brings forth bread from the earth.

(Pass the bread for all to share.)

Blessed art thou, Lord our God, King of the universe, who has broken the bonds of slavery, sin, and death and gives us this precious day of rest. Blessed are you, Lord, who makes the Sabbath day holy.

You can say these blessings on Sabbath eve or at a meal on Sabbath day.

Hand washing

Some families perform a ritual hand washing before the meal. Wash off the cares of the week, and enter into the Sabbath space clean and holy.

Before bed

To close the meal, you may want to ask each member of the family to take a turn picking out a psalm to read. Try starting with Psalm 23, 24, 29, 93, 126, and 148.

If you have young children, you might want to make a Sabbath

bath a special time after the meal. Remind your children of the stories in the Bible where God used water to cleanse and renew—such as the Flood, Exodus, and baptism.

Say a Sabbath good-night prayer, praising God for the gift of rest and asking for peace and renewal in the day ahead.

Solo Sabbath

Keep my Sabbaths holy, that they may be a sign between us. Then you will know that I am the Lord your God. —EZEKIEL 20:20

With Matthew's speaking schedule and the kids both in college, I sometimes find myself celebrating Sabbath . . . alone. My Sabbath preparations begin on Saturday morning, sharing breakfast with my spiritual group, a few women who laugh and pray together and hold me accountable. This pre-Sabbath time of reflection helps me to prepare my heart and mind for time with God, a warm-up for the main event that I so eagerly anticipate all week long.

Before rest, however, comes work—returning e-mails and phone calls, cleaning the house, washing dishes, sorting the recycling, hanging up the laundry—I don't want any undone business to lure me away from my honored guest. As I prepare my house for the Lord, the seventies song "Anticipation" plays in my head. I shut down the computer and feel my shoulders relax; just knowing that I won't be sitting in front of the screen for the next twenty-four hours fills me with extravagant joy.

Night comes at last. I light a candle, say a few prayers in Hebrew, and welcome the Sabbath bride. As I read in bed, enjoying books that have beckoned me all week, the flicker of the candle reminds me of the lovely day ahead—and the flicker of light that is our life. Matthew calls and we pray together. The Sabbath has begun!

LOOK

Worship

Many people begin their Sabbath day with church. Decide as a family how you want to experience your church time. Will all of you sit together? Is it okay for teens to sit with friends? Will you attend Sunday school? Do you prefer to worship at home in the morning and end your day at church? If you are involved in running the nursery, worship team, choir, worship service, or Sunday school, do you need to extend your day of rest into Saturday or Monday?

Errands

Many families, unfortunately, end their Sabbath the moment they leave the church parking lot. Though it might be tempting to stop at the store on the way home from church, avoid running errands on the Sabbath. Our family tries not to engage in any commerce; God wants *all* people to have a chance to rest. It is often minimum-wage earners, today's "menservants and maidservants," who have no choice—work on Sunday or lose their livelihoods. To cease is to let God be God and enjoy his presence.

Food

Sabbath is a time for feasting and celebration. Remember the Sunday chicken dinner? Start your own tradition, perhaps a soup, chili, or stew put together in a slow cooker the night before. For our main Sabbath meal, we usually make a loaf of bread and a pot of soup. The meal is expandable, especially if the fridge is stocked with salad fixings—making it easy to invite a friend or two (or three or four) to break bread with us after church.

Remember the Sabbath day by keeping it holy.
Exodus 20:8

As a special treat, consider making pancakes in the shape of your children's initials for breakfast or banana splits for dinner (use frozen yogurt and lots of berries—fruit and calcium!—if you want to make "dinner" more nutritious). Bread and spread (crackers, bread, hummus, cut-up fruit) can be a simple closing meal for your Sabbath, shared in the family room instead of the kitchen as a once-a-week exception. Your meals don't have to be fancy, but establishing traditions will make them stand out from the rest of the week.

Grace

Say grace over all your Sabbath meals, thanking God for the farmers who grew the food and the many hands that brought it to your table. You may also want to start a tradition of praying at the end of a Sabbath meal, based on Deuteronomy 8:10: "When you have eaten and are satisfied, praise the Lord your God for the good land he has given you."

Example of a closing prayer:

Blessed art thou, King of the universe, who sustains all living creatures with the fruit of the land. Thank you, Lord, for fulfilling your promise that while the earth remains, seedtime and harvest will not fail. Help us to remember that we do not live on bread alone. Teach us to feed on the true bread from heaven, Jesus Christ our Lord.

Praises and concerns

During or after a Sabbath meal, share praises and concerns from the week that just passed and for the week to come with your family. Encourage your children to recognize God's work in their everyday lives, including any answers to prayer, unexpected evidence of God's care, providential timing, and provisioning in service of others.

Sabbath talk

Parents of younger children might want to ask a Sabbath question to discuss over a meal. What Bible character would you like to have as a friend? If Jesus lived in your neighborhood today, what kind of car would he drive? What would he eat; what kinds of clothes would he wear; how would he earn his living? How would he celebrate the Sabbath? If you could spend a day with Jesus, where would you take him? What would you ask him? What would you do together?

Sabbath walk

One of our favorite Sabbath rituals is to take a Sabbath walk. Don't make it a power walk; instead, observe and investigate. Enjoy watching the caterpillar nibble a leaf; marvel at the new buds that are forming; watch a flock of birds peck for food in the ground. When you pass neighbors or acquaintances, stop and talk. Enjoy a special stroll with a child or grandchild. Because they are closer to the ground (and closer to God's sense of time), you are guaranteed to see things you normally would pass right by. There is no lack of wonder in the world, only wonderment.

Immersion in nature

Another Sabbath discipline is to spend at least ten minutes completely surrounded by nature. Some of our most memorable times as a couple have been experienced in silence: sitting on a sunny south-facing slope in winter; leaning against a tree at the edge of a cool forest in summer; watching streams flow by any time of year. Make sure you can see nothing man-made—even if you have to restrict your vision to one square foot of grass. Study God's creation, and see what it reveals to you about the nature of our Lord.

Technology

Make intentional choices about your Sabbath use of technology. Does your family want to eschew TV, or is renting a weekly movie that everyone can enjoy a Sabbath tradition? Is the computer taboo, or can siblings play a (nonviolent) game together?

If you do decide to make films part of the family tradition, consider a family movie, such as *Chariots of Fire*. Based on a true account of the British track and field team during the 1924 Olympic Games in Paris, Scottish runner Eric Liddell (who would later become a missionary) refuses to run any races on the Sabbath, the day he is scheduled for a preliminary heat in the 100-meter dash.

LISTEN

Sabbath is a time of coming to rest so that we can hear God more clearly. Prayer, meditation, studying God's Word, and reading books of Christian wisdom and devotionals all help us listen to the messages that our busyness drowns out the rest of the week. See if some of these ideas help you tune out the world and tune into God.

Morning prayer

When you wake up on Sabbath morning, ask God how he wants you to spend the day. Listen for his answer. Pray that this Sabbath time brings you closer to him and fills you with a sense of God's presence.

Then he said to them, "The Sabbath was made for man, not man for the Sabbath."
MARK 2:27

Another question you may want to ask: who should I minister to today? This person might be in your family or at church. He or she might be an old friend or an ailing relative. He might be the elderly man you see walking the dog each morning. It might be the earth itself or one of the Lord's creatures. Listen, and God will let you know.

Quiet

Our lives are filled with noise. Give at least one noisy appliance or device—the dishwasher, your washing machine or dryer, the TV, your telephone—a day of rest, and experience the quiet.

Go one step farther: unplug *everything* electronic except the refrigerator. Sound radical? Jesus didn't use text messaging or PowerPoint—and his ministry is still going strong two thousand years later.

Consider including an hour of silence in your Sabbath day. If you have young children, make each child a Sabbath box that is only brought out once a week. Fill it with watercolors, new books from the library, a journal, and other age-appropriate treats.

Here are some prayer exercises that you might want to try during your hour of silence. Choose a different one each week, or find a favorite and do it weekly:

- Write a short letter to God, as you would write to a friend. Share your week. Let go of grievances. Talk about an attribute of God that you want to imitate in the coming week.
- Listen to a praise song or read a hymn repeatedly. Let the music seep in and guide your meditations.
- Set aside a time of adoration. Place yourself in a posture of humility—kneeling, sitting, or standing. Praise God for all he has done in your life and the lives of those you love. Think about all the times that God has saved you from yourself, mistakes, and choices that could have had bitter consequences. Praise him for his many and glorious attributes.
- Find a favorite poem or psalm. Read it repeatedly. Or write your own. Let the words guide your Sabbath worship and prayer throughout the day.

Forgiveness

Ask the Lord if there is someone you need to apologize to for something you said or did in the past week. Clearing the air and making amends will do wonders for family relationships.

Meditation

Meditate on Scripture. Select a short piece of Scripture for reflection. Read it a few times and then choose a phrase that speaks to you. Sit still or go for a walk. Repeat the phrase until it flows in and out with each breath. If your mind wanders—if it's like mine, it will—use the phrase to bring you back to God's wisdom.

Here's another form of meditation that I often use: every time I breathe in, I silently say, *Abide in me*. Then I slowly exhale, *And I will abide in you*. I use this meditation any time I need to calm myself, grow still, or converse with God.

I also meditate on the Lord's Prayer, repeating it dozens and dozens of times when I go for a walk or for a swim.

One more tool that has been helpful to me is to say, "Be still, and know that I am God." Then I take one word off the end of the sentence: "Be still, and know that I am." Then I take another couple of words off: "Be still, and know." Then, "Be still." And finally, "Be." I repeat it until the words draw me into that silent space in all of us that can only be filled by God.

Devotional

Some couples find that reading a devotional together on the Sabbath brings them closer as a couple throughout the week. Try doing a weekly devotional as a couple or a family. After reading the devotional, set aside time to pray together as a couple. If you don't pray weekly for your children and family, who will? Nobody knows their inner lives, hurts, and needs better than you do. Bring your concerns before the Lord, and watch him move in miraculous ways. I cannot tell you how many of my seemingly impossible Sabbath prayers have been answered. Often I am simply praying for help, and God works out the details.

> Blessed be to God for the day of rest and religious occupation wherein earthly things assume their true size.
> —*William Wilberforce, British statesman and abolitionist, in his journal about his Sundays*

Sabbath also can be a time to pray regularly for the church, pastors, worship team, choir, Sunday school teachers, and church elders who serve the Lord and others. Ask God how he can use you in the coming week to serve your church community.

Here's another well-known prayer tool that I've adapted for

the Sabbath, based on the pattern of the Lord's Prayer. It focuses on the acronym ACTS: adoration, confession, thanksgiving, and supplication.

- Start by *adoring* your heavenly Father for all of his gifts, including this Sabbath day and the glorious creation he has put in our trust.
- *Confess* your unkind thoughts, words, and deeds from the previous week, and any ways in which you have been careless in your stewardship of his creation. Be specific!
- *Thank* him for the many blessings he has bestowed on you in the last week. Be sure to include the physical gifts that sustain our lives, but which we often take for granted: ready access to clean water, gasoline to transport our food and take us to work, the forests that provide the very oxygen we breathe.
- Finally, *supplicate* God with specific requests for yourself and others in the week to come.

Sabbath Retreat

I was feeling guilty. I had picked up a nasty case of poison ivy and passed it along—like an unwanted fruitcake—to my husband. An angry, oozing band of red blisters now encircled his waist, where I had hugged him.

We both were pretty miserable—and miserable to be around. My left eye had swollen shut, and I had a sack of edema protruding from the middle of my cheek. I looked like a monster and was acting like one too—running on less than three itchy hours of sleep per night for over a week. We were washing sheets and towels frequently and changing clothes several times a day. Both of us were crazy-busy with work commitments and crazy-grumpy because of the steroids we were taking.

Friday night we both turned a corner with our poison ivy, but our emotional wounds were still raw. Around midnight, I got online, found a state park with a lodge about an hour away, and reserved a room. We needed a change of scenery. We needed a Sabbath retreat.

On Saturday morning, we put the house in order, packed up, and headed north in our Prius through horse country—an area of the state we had never seen. We stopped at a drugstore on the way and bought some camphor itch cream that I had read about online the night before. The stuff stung like crazy for a few minutes, and then it began to work a miracle. The itching was barely noticeable. Things were already looking better, and we hadn't even arrived at the park yet!

The next twenty-four hours were everything a Sabbath retreat should be. We read the Bible. We napped. We took walks. I swam outdoors. We talked. We prayed. It was as if the heavens opened and the Lord descended. By Sunday afternoon, Sabbath peace had restored us—mind, body, and spirit.

It took a bad case of poison ivy to heal us.

That Sabbath retreat, just twenty-four hours, drew us closer to God, to each other, and to the holy rhythm of work and rest.

Music

When God passed out talents, he blessed our family with many gifts; however, no one in our family received the gift of an angelic singing voice. God did, however, give us a great appreciation of music. Handel's *Messiah* is a family favorite. If you are fortunate enough to have someone in your family who plays a musical instrument, enjoy a family concert. If you like to sing, do so with a full heart.

Scripture

Select a weekly Scriptural passage for family reflection throughout the week. If your family is focusing on using less resources and caring for the earth, consider one of the following:

> *Why do you look at the speck of sawdust in your brother's eye and pay no attention to the plank in your own eye?*
> — Matthew 7:3

Small is the gate and narrow the road that leads to life, and only a few find it.   —MATTHEW 7:14

No one can serve two masters. Either he will hate the one and love the other, or he will be devoted to the one and despise the other. You cannot serve both God and Money.
— MATTHEW 6:24

Here are a couple of passages that may help you celebrate the Sabbath more intentionally:

Come to me, all you who are weary and burdened, and I will give you rest.   —MATTHEW 11:28

My times are in your hands.   —PSALM 31:15

Put the Scripture on the refrigerator, bathroom mirror, or family bulletin board—or make copies to hang in your bedrooms or place in your Bibles.

Fellowship
One of the great blessings of Sabbath time is fellowship and conversation. Talk to your spouse, your children, your parents, and your siblings. Invite friends over for a bowl of soup and a cup of conversation.

Family read-aloud
Some families have a book that they read aloud together only on the Sabbath. Consider reading C. S. Lewis's entire Chronicles of Narnia series over several months of Sabbaths.

Telephone calls
We use the answering machine to screen phone calls on the Sabbath. If possible, avoid any calls that relate to work. For some, a Sabbath discipline might be to avoid all use of the phone. For

others, a weekly call to an elderly relative or faraway friend might enhance your Sabbath rhythm.

The hearth

We love fires in the winter. Turn the heat way down, and gather near the warmth. The hearth is traditionally the center of the home. It brings people together. Looking at the flames and reflecting on that day's sermon or devotional reading can become a simple form of meditation, bringing you in harmony with God's presence. (Unlike most of the other suggestions in this chapter, this one requires some energy. We get our firewood from fallen trees. If at all possible, burn the wood in an efficient woodstove. And always give thanks for the warmth that the Lord has provided.)

> Thou art my single day,
> God lends to leaven
> What were all earth else,
> With a feel of heaven.
>
> —Robert Browning, British poet

Hammock times

For years, Matthew has joked about starting a new magazine called *Hammock Times*. In the summertime, we like to sit out on the back deck and just hang out together. I cannot count how many hours Matthew spent swinging in the hammock on Sunday afternoons with the kids snuggled in on either side.

Bible study by osmosis

After church, we have a ritual of Bible study by osmosis. We get into comfortable clothes, open the Bible, read a few passages, and then take a nap. In our busy lives, a nap feels like a luxurious indulgence, costs nothing, uses no energy, and charges us up for the week ahead.

Rest in love

Most of all, Sabbath is about resting in love: love of God, love of his creation, love of his living Word. The Sabbath is a time for loving our families and loving our friends. It's about embracing our church families, especially those who are struggling or feeling alone. It's about caring for strangers, inviting them into our homes and our lives. It's about loving his commandments, including the commandment to rest. And it's about going into the week ahead, overflowing with Christ's love.

Blessing your children

Love begins at home. Express that love by blessing your children. Saying a weekly blessing for your children, even if they resist at first, is an act that will be remembered and treasured long after they leave home. Lay your hands on their shoulders or heads, and pray for them in silence or out loud:

> *The Lord bless you and keep you;*
> *The Lord make His face shine upon you,*
> *And be gracious to you;*
> *The Lord lift up His countenance upon you,*
> *And give you peace.*
> — NUMBERS 6:24-26, NKJV

Blessing your marriage

Marriage can be the ultimate mission field, where our patience, ability to forgive, and willingness to sacrifice for the benefit of another is put to a daily test. If you are working together on becoming better stewards of creation, praise each other for the efforts made during the past week, and encourage each other for the week ahead. Check out *The Power of a Praying Husband Book of Prayers* and *The Power of a Praying Wife Book of Prayers* by Stormie Omartian or a similar prayer resource. Read one prayer to your spouse each Sabbath—or say your own prayer right from the heart.

Criticism oasis

Make it a rule that no one can criticize another family member on the Sabbath. Taking a rest from judgment and criticism will make your Sabbath home a loving haven. You may be surprised at how others sense this and stop by to bathe in an atmosphere of acceptance.

Gratitude

Show your love for family members with this gratitude exercise. Have each person pick a name out of a hat. Then answer the following questions:

- What verse comes to mind when you think of this person?
- What do you think most pleases God about this person?
- How do you think this person might benefit the Kingdom someday?

Or simply think about these questions and write your answers in a journal or letter. Your reflections will affect how you treat that loved one throughout the week.

Another way to show your love for God is to start a gratitude journal. Commit to writing down at least five things that happened during the past week for which you are thankful.

Read Psalm 92, entitled "A psalm. A song. For the Sabbath day." The psalmist is full of love for the Lord, making music and proclaiming God's love and faithfulness. Write a prayer in which you share your love for the Lord and all he created.

Reaching out

In church, be generous with your hugs and greetings, especially to those who are sitting alone or may not have much contact with others during the week. A few minutes of conversation, a squeeze of the hand, and a welcoming smile could be the highlight of someone's week.

When I worked for AmeriCorps, one of the best parts of my job was bringing library books to shut-ins. For many, the *only* time they ever got out of the apartment was for church. If you have elderly friends, make a point of finding them in their pews and giving them a hug. The smile you receive in return will stay with you all week.

St. Francis

Follow the example of St. Francis: preach to the birds. The neighbors might think you are, well, a bit eccentric. Tell them that it's biblical—who knows where the conversation may lead.

My brothers, birds, you should praise your Creator very much and always love him; he gave you feathers to clothe you, wings so that you can fly, and whatever else was necessary for you. God made you noble among his creatures, and he gave you a home in the purity of the air.

You can also show love for our feathered friends by hanging up a bird feeder and filling it with seed. Make feeding the birds a Sabbath ritual that you share with your children. This Sabbath delight will spill over into the week ahead.

Trash

Demonstrate your love of creation by bringing a trash bag on your Sabbath walk. If you have kids, ask one to carry a bag for plastics, one for cans, and one for glass that you will later recycle. Is this "work"? In large part, that depends on the spirit behind the act. If you are healing the land, just as Jesus healed the withered hand, you're probably walking on safe ground.

Service

Look for ways your Sabbath day can help others. Perhaps you and your family can start a box of giveaway items. Do you have an unread book on your shelf that a friend, your church, or the library could use? Do you have outgrown coats or shoes that a refugee from warmer climes might need? Does your child have a toy, unused and underappreciated, at the bottom of the closet? Place at least one item each Sabbath in the

> As we keep or break the Sabbath day, we nobly save or meanly lose the last and best hope by which man arises.
> —*Abraham Lincoln*

giveaway box, and make it a point to find them good homes in the coming week.

Making a family ritual of visiting a hospital, prison, or nursing home on your way to or from church can enrich your Sabbath day. The slower pace of Sabbath allows us to give the gift of time to those who do not have the freedom to move about.

I have one friend who sets aside five things every week to give to charity. This Sabbath discipline helps her focus on giving to others and conserving, rather than consuming, God's resources.

Laughter

Laughter is a form of love. Consider watching a video of a Christian comedian. Share family stories. Walk to a playground and swing on the swing set; tunnel into a pile of leaves in your yard. See who can make up the most ridiculously self-pitying lyrics to a country western melody. Lighten the mood and your laughter will spill over into the week ahead.

Sabbath good-bye

Saying good-bye to the Sabbath is another way to express your love. The traditional Jewish service is called Havdalah, meaning "separation." Take an extra saltshaker or small jar and fill it with cinnamon, allspice, nutmeg, and cloves. Pass the spice box around during your closing Sabbath meal, a reminder of the sweet savor

What's Wrong with This Picture?

Americans go to church, then go to the mall:
   Sunday is the second biggest shopping day of the week in America.

Europeans stay home:
   In most European countries, where church attendance is far lower than in America, laws either completely ban or restrict Sunday shopping hours.

of this day of rest. Keep the spice box someplace handy where you can pause and breathe in the smell of Sabbath rest throughout the week.

Monday through Saturday

Another way to hold on to the spirit of Sabbath in the weekday rush is to pick a cue—the phone ringing, a glance at the clock, your e-mail delivery chime. Every time you hear this cue, take three mindful breaths. This simple act, a Sabbath pause, makes space for grace and peace to seep into every day of the week.

How to Save Money This Year

What would happen if you stopped shopping on Sunday? You could save as much as 14 percent of your annual spending, while reducing your fossil fuel use by 10 percent or more! The average American household spends over $48,000 per year. More than half of that goes toward food, apparel, transportation, entertainment, and other purchases. Suppose you eliminate one-seventh of that spending by not going to stores or driving anywhere (except church) on the Sabbath? You could save $3,429 per year by coming to rest, while enriching your spiritual, physical, and relational life.

. . . And Share It with Those in Need

How could you better use that $3,429? The American Institute of Philanthropy helps you "give wisely to charity" by ranking charities by category, such as International Relief and Development, Environmental, and Child Sponsorship. To make the Top Rated Charities List, all organizations must dedicate at least 75 percent of their income toward program costs. You can access their recommendations at http://www.charitywatch.org/toprated.html.

Looking for a specifically Christian charity? Of the top one hundred charities ranked by the *Nonprofit Times* for financial integrity, nearly a quarter were Christian. Catholic Charities, the Salvation Army, and Habitat for Humanity International were ranked among the top ten best charities.

Another excellent resource for choosing a worthy cause is http://www.charitynavigator.org—America's largest independent charity evaluator. Charity Navigator provides free financial evaluations of America's charities so that you know that your Sabbath savings are going toward a worthy cause.

At its best, however, Sabbath giving can be very personal—the teenager who needs help paying for college, the family down the street that lost a job and is struggling to get by, the food pantry that has trouble keeping their shelves stocked during an economic downturn. When Matthew and I were starting our nonprofit, Blessed Earth, we were deeply moved by friends who supported us with open hearts. Giving to people and organizations that you know can be one of the most grace-filled experiences in life.

↗ Putting Your Faith into Action

Dear heavenly Father, still my mind, my body, and my soul. Teach me to come to rest and behold the wonder of your creation. Remind me that the Sabbath way of life is not one of endless toil, but a holy cycle of work and rest, fellowship and solitude, laughter and silence. Teach me, glorious Creator, to pattern the rhythms of my life on yours, to remember my deliverance from bondage, and to accept the sacred gifts of peace and balance.

Lord, help me *today* to:

- talk with my family about how we want to celebrate the Sabbath
- pick a cue (my e-mail delivery chime, a glance at my watch) to breathe in three times and focus on grateful thoughts
- read Psalm 92, the psalm for the Sabbath Day
- resolve not to run errands on my next Sabbath
- select a family read-aloud book or devotional that I can share on the next Sabbath

Lord, help me *this week* to:

- clean the house before the Sabbath
- get all my errands done before the Sabbath
- take off my watch and remove all reminders of work during the Sabbath day
- prepare a special Sabbath meal
- light Sabbath candles
- turn off my computer, and keep it off all day
- use the answering machine to screen calls on the Sabbath
- bake challah
- bless my children and spouse
- encourage my family to rest on the Sabbath day
- observe some quiet time on the Sabbath
- read Psalm 23, 24, 29, 93, 126, and 148

Lord, help me *this month* to:

- find a church home, if I don't have one already
- say grace before every meal on the Sabbath
- share praises and concerns with family or friends on the Sabbath
- take a Sabbath walk
- spend at least ten minutes completely surrounded by nature each Sabbath
- reduce my use of technology on the Sabbath
- spend at least half an hour in silence on the Sabbath
- ask forgiveness from anyone I may have hurt or offended this week

Lord, help me *this year* to:

- engage in a plan for reading the entire Bible
- make most Sabbath meals with local or organic foods
- invite someone to share a Sabbath meal
- read a book aloud on the Sabbath
- take a criticism break
- write a letter of appreciation
- engage in service outreach
- avoid driving on the Sabbath, except to church
- avoid eating out and buying things on the Sabbath

Summing It Up

Getting Started

I have:

- ○ asked God how he wants me to spend my Sabbath
- ○ looked up *Sabbath* in my Bible concordance and read what Scripture says about Sabbath observances
- ○ discussed with my family how to make my Sabbath less consumer centered and more God centered
- ○ added at least five minutes of silence, meditation, or Scripture reading to my Sabbath practice
- ○ spent at least five minutes in nature
- ○ cut back on my driving and consumer purchases on the Sabbath by at least 20 percent

On the Journey

I have:

- ○ invited neighbors or friends to share a Sabbath meal
- ○ added at least fifteen minutes of silence, meditation, or Scripture reading to my Sabbath practice
- ○ spent at least fifteen minutes in nature
- ○ cut back on my driving and consumer purchases on the Sabbath by at least 40 percent

Green Superstar

I have:

- ○ added at least thirty minutes of silence, meditation, or Scripture reading to my Sabbath practice
- ○ spent at least thirty minutes in nature
- ○ cut back on my driving and consumer purchases on the Sabbath by at least 60 percent
- ○ donated the money I've saved from reduced consumption to a good cause

Do America's living rooms overflow with presents because we really need them, or out of a need to impress, or from a sense of guilt and obligation? Would a calm, divinely centered, debt-free, peaceful Christmas do us more good than a buying spree on credit? Instead of exchanging gifts in the workplace, why not take up a collection to give farm animals to poor people, plant trees in devastated countries, or provide health care to orphans? The spirit of giving that comes through the example of Jesus is about meeting the spiritual and material needs of others. Do you or your spouse need another sweater, tie, or scarf more than a child in Bosnia or Iraq needs a pair of good-fitting shoes? A wonderful life isn't about having more; it's about appreciating what we have and sharing our abundance.

    —*Serve God, Save the Planet*

I love holidays—but the rampant consumerism that's so often part of our holiday celebrations is disastrous for the environment. . . . Give the gift of your time. Make certificates entitling your parents to a night out while you watch your younger siblings, or make breakfast in bed. . . . Start a family Christmas tradition that doesn't focus on presents—go ice-skating, read the Christmas story aloud from the Bible, or play a board game together. . . . Give the gift of a better world. Instead of a trinket, donate to a charity or environmental organization.

    —*It's Easy Being Green*

Holidays and Special Events

Having Fun for Less

*They will celebrate your abundant goodness and
joyfully sing of your righteousness.*

PSALM 145:7

I BELIEVED IN CHRISTMAS even before I believed in Christ.

First, some personal history: Matthew was raised in a church-on-Sundays Protestant home. His Christmas celebrations were small because there were five kids and not much money to spare. I was raised in a conservative Jewish home. My Christmas celebrations were nonexistent—we lit the menorah and played games with a spinning top called a dreidel.

I met Matthew when he was a carpenter putting a bay window in my parents' house. I was a rather spoiled college freshman, home for December study week just before my first set of finals. Matthew says that my parents' worst nightmare came true: their daughter fell in love with the carpenter. By February, we were dating. In April, he asked me to marry him. I told him I needed to ask my mother.

Two years later, we married. I had been telling Matthew that he was the smartest person I'd ever met and that maybe he should think about going to college. So he did. Because of a severe case of dyslexia and a lack of direction, he had graduated third from *last* in his high school class—and that was in the vocational program. But the calculator was invented in the meantime, so math and science were no longer stumbling blocks. Now Matthew had a clear goal: to become a doctor. He enrolled in a state college, worked hard, and excelled.

Fast forward seven years. Clark, our son, was born the month Matthew graduated from medical school. And still, we didn't have any clear anchor, no faith traditions to harbor the storms. So we made it up as we went along—candy-filled baskets at Easter, matzo-ball soup for Passover, stockings at Christmas, and potato pancakes for Hanukkah. By the time our kids were in elementary school, they were so confused they thought the "fiddler on the roof" slid down the chimney, and if he saw his shadow, he laid an Easter egg.

> All that is sweet, delightful, and amiable in this world, in the serenity of the air, the fineness of seasons, the joy of light, the melody of sounds, the beauty of colors, the fragrancy of smells, the splendor of precious stones, is nothing else but Heaven breaking through the veil of this world.
>
> —William Law (1686–1761), Rules for Living a Holy Life

My fondest Christmas memory from those early years occurred when Clark was three and Emma was one. Matthew's parents had sent a tin of cookies packed in a box with lots of newspaper. At the time, one of Clark's chores was to crumple newspaper each evening to start our fire. While Emma happily sampled each type of cookie, Clark smiled up at me, his face shining: "Look at what Santa gave me! Lots of newspaper already crumpled up!"

Our Christmas traditions grew along with the children. When Clark was five, some kindly neighbors felt sorry for him and gave us a small artificial Christmas tree and some decorations. A year later, we moved to our doctor's-sized house and bought a doctor's-sized spruce. Christmas Eve was always spent at our next-door neighbor's, along with several dozen other families and a never-ending supply of jumbo shrimp and champagne. Because my friends all dropped by with picture-perfect handcrafted presents, I reciprocated. We exchanged artsy Christmas cards—more beautiful than anything Martha Stewart could ever dream up. We caroled, wrote letters to Santa, left food for the reindeer, woke up at dawn to open presents, and ate a Christmas breakfast big enough to feed an army of angels. But still, my family did not know God's Son.

Eventually, some bad stuff happened to my family—as it does to everyone. These storms pushed us to reevaluate our lives. Matthew turned back to the faith of his youth, and this time it stuck. Jesus was alive and ready to share our burdens. One by one, everyone in our family came to Christ.

The funny thing is, the more we believed in Jesus, the less complicated our Christmas celebrations became. We stopped going to parties on Christmas Eve and started going to church. We stopped buying elaborate presents and started giving to special charities in each other's names. Instead of designing the most impressive Christmas card, we made just one, stuffing its envelope with cash—the kids contributing from their piggy banks—and leaving it anonymously taped to the door of a needy family. We even convinced our extended family to exchange gifts with only one person, picking names out of a hat after the Thanksgiving meal.

Last Christmas was our best ever, and our simplest. I did *no* Christmas shopping. Emma asked if she could fill the stockings. She delighted in choosing a charity for each of us, finding used copies of the Woodland Folk series that we used to read when the kids were little, making gift certificates for breakfast in bed or a back rub, and ordering a favorite Christian comedian's DVD for the whole family. We still made a big breakfast—just not quite so big. The Christmas cards, traveling, Christmas tree—all gone—along with the stress, trips to the mall, credit-card debt, and hectic holiday schedules. Instead, we read aloud the account of Christ's birth. We stayed in our pajamas and watched the new DVD together.

Putting Christ back at the center of our Christmas has meant choosing a road less traveled—a choice that has truly made all the difference.

GETTING STARTED

Reflect on Psalm 145. Do your holidays celebrate God's goodness and joyfully sing of his righteousness, or have they become a mad dash of gifts, glitter, and (for too many of us between Thanksgiving and Christmas) material gluttony? The simple truth of Jesus Christ's love is not always simple to communicate, but can be most effectively displayed in the lives of believers. Holiday celebrations are one way of expressing Christ's love and giving thanks for his blessings.

If gratitude is your goal, start by finding ways to simplify. Volunteering at a soup kitchen on Thanksgiving, sponsoring a child to honor a relative's birthday, or planting a tree to mark an anniversary will be remembered long after that tie or sweater gets lost in the back of the closet. Though the transition from exchanging piles of presents to giving fewer gifts with greater meaning may not be easy at first, it will speak a powerful message about who you are— and whose you are.

CHRISTMAS

Most people say they would love to simplify Christmas but don't know where to start. With a few simple steps, you can save money and lessen your impact on the planet.

'Tis a gift to be simple

The first step toward celebrating the holiday in a way that respects creation and honors the Creator is changing your mind-set. Yes, advertisers want you to believe that a true Christmas celebration requires a mountain of gifts under an ornately decorated tree.

Even friends and family may pressure you to indulge in holiday excess just because that's what you have always done.

If you're like me, you have experienced Christmas stress first-hand—braving the malls to find the perfect gift, jumping from party to party, and cringing at the January credit-card bills. Studies show that the "season to be jolly" has become the most depressing time of year for some people.

To get back to the heart of Christmas, start by simplifying. Sit down with your family this summer or fall—before the holiday craziness begins—and discuss what kind of Christmas celebration would truly capture the meaning of the holiday. Which activities have meant the most in years past? Who helps you experience Christ's love around Christmas time? Instead of creating a Christmas gift wish list, think of ways you can reach out to others. Your goal should be to end the holiday with deeper relationships rather than mounds of wrapping paper, ribbons, and bows. You will spend less money, create less waste, and have more stories to share in the future.

Experiencing Christmas in a new way, however, doesn't mean you have to drop all of the traditions that have made the holiday so meaningful. Scaling back, prioritizing, and eliminating some of the excess is the key.

> **SAVE GREEN**
>
> It takes an average of six months for a credit card user to pay off holiday debt.

Use Less Stuff Day

What better way to gear up for a simpler, more meaningful holiday season than celebrating Use Less Stuff Day? Usually set during the third week in November, the purpose of this day is to encourage consumers to create less waste; reducing in the first place lessens the need for recycling and reusing. Join the Environmental Protection

Agency, Keep America Beautiful, and over two hundred other organizations across the country in this celebration of simplifying. Find out more at http://use-less-stuff.com.

Christmas cards

If sending out Christmas cards only elevates your stress level, skip them altogether. There are other ways to let loved ones know that you remember them this Christmas, like e-cards. Not ready to give up traditional cards yet? Make your own cards using recycled paper and other materials and recruit your kids to help. Use the fronts of cards you've received in the past. Your one-of-a-kind creations are sure to stand out among the piles of mass-produced cards your friends receive. Or consider purchasing cards directly from your favorite charity. Choose an organization that sends a message you support and uses recycled materials. Visit http://www.cards thatgive.org for a list of charities that offer greeting cards and links to each of those Web sites.

Many recycling facilities accept greeting cards along with office paper and paperboard, so be sure to recycle your old, unwanted cards. The environmental site http://www.earth911.org allows you to enter your zip code and locate your local recycling resources.

> GO GREEN
>
> If everyone sent just one less card per year, we could save 50,000 cubic yards of paper.

O Christmas tree, O Christmas tree

In many households, the Christmas tree is the focal point of holiday magic. If you live in a warm area of the country, consider purchasing a living tree from a nursery and replanting it after the holiday or buying your tree from a local organic or sustainable farm. Buying locally minimizes CO_2 emissions from shipping long distances, and supporting sustainable and organic farms prevents environmental degradation. Visit http://www.localharvest.org for a list of live Christmas tree providers across the country. When it's time to take your tree down, be sure to recycle it. Find the Christmas tree collection point nearest you so your old tree can be shredded for composting or mulch. In some communities, trees are sunk in local lakes to create fish habitats or used for stabilizing sand dunes in coastal areas.

Purchasing an artificial tree also can be a good option. The one-time purchase cuts costs and saves gas on annual trips to a tree farm; also, artificial trees do not require pesticides. If you opt for an artificial tree, try to find one made in the United States, which will greatly decrease the distance that the tree traveled and lessen the chances of contamination from lead and other toxins. Down the road, when you're ready to get rid of your artificial tree, donate it to a local charity, school, or church.

The cheapest alternative is to simply decorate an outdoor tree for Christmas. It may seem a little strange at first, but you'll have more money to share with others over the holidays. If you decorate one close to your front window, you can still admire it from inside your house.

> **GO GREEN**
>
> For several years, Emma has decorated an indoor houseplant instead of a Christmas tree. Her creations usually have a theme (a few years back, we had a Hawaiian Christmas) and always come from the heart—far more original than anything you'll find in a magazine.

Trimming your tree

Do you really need the newest Hallmark collectible ornament this year? Instead, opt for edible or compostable items like stringing popcorn or cranberries for garland. Making ornaments and

Christmas decorations—especially with kids—can be a fun holiday tradition. Use flour, water, and a little salt to make dough for tree decorations. Form Christmas shapes with cookie cutters, and make a small hole near the top to loop string or ribbon through. Then bake them in the oven until they are hard. Decorate your new creations with paint, seeds, feathers, or glitter. And if you carefully wrap and store them, they should last for years.

Decorations

Create your own winter wonderland right inside your home. Cut out circular pieces of used white paper, and fold each one in half three times. Cut v-shaped notches into the triangle you've made. Unfold it and you'll discover a beautiful snowflake. Use various sizes to decorate your tree, or hang them from the ceiling. You can also cut discarded magazines and old wrapping paper to form colorful paper chains.

Lights

If lights are non-negotiable for your family, LED holiday lights could be a better option for illuminating your home. They cost about $8 more per strand than standard lights, but use up to 100 times less energy and will last about ten years or one hundred thousand hours when used indoors. LED lights could save your family up to $50 on energy bills this holiday season. Unlike their traditional counterparts, if one of the LED lights burns out, the rest of the strand will stay lit, so you'll never have a problem identifying the faulty bulb.

Gifts

For many families, gift giving is the area with the most room for change during the holidays. Culture—not to mention our selfish nature—encourages us to constantly want more and never to be satisfied with what we have. The average American adult spent $860 last year on Christmas gifts. This Christmas, shift your focus from what you want to receive to what you can give others.

In our family, we do stockings only—mostly practical items, gift certificates for help around the house, and gifts to charity. My favorite gift last year was a package of calligraphy pens—something I would not buy myself, but always wanted and now use nearly every day. A simple attitude adjustment will lead your family toward a more economical, environmentally friendly, and Christ-centered Christmas.

> **GO GREEN**
>
> Agree as a family what you're going to do for gifts. I know a family who decided that each person would receive three gifts each year to symbolize the gold, frankincense, and myrrh the wise men gave Jesus. They each receive one thing they need, one thing they want, and one small surprise.

Useful gifts

Don't buy a useless gift just because you feel obligated. Ask yourself what your loved one needs or will actually use. Consider buying friends and family canvas shopping bags, high-efficiency light-bulbs, a battery recharger, a dozen handkerchiefs, a refillable thermos bottle, or seeds for next year's garden. Consumable gifts are another great option. Give organic teas, fair-trade coffee, a gift card to the local natural food store, or homemade baked goods. Many a time, I've filled a nice canvas bag with an "environmental starter kit," including practical items the recipient will use and enjoy rather than toss on a closet shelf to collect dust.

> " And he puzzled three hours, till his puzzler was sore. Then the Grinch thought of something he hadn't before. Maybe Christmas, he thought, doesn't come from a store. Maybe Christmas perhaps means a little bit more!
> —*Dr. Seuss,* How the Grinch Stole Christmas "

Homemade gifts

Create personalized, unique gifts using recycled objects. Re-cover a journal, make a photo collage, or design earrings for a friend. For my birthday this year, Emma made me a mother-daughter scrapbook—a gift I look at frequently and will treasure always.

Local gifts

Check your area for locally made gifts like ceramics, sweaters, and furniture. Your gift will cut back on emissions involved in shipping, support local artisans, and provide a memorable story.

The gift of yourself

When you'd like to show love to friends or neighbors, give an act of service. Shovel a snow-covered driveway. Offer to babysit for young couple that needs a night out. Give coupons to mow a yard when spring and summer arrive. Prepare and deliver a meal or a loaf of fresh bread.

Re-gifting

Some people might disagree with this, but I'm okay with passing on nice items I don't need to someone who does. Also, consider trading or giving away unneeded items on http://www.freecycle.org.

Gifts for people in need

Many churches, malls, and charitable organizations serve as collection sites for Christmas gift projects such as Operation Christmas Child and Angel Tree. Instead of buying gifts for each other, shop as a family for a child whose parent is in prison this Christmas. Or send a gift overseas. Many charities allow you to distribute monetary gifts to developing countries on behalf of a friend or family member. Give everything from a goat, pig, or chicken to a water purification system through sites like http://worldgifts.cafod.org.uk and http://www.heifer.org. For another gift idea that keeps on giving, visit http://www.kiva.org/about. Kiva offers microloans to help people in third-world countries start small businesses, providing income to help meet basic needs.

Share your celebration

If you know a needy family—or anyone who may be celebrating alone—invite them to share Christmas dinner with you in your home. Practicing hospitality fills us with thankfulness and takes the focus off ourselves and on to caring for others.

GO GREEN

My favorite Christmas gift ever? R-60 insulation in the attic from a loving husband who knows I get cold easily in the winter. His gift will keep my heart (and my fingers, toes, and nose) warm all winter long, for years to come.

Shopping smart for the holidays

As you simplify your holiday season step-by-step, you may find that some shopping is inevitable. Making minor changes and wise decisions can keep you on the straight road to true holiday celebration.

Shop online

Save gas and time (and possibly avoid a nervous breakdown) by shopping online through an Internet shopping portal such as http://www.greatergood.com. When you start from these Web sites and link to your shopping sites, 5 to 15 percent of your purchase price goes to an organization of your choice, with no extra cost to you. Remember to look for items that won't be excessively packaged.

Plan ahead

When a mall run is unavoidable, save gas by planning ahead and consolidating shopping trips. Bring your own reusable tote bags to cut down on paper and plastic bag use. Also, beware of sales.

Resist the urge to buy things you don't need just because they are "affordably priced."

Buy responsible, high-quality products

Shop at flea markets and vintage and secondhand stores for affordable, quality goods. Then add your own personal touch to make the gift "new," like a fresh paint job for a chair or table.

Sometimes paying a little more up front will assure a longer life span for your gift. When choosing what stores to patronize, research the company's record. Does your choice to shop at a certain store show love for your neighbors? Is child labor used to make the products? What is the company's environmental record? Visit http://www.betterworldshopper.org to see an extensive set of product ratings.

Wrapping paper

Drastically reduce wrapping paper waste by using reusable bags or boxes to wrap presents. If opened gently, wrapping paper can be used again on another gift. Look for gift wrap made from recycled

Be a Better Shopper

Want to support "good for the planet" merchandisers, but don't have time to do the research? Check out the *Better World Shopping Guide* online (http://www.betterworldshopper.org), and try to patronize stores near the top of the list. Searchable categories include the following:

airlines, audio equipment, baking supplies, bread, butter & margarine, candy, canned fruit & vegetables, cars, cereal, chips, chocolate, cleaning supplies, clothing, coffee, computers, condiments, cookies, cosmetics, crackers, credit cards, dairy alternatives, dairy products, desserts, eggs, electronics, energy bars, energy drinks, frozen dinners, fruits & vegetables, gas stations, gum & mints, ice cream, juice, meat alternatives, meat products, milk & alternatives, oil & vinegar, olives & pickles, paper, paper towels, pasta sauce, peanut butter & jelly, pizza, popcorn, nuts & pretzels, retail stores, rice & other grains, salad dressing, salsa, spreads & dips, seafood, soap, soft drinks, soup & noodles, sugar, spices & sweeteners, supermarkets, tea.

GO GREEN

If every family reused just 2 feet of holiday ribbon, the 38,000 miles of ribbon saved could tie a bow around the entire planet.

paper, and secure it using string or ribbons instead of tape. Since our family only does stockings, very little or no wrapping paper is needed.

If you haven't already purchased holiday gift wrap, don't buy it this year. Instead, wrap gifts in newspaper comics, maps, or your child's artwork. Go one step further by making the wrapping part of the gift, like a scarf, flowerpot, brightly colored towel, or dish. For gift tags, cut up used Christmas cards and write the recipient's name on the back. To cover previous handwritten greetings, glue a piece of paper on the back with your message over it.

Why wrap gifts when you could make a game for your children? For kids—or kids at heart—hide clues around the house that will lead them to the present. This not only eliminates the need for wrapping but also sends your child on an adventurous gift search.

GO GREEN

Think reusing your wrapping paper won't make a difference? Think again! If every household in America wrapped just three presents in reused materials, it would save enough paper to cover forty-five thousand football fields.

Holiday travel

If there's "no place like home for the holidays," why do we complicate our holiday season with travel? By staying home, you reduce the amount of gas used during one of the year's heaviest travel times. Staying home also helps keep your local economy strong. Take advantage of time off from school and work to enjoy your family in a relaxed setting.

Holiday entertaining

From Thanksgiving to New Year's, we open our homes and celebrate the season with friends and family. Here are some practical ways to entertain while leaving you more cash and giving the environment a break.

Energy use

If you're hosting the party, turn the heat down before your guests arrive. For each degree above 68, your furnace uses 3 to 5 percent more energy. The extra body heat of your guests will warm up the room while you save energy.

Formal wear

For formal affairs, don't buy a new outfit. Check consignment shops or borrow from a friend.

Food

When the party is over, save the leftovers. Send them home in containers with guests. For large parties or church functions, leftovers can be donated to Second Harvest, an organization whose goal is to end hunger in America. Visit their Web site at http://www .secondharvest.org.

Plan ahead to minimize waste. This chart can help you estimate portion sizes.

FOOD/DRINK	PORTION PER PERSON
Eggnog	1/2 cup
Turkey	1.2–1.4 pounds
Stuffing	1/4 pound
Sweet potato casserole	1/4 pound
Green beans	1/4 pound
Cranberry relish	3 tablespoons
Pumpkin pie	1/8 of a 9-inch pie

Adapted from "42 Ways to Trim Your Holiday Wasteline"

Party gifts

Consider swapping cookies instead of gifts. For a cookie exchange, ask guests to share the story behind the recipe.

How to Save a Bundle This Christmas

Business-as-usual Christmas

ITEM	INITIAL COST	COST OVER FIVE YEARS
Christmas tree, fresh cut	$75	$375
Ornaments, Hallmark	$175/25 ornaments	$175
Lights, standard	$80/350 count	$160
Decorations, fancy	$250	$250
Electric utilities	$120/month of Dec.	$600
Cards and postage	$50	$250
Travel (long distance average 275 miles)	$150	$750
Gifts	$1,800	$9,000
TOTAL	**$2,700**	**$11,560**

Simplified Christmas

ITEM	INITIAL COST	COST OVER FIVE YEARS
Christmas tree, existing plant or outside tree	$0	$0
Ornaments, homemade	$25	$25
Lights, LED	$140/400 + $10 adapter	$150
Decorations, handmade	$10	$10
Electric utilities	$60/month of Dec.	$300
E-card	$0	$0
Travel (local)	$25	$125
Cut spending on gifts in half	$900	$4,500
TOTAL	**$1,170**	**$5,110**

TOTAL SAVINGS ON CHRISTMAS OVER FIVE YEARS: $6,450

If each family in America consumed one less gallon of gasoline this holiday season (cutting out about 20 miles of travel), we'd reduce greenhouse gas emissions by one million tons.

VALENTINE'S DAY AND ANNIVERSARIES

When telling the one you love how much he or she means to you on Valentine's Day or an anniversary, consider the following environmentally friendly practices.

Cards

Why pay as much as $4 or $5 for a card that someone else wrote when you could lovingly make your own for little or no cost? Pick up your scissors, grab an old magazine, and create a card made from paper you find lying around your house or office. Chances are it will capture your loved one's attention more than a mass-produced greeting card.

Flowers

The floral industry uses the highest level of pesticides of all agricultural sectors. Long before that beautiful bouquet reaches your sweetheart, pesticide runoff from flower farms pollutes waterways. So if you choose to say "I love you" with flowers, buy fresh or dried flowers at your local farmers' market. Even more local: grow your own!

Wild for Wildflowers

When we lived in New England, our yard was two-thirds of an acre of wildflowers. We invited the church and neighbors to pick bouquets any time they wanted to. Our wildflower meadow even provided bridesmaid bouquets and centerpieces for a summer wedding.

One day when Emma was outside hanging laundry, a man stopped and asked if he could pick flowers for his wife—he had forgotten their anniversary. Anything to help keep the romance alive!

Buy fair-trade and organic

This is one case where good-for-the-environment is going to cost more; however, once you learn about the human price of child labor and shortsighted agricultural practices that leave the land devastated, fair-trade and organic products make the higher cost seem like an ethical bargain.

Although it is more expensive, certified fair-trade chocolate does not use child labor and pays a living wage to workers on plantations, helping them meet their basic human needs. Try to support fair-trade companies such as Newman's Own Organics, Rapunzel Pure Organics, and Green & Black's Organic Chocolate. While you're at it, oppose child labor by joining Global Exchange's Cocoa Campaign online at http://www.globalexchange.org/cocoa.

Fair-Trade and Organic Chocolate

NAME	ORGANIC	FAIR TRADE	PRICE	PURCHASING INFO
Art Bar	X	X	$12.00/ 4 bars	http://www.globalexchange.org (800) 505-4410
Betty Lou's Organic Patties	X		$30.72/ 24 pieces	http://www.bettylousinc.com (800) 242-5205
Ecco Bella's Health by Chocolate	X	X	$21.99/ 50 minis	http://www.eccobella.com (877) 696-2220
Equal Exchange	X	X	$4.25/bar	http://www.equalexchange.com (774) 776-7333
Gaia Organic Chocolate Drops	X	X	$18.99/ 3 boxes	http://www.ecoexpress.com (800) 733-3495
Theo's 3400 Phinney Chocolate	X	X	$3.25/bar	http://www.theochocolate.com (206) 632-5100
Yachana Gourmet Chocolate		X	$19.95/ 6 boxes	http://www.yachanagourmet.com (800) 637-7614

Adapted from http://www.thegreenguide.com

Say it with pictures

Want to express your love creatively and score some bonus points in the love department? If your computer has simple video-editing equipment, make a three-minute film or slideshow that tells the story of your love. Be creative and find pictures that highlight special memories and landmarks of your relationship. Your significant other will surely treasure this original creation—throw in humorous photos and share a few laughs.

You may think this is taking frugal to an extreme, but I've had no complaints in our family. Several years ago I bought Matthew a simple but nice Valentine's card for one dollar. It says, "God is love; and he that dwelleth in love dwelleth in God, and God in him" (1 John 4:16, KJV). Each year, I put a new note in the card, written on recycled or reused paper. I keep the old notes in the back of the envelope, so we can see what was going on in our lives the year before. I've started the same tradition with a Father's Day card. God's love is eternal—so why buy a new card every year?

Then the angel spoke to the women. "Don't be afraid!" he said. "I know you are looking for Jesus, who was crucified. He isn't here! He is risen from the dead, just as he said would happen."
MATTHEW 28:5-6, NLT

EASTER

For Christians, Easter offers unlimited hope and reminds us that Jesus Christ died on Friday and rose from the grave Sunday morning. Too often that message is overshadowed by Easter baskets, Honey-Baked hams, and shiny fake grass. This Easter, don't forget what the holiday means. Focus on spending time as a family. Get in touch with the Creator by spending time outdoors or attending a sunrise service on Easter morning.

Below are some easy ways to deepen your current Easter traditions.

Sacrifice

Whether you are from a Catholic or Protestant background, encourage each member of your family to give up something for Lent. Pledge not to watch television, eat junk food, use plastic bags, or shop at the mall. One year our daughter, Emma, gave up bananas (because they have to be shipped so far from where they are grown) and meat (because it requires a more intense use of resources than a grain and vegetable–based diet). Giving up something that has become an addiction in your life will certainly loosen its stronghold on you, while saving you money and bringing you closer to God.

Easter eggs

Make your own natural dyes instead of using store-bought ones. The ingredients are easy to find, offer a wider range of colors, and are better for your children and the environment. Bring eggs to a boil in water with a small amount of vinegar and one of the natural dyes listed in the following chart. Let simmer for at least fifteen minutes and you'll have a rainbow of colors. Remember to make only as many hard-boiled eggs as your family can eat. If you make too many, share egg salad with a friend or neighbor.

Natural Dyes for Easter Eggs

DESIRED COLOR	INGREDIENT
Lavender	Purple grape juice
Blue	Red cabbage
Green	Spinach
Yellow	Carrot tops, orange peels, or lemon peels
Orange	Yellow onion skins
Pink	Beets or cranberries
Red	Red onion skins

U.S. consumers purchase more than 17 million egg coloring and dye kits during the week leading up to Easter. Chocolate candy chalks up about $318 million in sales, second only to Valentine's Day.

Easter baskets

When using plastic eggs, be sure to save them to refill the following year. Rather than plastic Easter grass, use a scrap of green fabric, a pretty green scarf, or shredded paper. If you already have plastic grass, continue to reuse it for as long as you can.

Instead of excessive candy and cheap plastic toys, consider gift cards, books, or coupons for rewards like "Pick and help make your favorite dinner," "Go out on a date with Mom or Dad," or "Get out of one chore for free." Also, plan to make decorated Easter cookies to take the place of at least one bag of individually wrapped Easter candy, which will eliminate packaging waste and reduce the money you'll spend on candy.

Since 2004, candy advertising has been greater during the Easter season than during the weeks leading up to Halloween. About $61.6 million was spent on candy advertising in September and October of 2007, versus $90.8 million during March and April of that same year. That's a lot of marshmallow chicks!

No More Jelly Beans

When Clark and Emma were growing up, they could have one dessert each day. Even if they had some candy of their own, they always knew to check in with us before eating a piece: "Can this count as my dessert of the day?" We always said yes, and that was that—no nagging, no whining, no food battles. The only exceptions were major holidays and birthdays.

When Clark was about eight years old, he collected quite a few jelly bean–filled plastic eggs on our neighborhood Easter egg hunt. Clark has never been a huge fan of sweets, and he has always been pretty good about "listening to his belly"—when he gets full, he stops eating. But the jelly beans must have been a novelty, and he (and his parents) lost track of how much candy he ate that Easter.

I can still picture Clark crawling up the stairs at bedtime, groaning, "My belly doesn't feel so good." Fortunately, the bathroom is located right at the top of the flight, and Clark made it to the toilet before getting sick.

Kids recover quickly. "I feel much better now," Clark said, flashing a relieved grin. He brushed his teeth and then headed right to bed.

What a cheap lesson in the price of excess. Just because you can have more, doesn't mean you should.

Clark has never had another jelly bean since. Not one.

SAVE GREEN

The average shopper who celebrates Easter (nearly 80 percent of Americans) spends $135.07 on the holiday. He or she spends the most on a new spring outfit ($26.03) and food for the Easter meal ($37.56). Other popular Easter purchases include candy ($18.53), gifts ($20.61), flowers ($9.63), and decorations ($7.63).

EARTH DAY

What better way to increase our appreciation for creation than to celebrate Earth Day? Since 1970, people around the world have set aside April 22 as a special day to care for the planet and raise awareness about environmental issues. As Christians, our environmental stewardship directly impacts how we love our neighbors. We can take the lead in encouraging our friends, neighbors, and churches to honor God by respecting and caring for his creation.

Creation care groups

Exploring Scripture together is the first step toward helping others realize that the condition of our environment is a spiritual issue that crosses all political boundaries. God deeply cares about the condition of his creation. This Earth Day, start a Bible or book study about caring for creation. Read *Serve God, Save the Planet* together (written by a wise and humorous doctor I've known for thirty years, J. Matthew Sleeth). You can find a free workbook at http://servegodsavetheplanet.org/download/workbook.htm.

Matthew and I have been part of many Earth Day celebrations. Nearly all of the best—and best attended—Earth Day celebrations have been organized by churches. One of Matthew's favorite experiences was an eco-picnic celebration in Texas. After the bands finished playing, Matthew led everyone to stand under a huge oak tree for five minutes of silence. The wind picked up and God spoke. They listened. By being still in the midst of a celebration, they heard God.

Serving others

Visit http://www.earthday.net to learn about events scheduled for your area, or plan your own celebration and plant a tree. Each tree you plant helps to reduce greenhouse gas emissions, cleanses the air, provides homes for living creatures, and holds soil in place to prevent erosion. Build a birdhouse with your family or make a bird feeder to support the local bird population. Pick up litter from a stretch of road, park, or railroad tracks. If you have a large group, ask your town's public works department to provide gloves, vests, and bags. Once you've collected the trash and placed it along the side of the roads, you can make arrangements to have it picked up.

The generous will prosper; those who refresh others will themselves be refreshed.
PROVERBS 11:25, NLT

Our creation care group meets twice a month. One week, we shared a picnic supper and then cleaned up a stream bed. The organizer contacted our city hall to make arrangements for trash disposal, and we all brought our own gloves and trash bags. It was a lovely way to share fellowship and good work on a weekday evening!

Earth Day meals

Plan a healthy menu that includes locally produced foods and has a minimal impact on the environment. Choose bean products and vegetables since these require fewer resources to produce than factory-farmed meat. Invite a few friends over for the meal and plan something that you can all *do* together to help the earth. Don't hesitate to let people know that God the Creator is the motivation behind your environmental action.

THE FOURTH OF JULY

What could be more patriotic than caring for the planet this Independence Day? Whether you're hosting a picnic at home for friends and family or simply marveling over your town's fireworks display, here are some simple ways to add green to your red, white, and blue celebration.

Food choices

Throwing a picnic or having a BBQ on the Fourth? Choose locally grown, organic produce. Also, consider offering a vegetarian option, such as veggie burgers. Want to know how the foods you are buying measure up? Visit the Center for Informed Food Choices' Web site at http://www.appetiteforprofit.com.

If your picnic involves grilling, consider using sustainably produced charcoal. Some varieties are made from industrial scrap wood, while others are produced using clean energy turbine heat. Look for eco-friendly brands like Wicked Good Charcoal and Kingsford Charwood.

Disposables

Disposable plastics can remain in the environment for hundreds of years. Your party can be just as much fun and more environmentally friendly when you serve food on regular reusable plates. Add a touch of patriotic color with red, white, or blue cloth napkins. Skip the plastic forks and opt for metal utensils instead. Ask a couple of teens to help you wash dishes after everyone has finished eating if you are worried about the mess. Most people are glad to help, especially when they know their small gestures are helping the environment.

Clearly label recycling bins and place them in an obvious spot so guests will use them. Avoid plastic and glass bottles; instead, have an abundance of filtered tap water and ice on hand.

Something to Celebrate

It was two weeks after the Fourth of July, but my friend Geoff was wearing a hat with two American flags waving in the breeze. "Today's *my* July 4th," Geoff explained. After attending seminary, marrying, having a child, and working in the United States for more than a decade, Geoff, a native of Australia, had been sworn in that morning as an American citizen. About seventy-five friends had gathered in his inner-city backyard to celebrate.

Geoff and his beautiful wife, Sherry, are urban pioneers, living and working among the poor and sharing the creation-care gospel wherever they go. Their latest project is an urban garden, part of a racial reconciliation effort by the local Episcopalian church, which centuries ago excluded African Americans from being buried in the adjoining cemetery. Now the garden plot is being shared by a diverse group of neighbors working together in the garden as God intended, while providing fresh, organic vegetables to a local after-school program.

For the citizenship celebration, Sherry and Geoff borrowed plates from their church to lessen the amount of trash, but more people from the neighborhood showed up than expected. Matthew and I scraped food waste into the compost and washed dishes, so we didn't have to resort to Styrofoam plates. With a little forethought by the hosts, and some great kitchen conversations while we washed and dried dishes, we were able to keep the environmental impact of the party to a minimum while celebrating Geoff's citizenship with an all-American barbecue.

Fireworks

Fireworks are bad for the planet. They fill the air with gunpowder, heavy metals, and accelerants. They are often unsafe as well as costly. A home fireworks display can cost anywhere from $500 to $1,000 for fifteen minutes.

This year, cut out fireworks and sparklers from your budget and enjoy a nearby display at a park. At home, make other colorful decorations like ribbon streamers, from recycled newspapers.

Ready to take action? Consider talking to your local fireworks authorities about using Sekon biodegradable fireworks next year. This is the gunpowder-free, compressed-air technology that Disney now uses in its fireworks displays.

HALLOWEEN

If you choose to celebrate Halloween as a family, it is possible to enjoy an inexpensive and environmentally friendly holiday by putting a few simple tips into practice.

Costumes

Before splurging on a costume that may only be worn once, check your closet for creative ideas. Overalls and an old plaid shirt make a great start for a scarecrow or farmer. Mix and match clothes from the 1970s or '80s for a retro costume. Can't find anything costume-worthy in your closets? Check out the local thrift store or borrow your neighbor's costume from last year.

Custom Costumes

I have many Proverbs 31 wifely skills, but sewing anything more complicated than curtains, buttons, and hems is beyond my abilities. Yet my kids always had great costumes, thanks to some generous and talented neighbors with older kids and a lot of imagination.

Emma's favorite costume was a calculator—all her idea and execution. She took two pieces of rectangular cardboard, punched holes at the top, and then inserted ribbon straps—

like a walking billboard. To make the push buttons, she cut up sponges, numbering them with a permanent marker. I have never seen a walking calculator before or since, but Emma's costume was quite the hit that year.

I think Clark's favorite year was when he dressed up like Bill Nye, the Science Guy. Matthew's lab coat, some glasses, a pocket protector, and a borrowed bow tie did the trick. Total cost: $0.

One fall when my nephews were visiting, they talked me into making them Three Musketeer capes. A few yards of blue felt and some ribbon and swords slung alongside a leather belt resulted in costumes that were used over and over for years to come. Not to be left out, Emma, the only girl cousin at the time, went along as d'Artagnan, the Three Musketeers' dashing young companion.

Jack-o'-lanterns

Think ahead and grow your own pumpkins, or buy your pumpkin at the local farmers' market. Keep the waste to a minimum: Clean, bake, and salt the seeds for a healthy snack. Instead of throwing your pumpkin's flesh away, make pumpkin muffins, cookies, or a pie. When his time comes to an end, add your jack-o'-lantern to the compost pile instead of sending him to the landfill.

SAVE GREEN

A frightening fact: The United States spends more on Halloween decorations than any other holiday except Christmas. In addition, we shell out $23.33 per costume and $20 on candy. Retailers also report a boom in sales of pet costumes, with 7.4 million households planning on dressing up their pets. Total Halloween spending: $5.07 billion, second only to the Christmas holiday.

When I Grow Up, I Want to Be Mary

I affectionately refer to my walking buddy as "Saint Mary." In the midst of caring for five adult children and a slew of young grandkids, Mary devotes herself to serving God and her neighbors. She is one of the most generous—and energetic—people I know.

Mary's special passion is caring for the environment. All summer long, she hauls 30 gallons of household wastewater per day from the sink and shower out to her garden.

Last week, after our very brisk walk (our other walking partner is a former volleyball player with legs about 10 feet long), Mary gave me a tour of her garden—the vegetable patch, the fruit trees and grape arbor, the new rain garden with perennials that will help to conserve water runoff. The pumpkins are especially impressive—and have a great story behind them: A dear friend of Mary's has an annual ritual of smashing a spent pumpkin as hard as she can against her barn wall and then allowing the seeds to self-sow on the fertile ground for a prolific pumpkin patch the following summer.

Last fall, Mary decided to follow suit, only she doesn't have a barn, so she smashed a large pumpkin in a corner of her garden. Now the pumpkin vines are growing everywhere, with beautiful flowers promising a bumper crop of jack-o'-lanterns. Since I did not plant pumpkins this year, but have more cucumbers, lettuce, dill, and parsley than our family can possibly eat, we are happily exchanging our excess produce.

If I am half as energetic, kind, and fruitful as Saint Mary when I reach my sixth decade of life, I will consider myself blessed beyond measure!

Candy

If you're handing out candy, don't go overboard. All those individually wrapped bars add up to a ghoulish amount of trash. Try passing out healthier snacks, like honey sticks or fruit leathers. Stores like Whole Foods and Trader Joe's offer fun and healthy alternatives to candy.

I admit it: merchandisers have got chocolate lovers like me all figured out. They put the Halloween displays up in the middle of September and then advertise a terrific sale. I used to purchase multiple bags of candy since "the price was so good," hiding them in the back of my closet. But those little packs of miniature chocolate bars kept calling my name. One little bar couldn't hurt, could it? Before I knew it, a family-sized bag had disappeared—and it wasn't the mice who were eating it!

I have a theory that the 15 pounds Americans reportedly gain between Thanksgiving and Christmas really starts with those pre-Halloween sales. Of course, the candy makers are happy: I ended up spending twice as much money while doubling the environmental cost to produce and transport that candy, creating twice as much trash, and eating more calories than I needed. Maybe it's not a coincidence that our waste and waists both grow significantly as we enter the holiday season.

So what's a mom to do? I ignore those September sales and don't buy candy until a day or two before Halloween—no matter how great the temptation!

Trick or treat

Rather than driving to other neighborhoods, stay local. Walk door-to-door with your kids to reduce fuel consumption and air pollution. Also, skip the special Halloween bags and let your kids collect candy using pillowcases or grocery bags.

THANKSGIVING

When did Thanksgiving become more about turkey, crescent rolls, and pumpkin pie than giving thanks to the Creator? This Thanksgiving, make a grateful heart your priority.

Counting your blessings

Thanksgiving is the perfect time to make a list of all the things you are thankful for. Thank God for everything from the religious freedom we enjoy to the beauty of his creation. Make time for prayer and sharing your gratitude as a family. Take a walk in the woods and give thanks for the majesty of nature. Focusing on your blessings will change your perspective and fill your heart with gratitude.

Sharing your meal

The Pilgrims of Plymouth Rock celebrated Thanksgiving with their Indian neighbors and gave thanks to God for an abundant harvest. Look for someone in your area to invite for Thanksgiving dinner—a young couple with no family nearby, an elderly friend, or next-door neighbors. Invite people who live close to reduce auto emissions, and thank them for what they have meant to you and your family.

Saying thank you

Don't let Thanksgiving pass without saying thank you to someone who has made a significant impact on your life. If you can't say it in person, write a letter (on recycled paper) or call and let that person know why you are thankful for his or her presence in your life. Your call or letter will likely become a treasured gift.

BIRTHDAYS

Whether for kids or adults, you can throw a first-rate birthday party without spending a fortune or hurting the planet.

Partying for a cause

Most American children already have too many toys. Try a different approach to parties this year. Ask your child to help pick a theme like animals, camping, or the rainforest. Then find a matching organization that would appreciate donations or gifts. Plan your party food and activities around the theme. Instead of bringing presents, guests can be encouraged to bring donations for the cause you are celebrating. Be sure to include the cause and type of donations you are collecting in the invitation. Partying for a cause is a great way to show your child the importance of helping others while still having fun.

Decorations

Instead of hanging mass-produced banners and decorations around the house, create your own banner on recycled newsprint to set the party's tone. Or make a photo collage of the person who is being celebrated. If you decorate with balloons, choose natural latex, which is fully biodegradable.

Cards and invitations

Consider giving friends and family Grow-A-Note recycled cards for their birthdays. These greeting cards have wildflower seeds embedded in the handmade, recycled paper. The card can be planted directly in the ground, with the paper acting as mulch. Each card includes instructions for planting and growing. A few months in the soil will produce a beautiful patch of flowers. You can purchase these earth-friendly cards online at http://www.good humans.com.

WEDDINGS

Weddings are times of joy, celebration, and fellowship—Jesus performed his first miracle at a wedding banquet recounted in John 2. But weddings also can create a tremendous financial drain and environmental waste. Making some small changes will place you on the road to marital bliss, while sharing a powerful testimony about your faith and your values.

Simplifying

Before you sign on for the pricey hors d'oeuvres trays and ever-flowing chocolate fountain, set a realistic budget for your wedding.

Remember, this day—although significant and special—is only one among many in your upcoming marriage. Don't create unnecessary pressure for yourself to dazzle your guests. Simple, tasteful alternatives to extravagant, costlier choices can demonstrate that it is the marriage—not the wedding—that counts most. Strive to point others toward Christ through the powerful testimony of your lives, not the fancy centerpieces at the reception. You'll save money and set a godly example for others.

> **GO GREEN**
>
> About five hundred thousand trees are used annually to support weddings in the United States.

Invitations

Paperless e-mail invitations are the most eco-friendly option for spreading the word to friends and family about an upcoming union. If you're looking for something more traditional, try recycled paper and ask for an online RSVP. Instead of printed directions, point your guests to a Web site. Don't forget to also use recycled paper for thank you notes.

Wedding Web sites like http://www.theknot.com can help you organize and manage a guest list and create a personalized wedding Web page where your guests can find up-to-date information about your big day.

The reception

Having your ceremony and reception at the same place eliminates the need to decorate two spots and reduces travel. Look for local sources for food and drinks, and encourage caterers to use organic ingredients. Borrow dishes and cutlery from a church or other organization. Use homemade tablecloths you can later turn into dinner napkins, pillowcases, and quilts. Recruit friends to help wash dishes and clean up after your guests have left. Donate leftover food to a local mission rather than throwing it out.

Transportation

The largest environmental impact will most likely come from travel to and from your wedding. Try to have the wedding in a town where the majority of your guests live. Organize guest car pools to the wedding from hotels and from the wedding to the reception site. Suggest that your guests "offset" their CO_2 emissions on a site like http://www.terrapass.com.

Flowers

Will heliconias shipped from Columbia really contribute to the quality of your wedding—or your marriage? If possible, choose flowers that are grown locally and organically, which will reduce emissions generated during transport. Also consider using flowers from your ceremony and from the bridal party to decorate your reception. At the reception, substitute traditional centerpieces with potted plants that can double as gifts to your guests or wedding party.

They will celebrate your abundant goodness and joyfully sing of your righteousness.
PSALM 145:7

Photographs

Request one formal wedding portrait before the event; then ask your photographer to keep the rest of the celebration proofs in digital form. This cuts down on chemicals and paper used in developing and ensures that the only prints made are the ones you actually want. If you have a friend with photography skills, talk to him or her about shooting the wedding for you.

Gifts

Instead of registering at a traditional gift registry, offer your guests the option of donating to a cause or organization in your name.

Need ideas for gifts that will make a difference? Check out http://www.alternativegiftregistry.org.

For most showers and weddings, I give a reusable shopping tote filled with practical things like homemade soaps, organic food, a blanket or quilt, environmentally friendly cleaning products, handkerchiefs, cloth shopping bags, and energy-efficient light-bulbs. One newlywed friend reported that when she got back from her two-week honeymoon camping trip, they were grateful to find so many of the things they needed to set up their new apartment in my gift bag.

Green Weddings

The average wedding in America costs nearly $30,000. Clark and Emma are friends with a couple who planned a terrific wedding for just over $4,000 *and* stayed green. How did they do it? With a little help from their friends. One room-mate was in charge of plates—most were borrowed from the local student mission center or from friends and fam-ily. Another set the tables. Tablecloths were borrowed. One family was put in charge of replenishing the veggie platters. While the young people were dancing, a couple of parents and I washed dishes, enjoying a blessed time of conversation and fellowship.

Several people (including our daughter) told me afterward that it was the most enjoyable wedding that they had ever attended because it was so clearly Christ-focused, with friends and family all pitching in and becoming one body. Throughout the night, the couple's love of the Creator was evident to all—a living testimony of how we can entertain joyfully without being wasteful of God's resources.

FUNERALS

As my physician-husband often says, one medical statistic has stayed stubbornly consistent: we all die. In fact, the stats have gotten worse: some of us die twice; Matthew has resuscitated more than a few patients in the ER who were clinically dead!

Although ending our stay on this planet is a touchy subject for some, we all must face death sooner or later—our own or the death of a loved one. As Christians, because we have confidence in our eternal home, death is not so daunting. I very clearly remember the moment, soon after I had become a Christian, when I stood up and my field of vision went pitch black—nothing critical, just a little late summer lightheadedness. What was unusual was a sudden conviction that I no longer feared death. I still strive to be a good steward of the gift of good health; however, if I found out tomorrow that I had a terminal form of cancer, I know now that I would be at peace and not feel bitter or afraid.

Traditional burial and cremation practices can negatively effect the environment, but green funerals and eco-friendly burials can lessen the impact. With a little planning, we can say good-bye with a message of hope, service, and environmental stewardship while lightening the financial burden on the ones we've left behind.

To learn what makes a green burial, check out http://www.greenburialcouncil.org. Talk to a funeral director about sustainable options, or seek out a green burial specialist. Then make sure your family knows how you feel about what happens to your remains after you're gone. Consider adding a clause to your living will or specifying your wishes in an advanced funeral document.

Cremation

Trying to decide between cremation and burial? It's a personal choice, but more and more people are choosing cremation.

SAVE GREEN

A typical U.S. funeral—including embalming, a metal casket, and cemetery charges—averages $8,500.

According to the Cremation Association of North America, one reason for the increase is that the Catholic faith now allows cremation. Other reasons include the environmental impact of burial (less room for new bodies) and the poisonous effects of embalming fluids, which ultimately find their way into our groundwater.

Cremation is not only green but also far less expensive, averaging $1,200—about $7,000 less than the typical burial. While the idea of cremation might not seem very eco-friendly—burning creates pollution—modern crematoriums have significantly reduced their emissions, with many now using "clean smokestacks." For more information, ask the owners of your local crematorium what steps they are taking to make the process greener.

Coffins

If you opt for a coffin, avoid concrete vaults. Instead, think biodegradable and consider a coffin made from locally harvested wood or wicker. A company called EcoffinsUSA crafts biodegradable coffins

Green Facts

- Funerals are the third largest personal expense, after a house and car.

- In five states—Connecticut, Indiana, Louisiana, Nebraska, and New York—green funerals are more difficult because laws require funeral directors to be involved to some degree.

- In forty-five states, citizens can legally bypass funeral homes and obtain permits to handle the body on their own.

from bamboo, willow, banana, and other materials assembled without any toxic glues in fair-trade certified manufacturing plants.

Alternative burial sites

Eco-friendly burials are becoming more popular. Places like Ramsey Creek Preserve in Westminster, South Carolina, serve as cemetery and land restoration sites. Greensprings Natural Cemetery near Toronto sits on 100 acres of land surrounded by 4,000 acres of forest and offers gravesites for $500 each. Compare that to $5,000 for an urban Toronto cemetery plot!

Preservation

Consider the environmental impact of toxic embalming chemicals like formaldehyde, a known human carcinogen associated with nasal cancer and leukemia, according to the World Health Organization. Chemical preservatives slow down the body's decomposition process; it takes longer for it to return to the soil. At one time, arsenic was used for embalming. Today, formaldehyde has replaced it as a major source of groundwater pollution. Following the Jewish tradition of a quick burial and closed-casket ceremony could eliminate the need for embalming and lessen your impact on the environment. Other alternatives to embalming include refrigeration and dry ice.

Green Funeral Web Sites

Want to take the next steps to make sure your funeral is environmentally friendly? Check out these Web sites for more information:

- http://www.memorialecosystems.com
- http://www.greenburialcouncil.org
- http://www.greenburials.org
- http://www.naturallegacies.org

Preserving or destroying? Nearly one million gallons of formaldehyde are buried in embalmed bodies each year in the United States.

Planting a tree

Planting a tree or other living memorial provides a tangible reminder of the deceased person, while giving back to the environment at the same time. Consider a living marker instead of a traditional headstone. Not only is it more affordable, but it also leaves a legacy for the planet.

Funeral service

It is already a common practice to request donations for a charitable organization in lieu of flowers for a funeral. If sending flowers, use an organic service such as http://www.organicbouquet.com or purchase them from a local grower that does not use pesticides. For programs or hymn sheets, use recycled paper and help guests to arrange a car pool from the service to the burial site.

$AVE

How to Save Money This Year

Cut spending in half for the following holidays and save big!

(Actual savings will vary from family to family and region to region.)

HOLIDAY	SIMPLIFY AND SAVE HALF
Christmas	$850
Easter	$66
Halloween	$70
Thanksgiving/Christmas travel	$625
Birthday/anniversary/shower/wedding/funeral gifts	$550
TOTAL SAVINGS	**$2,161**

$HARE

. . . And Share It with Those in Need

- Fill 72 shoeboxes with Christmas presents through Operation Christmas Child at http://www.samaritanspurse.org.

- Purchase 332 beautiful handmade crosses crafted by unemployed and homeless people and donated to the troops in Iraq and Afghanistan at http://www.crossesforthetroops.org.

- Donate $500 anonymously to four needy families. Contact your local refugee resettlement program for suggested recipients.

- Plant 2,161 trees and send beautiful tree donation cards (made from recycled paper) instead of gifts at http://www.floresta.org/treecards1.htm.

- Order 186 copies of *It's Easy Being Green: One Student's Guide to Serving God and Saving the Planet* (my daughter's book—a great gift for teens) and donate a dozen or more to church youth groups in your area.

Putting Your Faith into Action

Dear heavenly Father, help my holidays and celebrations to center on you rather than earthly desires. Fill my heart with gratitude for the blessings you've given me, and make me satisfied with what I have. Instead of seeking to receive, show me ways that I can give to others. Help me to spend less time getting and spending and more time enjoying friends and family. Strengthen my desire to honor you and protect your creation as I celebrate the gift of your Son and the spirit of new life in him.

Lord, help me *today* to:

- make a list of all the things I am thankful for
- visit http://www.appetiteforprofit.com to see how my holiday food choices measure up to the Center for Informed Food Choices' standards
- make a few cards for upcoming celebrations from used materials
- shop for gifts online using an Internet shopping portal like http://www.greatergood.com
- write a "just because" appreciation letter (on recycled paper) to someone who has made a difference in my life

Lord, help me *this week* to:

- stop using wrapping paper when giving gifts; try the comics section or an old map
- buy fair-trade or organic chocolate
- research charitable organizations online that match my family's and friends' interests
- go through my collection of old greeting cards and Christmas cards; salvage what can be used again and recycle the rest
- find out about local, unique gifts available in my area
- avoid getting sucked in by sales; stop buying things I don't need just because the price has been "drastically reduced"
- walk, bike, or carpool to a neighborhood, office, or church party

Lord, help me *this month* to:

- plant a tree in my yard or neighborhood to honor a special occasion
- pass along a treasured item as a gift to someone I love
- buy flowers at the local farmers' market instead of from a standard florist
- talk to my local fireworks authorities about using Sekon biodegradable fireworks for next year's show
- skip the disposable plates, napkins, and utensils at parties and opt for cloth napkins and reusable plates and silverware
- discuss with my family how to make Christmas and other holidays less stressful and materialistic

Lord, help me *this year* to:

- celebrate Use Less Stuff Day in November
- give useful gifts to friends and family members; make donations to causes they care about
- save gas and stay home on major holidays
- use http://www.betterworldshopper.org to make more informed shopping choices
- share a holiday meal with someone who needs encouragement
- dye Easter eggs using natural dyes instead of store-bought kits
- give up something for Lent
- celebrate Earth Day by picking up trash, making a craft out of recycled items, or serving a meatless, earth-friendly meal
- borrow or make costumes instead of buying new
- replace standard Christmas lights with LED holiday lights
- cut back on Christmas spending by at least 25 percent

Summing It Up

Getting Started

I have:

- ○ invited a local guest or family to share a holiday meal
- ○ given up an environmentally harmful practice for Lent
- ○ chosen locally grown, organic produce for celebrations
- ○ volunteered to help wash dishes at a holiday celebration
- ○ discussed how to simplify Christmas with my family

On the Journey

I have:

- ○ eliminated wrapping paper
- ○ stayed home on a holiday when I normally travel
- ○ purchased recycled Christmas cards from a charity
- ○ replaced at least three candy items with coupons in my child's Easter basket
- ○ made or borrowed a Halloween costume
- ○ stopped buying chocolate unless it's fair-trade and/or organic
- ○ talked to my family about green burial options

Green Superstar

I have:

- ○ stopped using disposable plates, cups, napkins, and utensils for parties
- ○ replaced many of my family's traditional gift exchanges with donations to charitable organizations
- ○ sent an e-mail holiday newsletter to friends and family instead of snail-mail Christmas cards
- ○ made my own tree trimmings and Christmas decorations
- ○ planted a tree on Earth Day

The three hundred million TV sets in the United States consume a lot of energy—five times more than is produced by all the geothermal, biomass, solar, and wind sources in the United States. They take energy and materials to manufacture. They are difficult to get rid of and to recycle. They convince us to buy things we don't need, which cost energy to produce, transport, and dispose of. But the real reason to worry about watching TV has to do with the part of us we can't see or measure: our spirit. Television separates us from our Creator while killing his creation.

—*Serve God, Save the Planet*

We're asking for more than we need instead of being content with what we have. It simply is not essential to always be on the cutting edge with the latest way of listening to music—or even the latest CD from our favorite artist. . . . We need to resist the advertising around us that tells us to buy, to feed the consumer market, and instead listen to God. Have you heard what he has to say?

—*It's Easy Being Green*

8

Entertainment

Low-Cost Family Fun

Finally, brothers, whatever is true, whatever is noble,
whatever is right, whatever is pure, whatever is lovely,
whatever is admirable—if anything is excellent or
praiseworthy—think about such things.

PHILIPPIANS 4:8

WHEN MATTHEW WAS IN COLLEGE, he had an English teacher who wore thick glasses and had a beehive hairdo. She wore blouses with frills up the front and she didn't have a PhD, but she was one of Matthew's wisest professors. The most important lessons she taught had little to do with comma splices or dangling modifiers—though she was a stickler for proper grammar. What really stayed with Matthew was her insistence that students guard what comes into their minds.

On several occasions, Miss Rousseau brought a newspaper to class and then led her students through the paper, section by section, article by article. She was teaching them how to recognize the 95 percent of the "news" that would be forgotten the next month. Miss Rousseau explained that in order to allow their brains time to think and ponder and grow, they needed to limit the amount of useless garbage going in.

With today's 24-7 onslaught of infotainment, Miss Rousseau's lesson is more valuable than ever, especially among young people. Last fall, Matthew and I were asked to teach a college leadership workshop entitled "Simple Living." The students at this Christian college are not, for the most part, the owners of a lot of stuff—yet. But nearly all of them spend a significant portion of their day hooked up to entertainment technology.

We opened the simplicity workshop with a question: How many hours did you spend this week watching TV or surfing the Internet? Then we asked how many wished they had spent that time doing something else. Nearly everyone's hand went up.

The two dorm resident directors who attended our simplicity workshop—one male and one female—both agreed that when students cut back on video games and Internet surfing, their social patterns change dramatically: They spend more time talking with friends. And more time outside.

At the end of the workshop, we asked for volunteers to state one change they hoped to make in the coming weeks; nearly all wanted to cut back on their use of entertainment technology and focus more on relationships.

Miss Rousseau would have been pleased.

Consider these stats:

- The average child in America spends six hours and twenty minutes *per day* in front of a TV or computer screen.
- By age seventy, the average American has spent *ten years* of his or her waking life in front of the television: Ten years that could have been spent fellowshipping with friends, helping others, conversing with God, praying, reading the Bible, walking in nature, gardening, volunteering at the library, playing with children. Ten years!

Unlike many problems the world faces, the solution to information overload can be quick and easy: as simple as canceling the cable, unplugging the TV, praying on the daily commute instead of listening to the radio, not renewing those magazine subscriptions, and staying off the Internet. Here's the bonus: many of these (in) actions will also save you money, as well as make you less anxious about things over which you have no control.

No matter what your age, the less time you spend plugged in, the more time you will have for family, friends, and God. The less garbage you allow into your head—and your heart—the more peace you will have in your soul.

Dear gracious Lord of heaven and earth, teach me to enjoy the silence of each day. Let me hear the song of the morning sun, the sigh of buds about to open, the whisper of pine needles falling. Give me the discipline that is only possible through your grace; gird me with fortitude to resist temptations. Let me read, think, watch, and hear thoughts that are pure and good and holy. Help me to tune out the material world and tune in to the simple rhythms of your creation.

GETTING STARTED

"I'm so busy!" My stomach clenches up when I hear that phrase, yet I find myself wearing it almost like a badge of honor. We Americans pride ourselves on working hard—and playing hard. The problem is not that we don't have enough family time; the problem is how we spend our time as a family. Extracurricular activities, television watching, organized sports, and church events add up to a schedule that is anything but relaxing. We expend massive amounts of energy and natural resources on entertainment, yet we reap little from the hours we spend playing video games, following Hollywood celebrities and sports stars, and filling our iPods with music. These addictions masquerade as recreation, but quickly become energy-consuming, life-draining idols.

Psalm 46:10 gives us a different directive: "Be still, and know that I am God." Though it may seem nearly impossible to "be still" in our ordinary lives, this commandment is central to God's extraordinary plan for us. The more we stop and enjoy silence, the more room there is for God to speak into our lives.

How do you start moving from an energy-consuming, energy-sapping social schedule to one that is life-giving? After a long day at work, packing the kids in the car and heading to the local pizza joint sounds tempting. Many of us resort to the same entertainment habits we've practiced for years, hardly considering the toll they take on the environment, our pocketbooks, or our relationship with Christ.

As our standards for acceptable media should differ from the world's, so can our entertainment *habits*. This chapter provides practical ways to "green" your current entertainment options as well as suggestions for new activities. From television, music, and Internet usage to dining out, reading, and playing organized sports, you can begin to make subtle changes that will yield long-term results for you and the planet.

As you plan your next weekend, try asking yourself this question: would Jesus participate in this activity, play this video game, or watch this show? If the answer is no, shut out the clutter and welcome whatever is true, noble, right, pure, lovely, and admirable.

Godly entertainment can be found everywhere—you just need to know where to look.

TELEVISION

For many Christians, television serves as a temporary escape from stress-filled, busy lives. In John 15, Jesus commands us to abide in him (not in the television set). He goes on to say that those who remain in him will produce much fruit, but apart from him, we

> **GO GREEN**
> According to the Kaiser Family Foundation, American children and adolescents spend twenty-two to twenty-eight hours per week viewing television, more than any other activity except sleeping.

can do nothing. How are your television viewing habits influencing your effectiveness for Christ—as well as your carbon footprint? Here are some ways to change your television viewing habits.

National Turn-Off-Your-TV Week

This year, children in the United States will spend well over one thousand hours in front of the television and only nine hundred hours in school. So who is really teaching our children? If you aren't quite ready to part with your TV, try unplugging it during National Turn-Off-Your-TV Week (around the end of April each year). Instead of plopping in front of the TV, go for a walk and pick up trash. Prepare a meal together as a family. Play games. Dare to resort to good old-fashioned family time.

Unplugged

I grew up with TV—Saturday mornings I watched *The Lone Ranger* on a little black-and-white TV in the kitchen, and after school it was *Batman* on our color console in the basement. In high school, I often fell asleep on the couch watching Johnny Carson banter with his sidekick, Ed McMahon. When I met Matthew, I felt sorry for him because he didn't have a TV—so I gave him one for his birthday.

He was the one who should have felt sorry for *me*. I was addicted. In the early years of our marriage, I rarely spent a whole day without turning on the tube. Then, when I was thirty weeks pregnant with Clark, I went into early labor and had to go on complete bed rest.

You would think that going on bed rest would lead to me watching *more* TV, not *less*. But those six weeks in bed marked a turning point in my life. It was the first time I had ever stopped. It was the first time I was forced to think beyond myself. I was completely responsible for this new life inside of me. What kind of life did I want my child to have?

Before bed rest, I had intended to go back to my corporate communications director position immediately after maternity leave. But God changed my heart. He made me realize that the most important gift I could give my child was time. I didn't want him raised by a babysitter. Or pop culture. Or the television.

Matthew graduated from medical school the month Clark was born—healthy and strong, an answer to many prayers. I arranged my schedule so that I could write part-time from home and be a full-time mom.

Gradually, very gradually, we phased out TV from our lives. I didn't want my children to pick up my old habit of turning on the TV "just to see what's on."

It worked: Besides an occasional episode of *MythBusters* from the library, my kids never watch TV. It's simply not part of their lives.

Like so many painful episodes in life, I now know that bed rest was a blessing, not a curse. If I had not had that time to "be still," my kids most likely would not be the big readers, curious learners, independent thinking young adults they are today. *Not* owning a TV has been one of the greatest gifts we've ever given our children.

Phantom loads

Television sets, when combined with DVD players and set-top boxes, probably account for about 10 percent of a household's annual electricity bill. Even when powered "off," a TV still uses between 10 and 15 percent of its energy. When nobody is around, these devices can be turned completely off by plugging them into a smart outlet strip or by connecting the TV to a wall switch outlet.

Next time you're tempted to veg out in front of the TV set, thank the Lord for downtime and the chance to relax. Ask him to help you use your free time in a way that doesn't require so much electricity and that will draw you closer to him. Spend time talking as a family, not just staring at the same big box.

GO GREEN

The average U.S. parent spends over thirty-one hours each week watching TV but only thirty-eight minutes per week actively engaging their children.

Want to Turn Off Your TV?

Try one of these fun and educational alternatives to channel surfing:

- **Collect cans and bottles.** Go on a walk through town with your kids and collect bottles and cans. Your kids will get exercise and help the environment all at the same time. If you live in a state that offers return deposits, let your children pick out a good cause and donate the "found" money.

- **Creation scavenger hunt.** Create a list of natural things that can be seen outside where you live—pinecones, acorns, flowers, leaves, feathers, insects, rocks. Have your children search for each item on the list.

- **Camp out.** You don't have to drive to Yellowstone or even a state park to go camping. Pitch a tent in the backyard and discover the sights and sounds of the night.

- **Visit a local farm.** Find a nearby strawberry patch in early summer or an apple orchard in the fall. Some farms in our area also offer hayrides and horseback riding.

- **Stargaze.** Relax on a blanket in your yard with an astronomy guide. Look for constellations and planets and teach your children about the night sky.

- **Dine in.** Set up a restaurant in your home. Let your kids create menu items using only things you have in your kitchen. Take turns filling the roles of wait-staff, chef, and cleanup crew.

- **Make gifts for friends and family.** Homemade gifts save resources and are often more meaningful than the standard ones. Make photo frames, miniscrapbooks, and craft items to give throughout the year. Think of all the money you'll save, too!

- **Organize a block party.** Get friends and neighbors on your street together for a potluck. Back when we lived on the middle of Middle Street, every Fourth of July we'd place a few sawhorses at both ends of the road and pull out our grills. Every family brought their own dishes and silverware, something to grill, and a salad or dessert to share.

- **Volunteer.** Many retirement homes and hospitals need volunteers to serve lunch or read to patients. Pitch in and make some new friends.

- **Write a note.** Write letters (on recycled paper or cards) to friends, grandparents, and mentors, letting them know how much you appreciate them.

Add Ten Years to Your
Child's Life—Guaranteed!

Televisions are everywhere—the airport, gym, doctor's waiting room, student cafeteria, the mall. But they don't have to be in your house.

When our kids were still in elementary school, we canceled our cable service. Matthew had urged me to keep the TV off when the kids were young, but I confess that I resorted to taped episodes of *Wishbone* while preparing dinner at the end of the day—especially when Matthew was working his twenty-four-hour shifts in the emergency room. The kids were tired, and turning on the electronic babysitter was so easy. And then there was that whole year when Clark would not go to bed without watching one of our three Thomas the Tank Engine videos.

Short-term thinking on my part, with long-term consequences. Christianity teaches us to focus on the big picture, the eternal. I opted for a few minutes of peace when I should have been teaching them (and myself) a lesson in self-discipline.

Television is new, very new. At the end of World War II there were fewer television sets in America than the number of people who live in my small town of seven thousand. Just fifty years later, over 98 percent of American homes have a TV and over 40 percent own three or more televisions. When surveyed, about one-half of Americans report they watch too much TV, eat dinner in front of the TV, regularly fall asleep with the TV on, and have purchased a TV for their first grader's bedroom. Is it any wonder that over half of these first graders, when surveyed, said they would rather spend their time watching TV than being with their moms or dads?

Television exists so that advertisers have a place to sell stuff. The average seventy-year-old has watched well over two million TV commercials and has spent ten years of his life watching television. And although U.S. children have about five minutes of conversation with their parents each day, they will spend over 240 minutes with the television. The biggest influences in many children's lives are television shows and the commercials that sponsor them. If you believe that PBS is different or commercial free, ask a child about the advertisements on PBS. My kids can still rattle off the advertisers from their youth: Cheerios, Chuck E. Cheese, Juicy Juice.

Despite warnings by organizations such as the American Academy of Pediatrics (which recommends no TV before age two), access to and time spent watching television continues to increase. The weight of evidence is similar to that which was known, but ignored, regarding the risks of smoking cigarettes. Television viewing has been linked to depression, attention deficit disorder, poor school performance, obesity, diabetes, and increased feelings of isolation and vulnerability. Even eight out of ten Hollywood executives believe that television promotes violent actions in its viewers. We teach our children not to take candy or accept rides from strangers, yet we entrust their very souls to anonymous advertisers and producers in Hollywood and on Madison Avenue.

If you do watch television, talk with your kids about what is promised in ads versus reality. When a SUV ad shows families charging up the side of a rugged mountain, remind them that these vehicles are not trailblazers or pathfinders or explorers, but rather mall finders and traffic sitters. When an ad shows cool kids staying connected via cell phones, invite your children to spend an hour observing shoppers in the local mall talking on cell phones. For every person seen smiling, twenty will have an anxious or blank expression.

The bottom line: If you want to add a decade to your child's life, get rid of the TV. They will have ten years freed up to serve the Lord and experience life, not just watch it happening to someone else.

GO GREEN

Plasma TVs use three times as much electricity as standard models, and twice as much as LCD screen TVs.

MOVIES/DVDS

Watching a movie as a family can be a relaxing way to spend time together and encourage young people to develop critical viewing skills. With today's increasing market for family-friendly, faith-based films from production companies like Walden Media and Fox Faith, more options exist for Christians who want to fix their thoughts on what is noble and true, as Paul commands in Philippians 4:8.

But must we regularly shell out top dollar for tickets and drive our cars long distances just to satisfy our appetite for entertain-

The 23rd Channel (Instead of the 23rd Psalm)

The TV is my shepherd, I shall want.
It makes me lie down on the sofa.
It leads me away from the Scriptures.
It destroys my soul.
It leads me in the path of sex and violence,
For the sponsor's sake.
Yea, though I walk in the shadow of my
Christian responsibilities,
There will be no interruption,
For the TV is with me.
Its cable and remote, they control me.
It prepares a commercial before me in
The presence of worldliness;
It anoints my head with humanism,
My coveting runneth over.
Surely laziness and ignorance shall
Follow me all the days of my life:
And I shall dwell in the house
Watching TV forever.   —AUTHOR UNKNOWN

ment? With a few simple changes, we can keep movies on the menu and still honor our Creator.

Movie theaters

Heading to the theater every week to catch the newest box-office smash is guaranteed to hurt your pocketbook—and the environment. To see one movie, a family of four can pay $28 for tickets alone. Add popcorn and a soda for each person and the cost of one movie-watching experience can easily top $50. Visiting the theater weekly for a year would drain over $2,600 from your family's bank account, not to mention the pollution caused by your car.

Pajama party

Why pay all that money to be crammed into a room that's too hot—or too cold—and full of chatty people and ringing cell phones? Our family has more fun snuggled on a couch while wearing pajama pants and sharing a bowl of popcorn than we ever do in a movie theater.

Waiting for the DVD

Perhaps we are too extreme, but I can only recall two movies that our whole family has seen together in the theater. We saw *The Lion, the Witch and the Wardrobe* for a Christmas treat. And we watched *Prince Caspian* together for my birthday.

Here's my promise: your family will survive if you don't see *Chronicles of the Potter Pirate Comic Book Hero IV* on opening night! Teach your children a lesson in patience and kick our culture's immediate gratification habit by waiting until movies are released on DVD. With rental programs like Netflix and Blockbuster Online, you can save gas and trips to the video store, not to mention all the time wasted agonizing over which movie to rent and the inevitable late fees.

Be still, and know that I am God!
PSALM 46:10

Borrowed not bought

Better yet, look for other, more economical places to find DVDs. Borrow from a movie-buff friend. Start a movie exchange with friends at school, church, or work. Or visit your library. Many public and church libraries lend movies for little or no charge and offer family-friendly titles as well as current new releases. Our library allows three DVDs and three videos per adult—and they can be renewed over the phone. In Emma's dorm, they have a semiofficial lending library, as well as room-to-room exchanges going on all the time.

Those $4 rentals from Blockbuster sure add up! According to a report from the Entertainment Merchants Association:

- Home videos generated $15.9 billion in sales and $8.2 billion in rentals in 2007.
- Nearly 9 million high-definition discs were sold in 2007, for which consumers spent more than $260 million.
- More than twelve thousand DVDs were released in 2007.
- It is estimated that in 2012, sales of Blu-ray Discs will exceed those of standard DVDs and will generate sales of $9.5 billion.
- Home-video spending is projected to increase to $25.6 billion in 2012.

Green Movies

Looking for something to watch this weekend? Check out these movies with environmental themes.

Baraka (1992)

Baraka is an ancient word that translates as "a blessing." This movie has truly been a blessing to our family—lent out and watched perhaps more than any other movie we own. (Okay, we don't own many movies, but that just makes this one even more special.) With images from twenty-four countries and six continents, and music by Michael Stearns (one of my husband's favorite composers), this film shows some of the best—and worst—parts of nature and human life. The film has no plot, no actors, and no script but is guaranteed to move your spirit more than just about any Hollywood film. Five stars!

Hoot (2006)

Based on Carl Hiaasen's Newberry Award–winning novel for young adults, *Hoot* follows the adventures of three kids and their fight to save a local population of endangered burrowing owls.
Rating: PG (Mild bullying and brief language)

WALL•E (2008)

An animated gem with an environmental message. The title character is a little robot trash compactor who continues to clean Earth seven hundred years after people left due to pollution. When a probe-droid named EVE arrives and finds plant life, the robots are whisked into space to a ship that has been housing what's left of the human race. Hailed as one of the best animated films ever made, this movie is sure to get your kids to think about recycling while sharing a very human story of loneliness, obligation, and love.
Rating: G

Winged Migration (2001)

This documentary is a Sleeth family favorite. It follows the migrations of more than a dozen bird species over four years, through forty countries and all seven continents. French filmmaker Jacques Perrin used planes, gliders, helicopters, and hot-air balloons to capture a feeling of flying right alongside the birds. Little kids, teens, and adults will all enjoy this nearly wordless masterpiece with unforgettable imagery.
Rating: G

- Traditional rental stores, dominated by Blockbuster, accounted for 73 percent of the rental business in 2007—which means most people are still driving to get their movie fix.

MUSIC

The Creator of our universe loves listening to music. Psalm 33:1-3 (NLT) says, "Let the godly sing for joy to the Lord; it is fitting for the pure to praise him. Praise the Lord with melodies on the lyre; make music for him on the ten-stringed harp. Sing a new song of praise to him; play skillfully on the harp, and sing with joy."

Music—and the ability to reproduce it at any time—are on the "top five" list of things my family would least want to give up. Music sets the tone for our lives and often draws us closer to God. We sing to him in corporate worship, and at home we enjoy our favorite music collections.

Adding beauty to life, however, must be balanced with the obsession for the new and novel. Would God frown on an impulse purchase of the latest and greatest iPod when a simple MP3 player would do? Does God care what we do with the old CDs we never listen to anymore? When our actions negatively impact his creation, the answer, I believe, is yes.

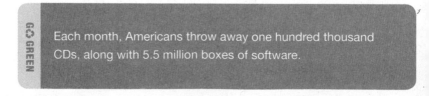

Digital music

Can't wait to hear Casting Crowns' newest album? Instead of driving to the store to buy a copy, download it online. Downloading an album will usually save you about $5 compared to buying the same CD from a store. You also eliminate the need for plastic and paper resources associated with packaging.

Rewritable CDs

Buy rewritable format CDs and DVDs for storing music, pictures, and documents. You'll save money and eliminate waste.

Shared music

Donate your unwanted CDs to your church, school, library, or a local charity. Buying used CDs or borrowing them from the library reduces the environmental impact of manufacturing new products.

CDs

Your old CDs can be recycled into a new product. Specialized electronic recycling companies clean, grind, blend, and compound the

Off or On?

Did you know that audio equipment in the United States uses more electricity when it is off than on?

The U.S. government reports that Americans spend more money to power audio equipment when it is off than when it is on. When audio equipment is off—which is most of the time—it is still using energy because it is in standby mode. The amount of current drawn in standby mode is small, at least in relation to the current drawn when the audio equipment is on. But because audio equipment is in standby mode most of the time, the cumulative effect is significant. If you don't know whether your audio equipment has a phantom load or draws current when it is off, here are two clues: If it has a remote control that can turn it on, or if it has an instant-on feature, then it constantly draws and uses electricity even when in the off mode. If it has a clock or LED lights, it is always on. Make sure to get power strips for audio equipment—or simply unplug it when not in use—so that the equipment can be turned completely off.

discs into a high-quality plastic for various uses, including office equipment, automotive industry parts, raw materials to make plastics, and jewel cases. Visit http://www.cdrecyclingcenter.com to find a recycling center in your area.

Vinyl records

When spring cleaning leads you to a box of your old vinyl LP records, don't just toss them in the garbage bin; check the Yellow Pages for a nearby used-record store. You may be able to sell them for about $10 each. Recycling them is also an option, but reselling them requires less energy.

> **SAVE GREEN**
>
> Moms spend 48 cents of every discretionary dollar on entertainment items, including music, movies, video games, and electronics.

ELECTRONICS

Batteries

Check around your house and take a quick battery inventory. If you're like the average American, you own about ten normal (A, AA, AAA, C, D, 9V) and two button batteries. For a family of four, that's forty-eight batteries, and you probably throw away most of these without a second thought. What happens to your discarded batteries after the garbage man hauls them away with the trash? Once in a landfill, batteries break down and release mercury, lead, and other toxic chemicals into the groundwater. This process hardly makes for springs of life-giving water that we read about in Revelation 7:17.

Given our frequent use of electronic devices, it makes sense both environmentally and financially to switch to rechargeable nickel metal hydride (NiMH) and lithium ion (Li-ion) batteries. Besides being less toxic, they quickly pay for themselves. The fastest battery chargers will have your AAs revamped and ready to go in as little as fifteen minutes.

Matthew has been recharging our batteries (literally and metaphorically) for a couple of decades. The new rechargeable batteries last much longer than their predecessors, and the chargers themselves are user-friendly and compact.

Here's my advice: After purchasing a battery charger and an assortment of rechargeable batteries, designate a battery-charging space in your home, close to a convenient outlet. Label one small box "uncharged" and another "charged" to encourage clear communications throughout the family. Not sure which batteries you need? Visit www.GreenBatteries.com for help finding the best fit for your electronics.

Advanced energy-saving battery chargers are now available that use about 35 percent less energy on average.

Also, remember to recycle the one-time-use batteries you already own. Visit www.earth911.org for a list of companies that participate in battery reclamation in your area.

> " Simplicity is the first cousin of contentment. Its motto is, "We brought nothing into this world, and we can certainly carry nothing out." It recognizes that we are pilgrims. It concentrates us on what we need, and measures this by what we use. It rejoices in the good things of creation, but hates waste and greed and clutter. It knows how easily the seed of the Word is smothered by the "cares and riches of this life." It wants to be free of distractions, in order to love and serve God and others.
> —*John Stott (1921–)*, "The Christian and the Poor"

SAVE GREEN

American consumers could save more than one billion kilowatt-hours of power annually if they used Energy Star battery chargers, which would also save more than $100 million each year while preventing the release of a million tons of greenhouse gases.

Three billion batteries are sold each year in the United States, averaging about thirty-two per family or ten per person. Almost as many batteries are thrown away each year as are purchased.

Computers

Before buying your next computer, resolve not to include more frills than necessary to do the job. Do you really need a 3-D graphics card for sending e-mails? Will it take 500 GB to store your photos from church events, typed sermon notes, and Sunday school lessons? Generally, the more powerful your computer and the more bells and whistles it has, the more energy it will consume, and the more it will cost. First decide what you *need* it to do, then find the right computer to meet your needs.

Buying used

On second thought, why buy new when used will do? If you'd rather not spend a small fortune on technology, check out Web sites like eBay and Craigslist for functional, high-quality used electronics. Buying used translates into using fewer resources for the production of more equipment. Plus, when you buy used, you help others safely recirculate electronics that they no longer need. We've been on both the giving and receiving end of used computers— only one of the four computers used by our family and our nonprofit was bought new.

Keeping up with the techno Joneses is expensive. A new Blu-ray player, HDTV, or next-generation gaming console can easily set you back $500 or more. Could you make do with your current system one more year, and instead donate that money to a worthy cause?

Extended use

Why do we feel the need to replace our electronic tools and toys every time a new model comes out? Although the newest technologies look enticing, the older versions usually will complete their tasks for much longer than advertisers would have us believe. Next time you step into Best Buy and find yourself drooling over the latest and greatest gadgets, slow down and take stock of what your real needs are.

Old electronics

Just the other day, my neighbor rescued two working monitors that had been left out on trash day and gave them to a charitable organization.

Before you throw out your old computer or cell phone, look for an organization or charity that recycles and reuses electronics. You might also consider selling them on an online auction site and putting the money toward your favorite charity or church's mission fund. Many computer manufacturers also sponsor take-back programs, where they accept and recycle their units when you're done with them.

Books, Music, Walks

Matthew and I are both avid readers. When I was a freshman in college, his first gift to me was a novella—*A River*

Dirty Habits

- Each year, we spend $250 billion powering computers worldwide, but only about 15 percent of that power is spent computing. The rest is wasted idling.

- Forty percent of the energy used for electronics in your home is used while these devices are turned off.

- Electronics make up 70 percent of all hazardous waste.

- Manufacturing the average PC requires ten times the weight of the product in chemicals and fossil fuels.

Runs Through It—by a little-known Presbyterian minister's son who taught English at the University of Chicago. My sweetheart's second gift to me was a record album—Willie Nelson singing "I Only Have Eyes for You" on vinyl remains one of my all-time favorites. (Yes, we still use the same record player!) And we fell in love taking walks through the fields and woods of Matthew's youth.

These are still our three favorite family activities—reading, listening to music together, and walking. We also like to borrow movies and have friends over to share a meal. That's about as exciting as it gets in the Sleeth household, beyond an occasional game of Uno or Parcheesi—Emma's favorites. Over dinner, we often talk about the books we are reading, reaching for the set of encyclopedias behind the dining room table or the *Oxford English Dictionary* to clarify a point of discussion. We still like to read books aloud to one another, and it's not unusual for the whole family to be reading the same series at the same time. (Family rule: you are *not* allowed to give away the ending.)

To some, these activities must sound rather tame (even nerdy), but they are all low on energy usage and high on relationship building—both with our neighbors and with God.

As our children grow older, the church and their Christian college community have become the center of their friendships. We are grateful to live just a couple of blocks from the school so that we can welcome our children's friends into our home. During our first year in Kentucky, we hosted a food-and-fellowship night at our house nearly every Friday night. The kids played board games, talked, ate, and laughed—music to any parent's ears, and I venture to say, to the heavens above.

Our son is now dating his first girlfriend. Their courtship began over an exchange of books and continued over long walks. For their first Christmas, Clark gave his girlfriend a couple of favorite novels; she gave him her mom's beginning piano books and the promise of weekly lessons. Books, music, and walks: it's beautiful to see these habits passing along to the next generation.

BOOKS, MAGAZINES, AND NEWSPAPERS
E-books

Borrow audio books from your library or purchase the digital versions online. Save money: ask your librarian if your public library offers downloadable books. Our local system offers free downloadable best sellers, book club favorites, award-winning authors, and audiobooks. The audiobooks, available through the system's NetLibrary, proved tremendously helpful when Clark needed to test out of his college's foreign language requirements. If your library doesn't offer downloadable books yet, keep asking.

The generous will prosper; those who refresh others will themselves be refreshed.
PROVERBS 11:25, NLT

The Kindle is another relatively new alternative. Launched in the United States by Amazon.com in 2007, the Kindle is a wireless reading device that allows you to purchase and store books without killing any trees. It can be used without a computer and holds over two hundred titles. The Kindle Store, which you can visit wirelessly via Amazon's Whispernet, offers more than 145,000 books, newspapers, magazines, and blogs for your reading enjoyment. Kindles aren't cheap—they currently cost about $360—but they can save you time and cut down on paper use.

Sharing books

Many libraries will gladly accept donations of gently used old books and even magazines. Rather than letting books collect dust on your shelf, consider sharing the knowledge with someone else by giving them away.

When we moved to Kentucky, I knew that we couldn't take all of our books. So I set up a free table at my school and let students take anything they promised to read. This was shortly after Hurricane Katrina, when many libraries had their collections completely washed away. A generous teacher at our school volunteered to pay for all of the shipping costs, so we donated many of our good quality books to our Louisiana neighbors—grateful that the books would be read by many families instead of just ours.

Used books and magazines

Millions of people in third-world countries want to learn English but have little or no access to written material. Ask your church or mission organization if their missionaries need books and magazines. You can help fulfill the great commission by providing resources for students who want to know Christ. Several organizations distribute books to other countries; the only cost to you is shipping the books to a U.S. facility. Be sure to contact the groups beforehand to find out what types of books they need.

Avid readers might also want to check out http://www.paper backswap.com. Swap your used books (*not* just paperbacks) with other book lovers for free. All you pay is postage. Members can swap CDs and DVDs as well. It only takes a minute to join, and membership is free.

Book Donations

For listings of organizations that coordinate book donations, visit the following Web sites:

- American Library Association at http://www.ala.org/ala/aboutala/hqops/library/libraryfactsheet/alalibraryfactsheet12.cfm

- Sabre Foundation at http://www.sabre.org/about/Links.php

- African Studies Association/Africana Studies Librarians Book Donation Committee at http://www.albany.edu/~dlafonde/Global/bookdonation.htm

- University at Buffalo, The State University of New York, Health Sciences Library at http://libweb.lib.buffalo.edu/dokuwiki/hslwiki/doku.php?id=book_donations

Slave to Sin

Jesus replied, "I tell you the truth, everyone who sins is a slave of sin." —John 8:34, NLT

"Who are the tyrants in your life?" our discussion leader asked the twenty-five people sitting in our town-wide interdenominational, intergenerational creation care gathering. The group had formed a short while after Matthew preached at a local church and has been meeting twice monthly ever since to work through tough questions like this.

One by one, we acknowledged the material addictions that enslave us: The TV. Our iPods. Video games. Starbucks coffee and Panera cinnamon-crunch bagels. Sports. Travel. Shopping. Entertainment. Comfort. Ease.

Are all of these indulgences necessarily sinful? Of course not. The d   ;er comes not when we own things, but when things own us.

Jeremy, a student at Asbury Seminary, shared a quick test for addiction that he learned from one of his professors. Try going without it for thirty days. If you can't make it—or if it's a bare-knuckled struggle—then you are addicted.

The only thing we should be dependent on is God. He is the source of everything. If we have faith in him, we will want for nothing.

Bible literacy in this group is high, so we never go long before someone brings in Scripture. Matthew 6:24 tells us that man cannot serve two masters, "for either he will hate the one, and love the other; or else he will hold to the one, and despise the other" (KJV). We are only fooling ourselves when we claim that our worship of money does not interfere with our worship of God. How is the pursuit of gold, which consumes so much of our waking lives, any different from the golden calf built by the Israelites in the wilderness? We are worshiping false idols when we spend an inordinate amount of time on things outside of God.

What is an inordinate amount of time? That's between you and Jesus. Each of us has our own addictions. I don't play video games. I hate shopping malls. But I love books—reading them, writing them, seeing how they look on my shelves. Sounds innocent enough, but the devil—pride—has a way of creeping in. The dark part of me subconsciously whispers, "Look! I've read all those books! Boy, I must be smart."

When we downsized, my book collection was the most difficult material possession for me to give up. It took prayer—lots and lots of prayer—before I could let go of "my" books. But God made the process easier by putting clear needs before me in my school, church, and community. When I knew that the books were going to specific students or specific groups, I was able to release them with gratitude. In the end, we gave away about two-thirds of our books, making our move much lighter and eliminating the need to build bookshelves in our new home.

Do bookstores still tempt me? Of course! But with support from my creation care group and the ever friendly services of interlibrary loan, I can save money *and* save some of God's trees.

Dear Lord, help me to recognize and confess the subtle tyrants that rule my life. Give me the will and the commitment to give up addictions; teach me to turn to you for help in my many moments of weakness. Pick me up when I falter; forgive me when I fail. Give me renewed hope and strength to form God-centered habits that rely on your saving grace.

Craft supplies
Use your old magazines as craft supplies or donate them to a children's Sunday school class, scrapbook club, or group that visits shut-ins.

NEWS AND INFOTAINMENT
Much of our news is really entertainment in disguise. Do you really need to read a physical newspaper every day to keep current? How much time do you spend ingesting sensational headlines that nobody will remember a month from now? And is all this news

addiction really helping solve world problems or just making you feel more anxious and helpless?

Consider canceling your newspaper subscription or going on a media fast for a week or more. You may find yourself becoming part of the solution instead of just worrying about the problem.

News Addiction

Newspapers have deep roots in my family: My grandfather spent most of his working life as a newspaper printer, and I grew up watching my father read the *Washington Post* from front to back every day. My own relationship with the paper began with the Sunday comics, and I started reading the full newspaper religiously in my early teen years—one of my first politically aware moments was watching the Watergate scandal unfold in print. The newspaper became a way for me to tune out for an hour or so at the end of the day, like the stereotypical 1950s father, in the guise of "staying informed."

When I moved away from the D.C. area, my dad gave me a subscription to the *Washington Post* national edition, a weekly newspaper containing highlights of the previous week. This cut back on the amount of paper I consumed and the time I spent reading the news by about 85 percent. After a decade, I let the subscription run out; I haven't subscribed to a newspaper now for at least fifteen years.

The same pattern applies to my addiction to radio news. In my early years of marriage, I listened to the radio news on my commute to and from work. The big change came after I had kids. It's not that I didn't want to stay informed; it's that I didn't want my kids to hear all the trash that comes along with the news.

The bus ride to school was the one place where they heard news unfiltered. Both my kids learned more than they needed to know about another presidential scandal—the Monica Lewinsky affair—on their way to school!

Emma has always been especially sensitive—and brilliant—about the news. When terrorists attacked on September 11, 2001, she asked us to tell her what was going on, but she didn't want to hear or see any of the reports directly. I think Emma was one of the few eleven-year-olds in the country who did not see images of the Twin Towers imploding, and all the horror that accompanied these terrorist acts, until many years after the event.

Some people might think we were sheltering the kids: I promise that they both have had extremely well-rounded educations, with a huge fund of knowledge from ancient history to current times. What I realize now is that I wasn't sheltering my kids; they were sheltering me. My children taught me that by changing my news habits, I could spend a lot less time "staying current" and a lot more time becoming part of the solution.

SPORTS

Let's face it: Americans are crazy about sports. In every city and suburb, kids are signing up for T-ball and soccer leagues before they even can spell their full names. But is this obsession healthy? Pediatricians have advised parents that competitive sports during elementary school—especially contact sports—can result in injuries with lifelong consequences. Many of these injuries, like bad knees and backs, don't show up for decades, but the damage is done. And then there are the emotional scars of those (the majority) who don't make the all-star teams.

So if competitive, organized sports are potentially harmful in the long term, why do we parents log thousands of miles a year and drive ourselves crazy towing kids to thrice weekly practices—and scrimmages on the Sabbath? The reasons all sound logical: we want our children to get exercise, be accepted, make friends, develop discipline. But at what cost to family life, emotional health, and spiritual growth?

Do an experiment. Ask a boy around age twelve, give or take a few years, what he wants to be when he grows up. Odds are he'll answer a professional football player or a pro basketball player. Now look at the way many of the elite players conduct their personal and public lives. Are they meek? humble? gentle in spirit?

chaste? faithful? peaceful? Are they stewarding their bodies as holy instruments for doing the Lord's work, or are they using (and often abusing) them for short-term fame and gain?

I'm not saying that all sports are bad or bad for you. I *am* saying that we need to be aware of how much time and money we spend on sports—both as spectators and as participants—and how running around to sporting events impacts our spiritual, relational, and environmental health. If sports begin to take our time, resources, and attention away from God, then we need to reevaluate the role they are taking in our lives—and our children's lives.

> Our present ecological crisis, the biggest single practical threat to our human existence in the middle to long term, has, religious people would say, a great deal to do with our failure to think of the world as existing in relation to the mystery of God, not just as a huge warehouse of stuff to be used for our convenience.
>
> —*Rowan Williams (1950–)*, Tokens of Trust

I recently read an article by a San Franciscan mom bemoaning the lack of quality family time because of her children's sports schedules. With four different sporting events every Saturday on opposite ends of the city, the only way this family could possibly get their two children where they "needed" to be was to divide and conquer—Dad take one kid, Mom the other—two separate vehicles zigzagging across town from early morning until late evening, changing uniforms in the car and grabbing fast food along the way. But compared to her neighbor's schedule, her weekends were relatively sane: The neighbor's kids had made the cut for the elite teams. They practiced on Sundays, too.

All this running around doesn't necessarily ease up when the kids get older. At the high school where I used to teach, one team boasted that they logged five thousand miles traveling to matches in *one year*. Now, think about the amount of hours those students spent devoted to just one sport—a minimum of 111 hours traveling, plus the competitions themselves, plus the practices, times seventy students—we're talking upwards of 7,770 hours for one team at one school! Now multiply that by the twenty-three thousand U.S. high schools, three or more sports per year. And then start to calculate all of the gallons of gasoline those buses use, plus all the fuel used by parents and fans who travel in private cars to attend those competitions. My calculator doesn't have enough digits to add up all the numbers.

Sports use resources—a lot of them. Many analysts agree that we have reached the apex of our finite oil supply, which means that the remaining oil will be harder to get to and more expensive to drill. This combination of shrinking supply and increasing demand, especially from India, China, and America, has many believing that gasoline will cost $7 to $10 per gallon in the not-so-

Green Fitness

How can you stay physically active while lowering your impact on God's creation? Here are a few ideas to get you started:

INSTEAD OF	DO THIS
Driving young kids to organized sports	Encourage unstructured outdoor play
Allowing older kids to join competitive teams year round	Limit to one sports season per year
Purchasing athletic equipment	Borrow or rent
Getting rid of used sporting goods	Pass them along to neighbors or donate them to a good cause (see http://www.sportsgift.org)
Buying sporting items made from aluminum, the most energy-intensive material manufactured in the United States	Choose steel (bikes) or wood or bamboo (bats)
Using equipment made from PVC plastic	Look for equipment such as tents and duffle bags, bike helmets, and yoga mats made from natural or recycled materials
Purchasing gym equipment	Use a gym within walking distance of your home or work, or along your regular commute

distant future—not surprising, since Europeans are already paying $9 per gallon at the pump.

As fuel prices rise, we are going to have to reevaluate many luxuries, including how many sports we allow our children to participate in. Perhaps spending that time playing in streams and backyards will prove better for them in the long run, as well as for the earth they will inherit.

Athletic equipment

Take a few minutes to check your garage, closets, attic, and maybe under the bed. How many old tennis rackets, baseball gloves, and soccer balls will you find? Now, here's the tough question: when is the last time you used them? Remember: many balls, helmets, and other types of sports gear are made from PVC, a common type of plastic that isn't easy to recycle. If you have equipment just sitting around, give it to someone who will put it to good use.

Sporting events

I never realized how much it costs to "take me out to the ball game" until I started doing research for this chapter. Professional sports charge anywhere from $20 to $200 per ticket, depending on where you want to sit. For a family of four, that can represent quite an investment, especially when you add the cost of driving to the stadium, parking, food, and drinks.

For those die-hard fans with season tickets, the cost is significantly higher. Season tickets to our closest pro football team cost $650 to $3,700. If we made this a family activity, that's $2,600 to $14,800—for just one sports season.

Working out

Instead of heading to the gym, consider physical activity in the great outdoors. Running through a park instead of on a treadmill or going for an actual bike ride saves electricity while improving your connection with both God's creation and your community. Depending on your climate and the season, you might opt for conservation activities such as gardening, hiking, or trail building. Many parks and public spaces depend on volunteers for regular upkeep—a great way to help maintain open spaces while staying in shape.

The gym

If you do use the gym, make your workout more environmentally mindful. To avoid unnecessary driving, be sure to select a gym that is either close to home or on the way to work. Some other questions to consider: Does the gym have a recycling program in place? Do they use water-conserving showerheads and low-wattage lightbulbs? Does the maintenance staff use biodegradable and natural cleaning products in the locker rooms and showers? Some gyms have programmed their televisions to automatically turn off when not in use—encourage your gym to do the same. Bring your own water bottle, and wear clothing made with organic cotton to keep your workout comfortable, fashionable, and green.

> We should remain within the limits imposed by our basic needs and strive with all our power not to exceed them. For once we are carried a little beyond these limits in our desire for the pleasures of life, there is then no criterion by which to check our onward movement, since no bounds can be set to that which exceeds the necessary.
>
> —*St. Nilus of Ancyra (407–494)*, Ascetic Discourses, *Vol I, Philokalia*

Home gyms

Home equipment is expensive, requires resources to manufacture and transport, and often ends up going unused after a short-lived burst of enthusiasm. In most cases, it is much more efficient to share gym equipment with hundreds of other people than to purchase your own home gym. The exception is if you would have to travel great distances by car to get to the closest gym facility. One low-cost option is to see if your local school or college opens their facilities to the public—for a small fee, you may have access to nearby, high-quality gym facilities for a fraction of the cost of a gym membership or home equipment.

Walking groups

Our town has an organized walking group that meets at noon— if you are new to town or are looking for walking buddies, groups

By the Numbers

- 350 million: number of new pairs of athletic shoes sold in the United States every year, which will eventually end up in landfills

- 2.5 billion gallons: amount of water used *per day* to water the world's golf courses—the same amount needed to support nearly five-sixths of the world's population

- 1,500 tons: amount of trash that could be removed from trails, beaches, forests, and oceans if every sports fan picked up just one piece of trash per year

- $500 million: amount saved if 10 percent of the money spent on new sporting equipment were diverted to used goods

- 22,500 gallons of gasoline: equivalent amount saved if tennis players chose racquets with natural strings instead of synthetic ones, which are usually made from petroleum

- 72,000 kWh of electricity: amount of electricity used by one baseball field with nighttime lighting, enough to keep your house lit for sixty years

like this offer built-in support, companionship, and accountability. Check with your town hall or city council to see if a group exists; if not, start your own.

Walking the Walk

Since I had children, walking has been the single best way that I have stayed in shape while spending time with friends. When my kids were little, I carried them in a front pack, then a backpack, then a stroller, and finally a double stroller for a heavy-duty workout, especially up hills! While I walked, I talked with other moms. We shared our lives while we worked our bodies.

Two decades later, I still walk with friends several times a week, *sans* kids. Some of the most important relationships in my life have been sustained by uninterrupted morning and late evening walks, where my spiritual sisters and I can pour our hearts out while breathing in fresh air.

The same goes for my relationship with Matthew and the kids. Matthew and I would likely not be in good shape as a couple, physically and relationally, without the sacred space of frequent walks. In the last few years, Clark often has called from his dorm room a couple of blocks away to ask if I wanted to go on a walk, especially in the morning since we are both early risers. So many of our unreserved mother-son conversations have occurred on those walks. Emma prefers to walk alone, but when we do walk together, I feel we are in step on every level. Walking the walk keeps our family healthy in ways that no other activity can replace.

Green athletic organizations

Consider joining a local group to support your green fitness program such as http://www.organicathlete.org. OrganicAthlete promotes health and ecological stewardship among athletes of all ages and abilities by sharing information, building community, and inspiring through athletic example.

Outdoor activities

It's a given that outdoorsy people love unspoiled, wild places—but too often we unintentionally love them to death. All that hiking, biking, fishing, hunting, skiing, white-water rafting, canoeing, and camping has an impact on the very wildlife we crave to restore our souls. Some ways to lessen your impact? Stay close to home, clean up behind yourself, purchase equipment made from recycled materials, borrow or rent instead of buying new, and stay on designated paths. For more ideas about how you can embrace nature without squeezing too hard, visit http://www.treehugger.com/files/2007/06/how-to-green-your-outdoor-sports.php.

DINING OUT

I grew up in a family where sharing meals was a daily activity, right up there with bathing and brushing our teeth before bed. Each night we would gather around the kitchen table, say grace, exchange news, and reconnect as a family. (We also took turns guessing what Dad ate for lunch—strange custom, but we four

Sport by Sport

INSTEAD OF	DO THIS
Playing baseball under the lights	Schedule day games
Playing basketball and tennis indoors or at night	Play outside during the day in natural light; purchase pressureless balls that come in a recyclable container
Throwing away bicycle tires	Recycle the tires
Playing soccer and football on artificial turf	Play on natural grass
Patronizing traditional golf courses	Seek out a conservation-minded course
Playing ice hockey during the day	Play at night to reduce cooling costs
Skiing or snowboarding off trail	Stay in designated areas to avoid ecologically sensitive terrain
Driving across dunes to surf	Stay on the road and marked pathways; use epoxy (recyclable polystyrene) surfboards rather than boards covered with polyester and fiberglass—they last five times longer too!

kids never tired of it!) Today, as we squeeze more and more activities into our calendars, the basic family ritual of eating together is vanishing from our homes.

Eating out may offer an easy answer to the age-old question, "What are we going to have for dinner?" But is this quick fix helping our budgets, our planet, or our walk with the Lord?

Eating in

Be adventurous and make eating at home more fun. Plan ethnic-themed nights where you cook international cuisine and experience various cultures—also a great way to learn about missionaries you or your church support. Pass along practical skills: get your children involved in planning and cooking the meals.

Effects of Eating Out

Physical effects

In 1 Corinthians 6:19-20, Paul charges us to honor God by the way we treat our bodies. Surprise, surprise: a Temple University study showed a direct correlation between the number of fast-food meals people eat per week and their body mass indexes and body weights. Several obesity studies report similar results: the more often we eat in restaurants, the heavier we become. Do we really need another scientific report to prove the obvious—America is getting fat. Perhaps our food has become *too* convenient!

Financial effects

If you're like the average American family, you probably eat out about three times a week. For a family of four, that can easily add up to $300 or $400 per month, or more than $4,000 per year.

Environmental effects

Sure, when it comes to dining out, you can have it your way, right away. But take a moment to consider the impact your food choices have on the environment. When you pull up to your favorite burger joint and order a hamburger, french fries, and soda, it takes an astounding 1,500 gallons of water to produce your value meal. This includes the water for growing potatoes, the grain for the bun and the cattle, and all ingredients for the soda.

Save dining out for special occasions, like anniversaries and graduations. When you want to celebrate with friends, share a hassle-free potluck meal.

Plates, flatware, and napkins

When you do eat out, try to patronize restaurants that use real plates and flatware. On the road, consider diners rather than fast-food restaurants; a meal at a diner costs about the same as Wendy's, but creates much less trash. Matthew and I usually share a meal when we go out because portions have gotten so big—and it costs half as much. Another money-saving tip: ask for water—better for your health and the earth.

Disposable paper products—cups, napkins, to-go bags—often end up in the landfill. So why grab a huge stack of napkins at McDonald's when one or two will do? If we each used one less napkin per day, we would save more than a billion pounds of napkins from landfills.

How to Save Money This Year

The average family of four spends more than $2,300 on entertainment and recreation each year, plus about $4,000 eating out. Here are some examples of how your family can save money this year, while saving the earth:

Cancel cable service	$720
Cancel two magazine subscriptions	$40
Cut movie theater attendance in half	$80
Eliminate one sport per child, per year (driving, equipment, lessons, etc.)	$400
Cut restaurant eating in half	$1,500
Borrow movies and books from the library	$160
Forgo one season of tickets to sporting events	$1,500
Replace one trip to a theme park with a picnic	$150
Avoid buying the latest Blu-ray player, HDTV, next-generation console, or Internet-enabled cell phone	$500

TOTAL SAVINGS PER YEAR   **$5,050**

. . . And Share It with Those in Need

Want to help others with some of your entertainment savings dollars? Here are some ideas to get you started:

- Purchase musical instruments for a low-income music program.

- Call your local high school arts department and offer to donate tickets to the theater, symphony, art museum, or dance performance.

- Donate sports equipment to your local Boys & Girls Club.

- Give generously to a museum that matches your interests—there are about 17,500 museums in the United States and nearly all are in need of additional funding.

- Support the Bard: the two hundred Shakespeare festivals held annually in the United States would welcome additional contributions of any size.

- Visit http://www.charitynavigator.org and click on the Arts, Culture, Humanities category. You will find hundreds of worthy charities throughout the country that are in need of your support.

Putting Your Faith into Action

Dear heavenly Father, thank you for the blessing of rest and relaxation, and for the joy that you provide in simple pleasures. I praise you for the creative spark that you have placed in each of us; inspire me to use that creativity to better serve you. Please help me be mindful of the monetary, relational, and environmental costs of the many ways that I seek entertainment, and to make decisions that honor your holy desires for my life. Break the tyrants that take away from my relationship with you and with those I love; teach me to replace them with habits that are true, noble, lovely, and pure.

Lord, help me *today* to:

- replace half an hour of television with a stroll around my neighborhood

- turn off all electronics when I leave the room, even when I think I'll just be gone for a few minutes

- avoid purchasing any food or drink in a disposable container

- turn off the radio when I'm in the car, and instead spend time talking with my spouse and children or fellowshiping with God

- memorize one Bible verse about godly entertainment, such as Philippians 4:8: "Finally, brothers, whatever is true, whatever is noble, whatever is right, whatever is pure, whatever is lovely, whatever is admirable—if anything is excellent or praiseworthy—think about such things"

Lord, help me *this week* to:

- keep track of how much time per week I spend in front of a TV or computer screen; do the same for each of my children

- eat at least one more meal at home instead of at a restaurant

- patronize only those restaurants that serve on washable dishes and flatware

- buy rechargeable batteries instead of disposables and set up a battery-charging center in my home

- buy smart power strips for the TV, audio equipment, and other electronics—especially anything that uses a remote

Lord, help me *this month* to:

- pledge to spend at least 10 percent less time in front of a TV or computer screen
- go on a three-day media fast—no radio, Internet, newspaper, or magazine infotainment—and use that time to pray for guidance on how to develop more godly habits
- unplug the TV and stereo when not in use, or turn them all the way off
- clean out my bookshelves and donate books I haven't read in the past year to the library or a charitable organization
- go through my sporting goods and sell or donate any items I no longer use
- tally up the total number of hours my family spent preparing for, driving to, watching, and participating in sports in the last month; discuss how this affects our relationships with each other and with God

Lord, help me *this year* to:

- go on a one-week TV fast
- donate my old cell phone and electronic appliances to a good cause
- kick the fast-food habit
- adjust my children's sports schedules so that I have more time with family and God
- modify at least one fitness or spectator sport habit to reflect my growing green awareness
- wait one month when I think I need a new iPod, computer, or TV; if I still believe I need one, consider buying used
- reduce the time I spend in front of a TV or computer screen by at least 20 percent
- donate at least half of the money I've saved to a good cause

Summing It Up

Getting Started

I have:

- ○ kept track of how much time I watch TV per week
- ○ borrowed books, CDs, and DVDs from the library instead of buying new
- ○ spent five fewer minutes listening to or reading infotainment news
- ○ used fewer paper napkins when I go out to eat
- ○ replaced one fast-food restaurant stop with an alternative that does not use disposable wares

On the Journey

I have:

- ○ cut back on my TV viewing by at least 20 percent
- ○ rented movies instead of driving to a movie theater
- ○ donated or sold unused books, CDs, and DVDs
- ○ purchased rechargeable batteries
- ○ placed TVs and audio equipment on smart power switches
- ○ gone on a media fast for at least one week
- ○ replaced two restaurant meals with two meals at home

Green Superstar

I have:

- ○ canceled cable and cut back my TV viewing by 40 percent
- ○ set up a battery-recharging center in my home
- ○ given away, sold, or recycled electronics and athletic equipment that my family no longer uses
- ○ gone on a media fast for at least one month
- ○ avoided nearly all restaurants that use disposable wares
- ○ donated the money I've saved to a good cause

Children do not belong to us. For a brief time, they are on loan to us from God, and we act as stewards and caretakers of them. If we have done our jobs well, in the end they will grow up and make us proud. . . . At no other time is our role of steward and our position of dominion of more importance than in childrearing.

—*Serve God, Save the Planet*

Taking care of God's creation can begin with small steps at your school. Pick your projects, don't lose motivation or get bogged down in bureaucracy, and remember who is guiding your efforts. Everything you do to save the environment is really part of your witness, showing the world how much you love God by respecting the gift of his creation.

—*It's Easy Being Green*

Schools

Equipping Kids for a Greener Future

*Let my teaching fall like rain and my words descend
like dew, like showers on new grass, like abundant
rain on tender plants.*

DEUTERONOMY 32:2

FOR A YEAR, I taught in a small primary school. I was responsible
for six children, ages five through eight. Because the school was
just getting started, and the class was small, it felt a lot like homeschooling. In fact, our building was a two-hundred-year-old Cape
Cod, and my classroom had served for many generations as the
front parlor.

When I started at the school, Matthew was just transitioning
out of medicine, and we were beginning our journey of down-
wardly mobile living. I took the job, in part, because of its proximity—a 3-mile bike ride from my home. Arriving on bike gave me
instant "cool" status in the eyes of my pupils.

The founder of the school was not particularly into green, but she
was open to my ideas—and the parents were extremely supportive.
Instead of doing a special unit on the environment, we incorporated
a respect for nature into everything we did. For physical education
and science, we removed garbage from the woods behind the school

and built a nature trail. For math, we counted pieces of trash we picked up on our walk through town, and then practiced our addition and subtraction at the cemetery, calculating how long each person lived. One of my students was fascinated with frogs, so we set up a classroom terrarium, and she wrote a research report on their habits and habitats. At story time, we read books about the rainforest, the desert, the Arctic, and the wetlands. During journal time, we sat outside and wrote about what we saw, heard, touched, and smelled. For art, we made crafts using objects from nature. At snack time, we learned how to cook healthful food, and during music we sang songs that celebrated the beauty outside our window. In the spring, we all participated in National Turn-Off-Your-TV Week, covering the monitor at school with the titles of all the books we read. Throughout the year, we wrote on the back of used paper and made sure that we recycled everything we could.

I know that teachers are not supposed to have favorites, but Josh was a very special boy. At age five, he was extremely inquisitive, honest, and affectionate. He also was obsessed with war. When he dictated stories to me, they always involved chivalric battles. When he looked through our children's encyclopedia, he always turned to the pages on weapons or battlefields. When I played Pachelbel's *Canon* during quiet time, he misheard me and later asked if we could please listen to that "popping cannons" song again.

One day, when Josh had just finished drawing yet another exquisitely detailed sword and shield, I decided to ask about his interest in war. Trying to be as gentle as possible, I said, "Josh, I can't help but notice that every time you draw pictures for me or take books out of the library, they always have something to do with war. I'm not saying that there's anything wrong with that—but I just don't understand. Why do you think that is?"

Josh was quiet for a full two minutes. A thoughtful boy, he clearly wanted to give me a truthful answer. Finally, he looked me straight in the eyes and replied, "It's because boys are boys and girls are girls."

So what does Josh's answer have to do with the environment? Last night, I finished reading *The Idiot* by the Russian novelist Fyodor Dostoevsky. His main character, the Christlike hero Prince Myshkin, has a special relationship with children, just as Jesus did. Young children love him because he is honest and never tries to deceive them. Further, Prince Myshkin has found, as I did with Josh, that "a child can give exceedingly good advice even in the most difficult case."

I will never forget what I learned from Josh about the differences between boys and girls, just as I will never forget the lessons my students taught me each time we went outdoors. Turn your face up to the first flakes of snow, watch a butterfly shake its wings dry, lie on your back and tell stories about the animals you see in the clouds—and you will understand that though we can share knowledge with children, they can teach us something even more valuable: wonderment.

Children instinctively understand that nature is precious—more valuable than anything humans can make. They live in the joy of the eternal present, neither ruminating on the past nor fretting themselves into paralysis about the future.

As adults, we must "train up a child in the way he should go," but at the same time be humble and patient enough to *receive* instruction, for the "kingdom of heaven belongs to such as these."

> Nature is school-mistress, the soul the pupil; and whatever one has taught or the other has learned has come from God—the Teacher of the teacher.
> —*Tertullian (160–230?),* De Testimonio Animae

When it comes to the environment, perhaps the best gift my students gave me was *hope*.

GETTING STARTED

Learning begins long before a child ever sets foot in school, in the biggest classroom of all—the wide realm of creation. During the transition from backyards to backpacks, we need to continue to foster a love for nature and a desire to become good stewards.

In America, the average student spends 16,380 hours in school from kindergarten through twelfth grade. We—as parents and teachers—can use this massive chunk of our children's lives to teach environmental principles and show firsthand how to love and care for God's creation. Yes, it will require time, resources, and creativity. But the long-term spiritual, financial, and environmental benefits will be well worth the effort—for us and for future generations.

Train a child in the way he should go, and when he is old he will not turn from it.
PROVERBS 22:6

Many schools all over the country are working to reduce their environmental impact. One program, the Green Schools Initiative, was started in 2004 by eco-minded parents who wanted to improve environmental stewardship at their kids' schools. You don't have to be a teacher or school board member to spur change. Visit the Green Schools Initiative Web site at http://www.greenschools.net to see how you can help.

Showing a child the transformation of food scraps into garden vegetables makes science come alive. Picking a favorite spot in nature and keeping a journal throughout the seasons teaches students to become keen observers. Conducting an energy audit on the school building and asking students to develop energy-saving recommendations develops teamwork, presentation skills, and a sense of stewardship.

Ask your schools to appoint a recycling representative for each classroom, start a worm composting bin, and create a school garden. Encourage unstructured after-school time to play and explore the green spaces in your neighborhood. Make it your assignment to educate students of all ages about caring for their first and most exciting classroom—God's creation.

START WITH A PLAN

Green team

If you are interested in helping with green initiatives at your school, start by talking to parents, teachers, students, and administrators.

Find out what their concerns are—and their hopes—and ask for recommendations on the best way for you to help make environmental stewardship a central part of the school culture.

At many schools, it's helpful to form an environmental task force, or green team. This group of teachers, students, custodians, parents, school board members, and other stakeholders makes recommendations for environmental activities at the school. Whether it is an elementary, middle, or high school, be sure to include at least one senior school administrator on the team.

Renewing Energy

When I worked at a boarding school, each teacher was responsible for participating on a committee. My first year, I was excited to learn that there was already an environmental faculty group in place, so I signed up.

The good news was that the school had a long history of initiating environmental programs. The bad news was that, like many schools, the leadership for these student-run programs graduated every four years. And with high turnover, especially among the younger faculty, after-school programs came and went with the teachers who served as their advisors.

From the very first meeting, I could see that one of the major tasks was to reenergize the committee members. Because so many programs—like recycling and cafeteria composting—had started and died away, they needed faith that a program could, and would, not only last but also grow beyond their tenure on the committee.

At my first meeting, teachers in my group shared some valuable history. I learned how a local hog farmer used to take all of their food scraps, until the Department of Health deemed that the empty barrels he returned were not sufficiently sanitized—even though they remained outdoors and were simply filled up again the next day. I also heard that the company running our food service program claimed that disposable dishes must be used at lunchtime because the school did not have enough dishwashing machines. When the green committee had drafted plans for expanding the dish-cleaning area, they encountered seemingly insurmountable roadblocks.

The false starts and disappointments were many, but there was hope. We clearly needed to focus on changes that would become standard operating procedure—integral to the campus culture—and not dependent on any one faculty member or student leader.

With the help of two other teachers, we started a paper recycling program. Students made recycling boxes and asked teachers if they would keep one in each of their rooms. A few teachers declined, but most were glad to help. On Thursdays, one of my colleagues arranged to park a school van in a central location, where teachers could then bring their paper to be recycled. The students in my last class of the morning went around campus offering to collect boxes that had not yet been emptied, and then I drove the van to the recycling center during my lunch break.

Not exactly rocket science, but it was a start.

The next fall, I purchased blue trash barrels to put around the campus. The industrial arts program drilled a hole in the center of each top, and my daughter painted "Cans and bottles only" around the hole. I also bought a few fire-resistant recycling containers for inside the buildings, placing them in the teachers' lounge and copier room where they would be used most frequently. These inside barrels were significantly more expensive because they had to meet fire code.

To make the can and bottle recycling a permanent feature of the campus, we invited the National Honor Society to take responsibility for the program. Because there is a 5-cent deposit on all beverage containers in the state, the club could collect the redemption money and donate it to a good cause. Members of the club wrote a humorous skit and performed it during an assembly to encourage student participation.

We then asked the dean of the freshmen if his class would

> *Teach them to their children, so the next generation might know them—even the children not yet born—and they in turn will teach their own children.*
>
> PSALM 78:5-6, NLT

take on paper recycling as an ongoing service project. He agreed, and thereafter the recycling program was handed down to each entering freshman class.

I also had the good fortune to pilot a senior capstone program. By then, a lot of people on campus knew that caring for the environment was my passion, so students with a green bent seemed to gravitate toward my class. The purpose of the senior capstone was to select an area of personal interest and complete a semester-long research project, "capped" by a practical, service-oriented project. One of my first students wrote a successful proposal to switch the entire campus to 30 percent recycled paper. When the student demonstrated that it would not cost the school any more money to be more environmentally responsible, the headmaster asked why no one had proposed this change before, and immediately approved the change. He also promised to switch to the slightly more expensive 100 percent postconsumer recycled content paper, once it could be demonstrated that paper usage on campus—and paper costs—had decreased.

The head librarian was a member of our faculty green team. She was great at keeping records and had a real heart for the environment. By switching the library printers from single-sided to double-sided printing default (another student initiative), she was able to show that paper costs in the library dropped from $9,000 to less than $4,500 in one year—more than twice the savings needed to make a campus switch to 100 percent recycled paper cost neutral.

Another advocate on the green team was a young physics teacher. I put her in touch with a nonprofit environmental education program in our state, and they helped her class conduct a campuswide energy audit. The class chose three lighting projects to research further and made recommendations in a formal PowerPoint presentation to the administration, with people from the campus, community, and local media invited to attend. All three of the recommended changes—switching to LED lights in exit signs, using motion-detector lighting in selected classrooms, and installing dimmers in the cafeteria where natural lighting was abundant—were immediately approved. The students were publicly commended for proposing changes that were cost effective as well as good for the environment—a lesson not only in physics but also in the rewards of civic involvement.

Even now, long after my departure from the school, new initiatives continue to be proposed and approved—including cutting back on the use of Styrofoam in the cafeteria and on-site composting of food waste. The entire waste disposal system was rebid, and large glass, plastics, and metal recycling collection sites were installed around campus. As a result, trash production on campus has been reduced by 50 percent.

Before leaving the school, I helped recruit and hire my replacement. I was thrilled not only that he had experience teaching my advanced placement classes but also that caring for the environment was a personal conviction for him.

Today, green is not only the school's official color—it's also an integral part of the campus culture. The school motto, *Semper Discens* (always learning), applies not only to what we know but also to how we live.

Environmental vision statement

Encourage your school to draft an environmental vision statement, detailing the goals that students, staff, and the community are striving to achieve. For a class art project, students can decorate the statement and display it in various places throughout the school. Talk to the school librarian about creating an environmental display in one of the library's showcases. Include your environmental vision on the school Web site and in communications with parents.

School energy audit

When we want to change any area of our lives, one of the first steps is to take an inventory. Encourage your school to complete an energy audit that measures the school's environmental impact. Many local utilities will perform an audit for little or no cost. Students can get involved by measuring the amount of waste produced from school lunches and checking the building for leaky faucets or electrical equipment that is left on overnight. View recommendations for a detailed environmental audit at http://www.recycleworks.org/schools/s_audits.html.

> And Nature, the old nurse, took
>   The child upon her knee,
> Saying: "Here is a story-book
>   Thy Father has written for thee."
> "Come, wander with me," she said,
>   "Into regions yet untrod;
> And read what is still unread
>   in the manuscripts of God"
> —*Henry Wadsworth Longfellow (1807–1882),*
> *"The Fiftieth Birthday of Agassiz"*

Another important measure is how much garbage your school produces daily. Collect all garbage produced in one day at the school and put it out on the school lawn. Wearing gloves, open the garbage bags on a tarp, and then sort it into piles. Items that can be recycled—glass, paper, plastic, metal, and cardboard—go into separate piles on one half of the tarp. Designate a separate corner for food waste that can be composted. Put garbage that must go to the landfill in the final corner. Weigh the amount of waste that could have been recycled or composted, as well as the trash destined for the dump, and then determine the percent that your trash production would decrease if everyone at school fully participated in a recycling program.

For more information on conducting a waste audit at your school, visit http://www.greenschools.net.

Plan of action

Your school's environmental audit will help you set priorities and develop a plan of action. The written plan should include short-term, realistic goals for environmental stewardship—like reducing trash production by one-quarter or having at least 75 percent of non-bus riders bike, walk, or carpool to school—as well as broader, long-term goals. Below are some suggestions to include in your action plan:

- Start a recycling program
- Use nontoxic cleaning products

- Establish a carpooling network
- Conserve energy by turning off lights, computer monitors, and printers when leaving the room and shutting them down completely after school
- Plant a school garden

AROUND THE BUILDING
Recycling

Recycling programs can significantly cut down on waste and lower disposal costs. The key to a truly successful recycling effort is

Eco-Friendly Suppliers

- Dolphin Blue (http://www.dolphinblue.com)
- Eco-Products (http://www.ecoproducts.com)
- Ecover (http://www.ecover.com/us/en)
- Green Earth Office Supply (http://www.greenearthofficesupply.com)
- Green Field Paper Company (http://www.greenfieldpaper.com)
- GreenLine Paper Company (http://www.greenlinepaper.com)
- New Leaf Paper (http://www.newleafpaper.com)
- Office Depot (http://www.officedepot.com)
- Office Max (http://www.officemax.com)
- Recycled Products Cooperative (http://www.recycledproducts.org)
- Seventh Generation (http://www.seventhgeneration.com)
- Staples (http://www.staples.com)
- The Real Earth, Inc. (http://www.treeco.com)
- Treecycle Recycled Paper (http://www.treecycle.com)

For more green ideas on green suppliers, visit http://www.grist.org. For additional green buying tips, visit http://www.greenseal.org.

involving all students and not leaving the work to a custodian or small group of dedicated enthusiasts. Most schools should be capable of recycling paper, plastic, aluminum, steel, cardboard, ink cartridges, and electronics. If your school only recycles a few of these items, investigate ways to expand your program.

Need fund-raising ideas for tree planting or other environmental school projects? Consider making your school a community drop-off point for old electronics, ink cartridges, and cell phones. Green School Project is one of several organizations that pays schools to recycle their ink-jet and laser printer cartridges as well as cell phones and PDAs. The organization provides prepaid shipping materials free of charge. Register online at http://www.green schoolproject.com.

Unbleached paper

Most standard paper products have been bleached with chlorine to achieve the "white paper" look. However, bleaching creates dioxins, which are highly toxic pollutants. Dioxins infiltrate the food chain; the higher up the food chain, the higher the concentration of toxins. Because dioxins accumulate in fat cells, they have a long half-life—seven to twelve years. Some forms of dioxins are considered "known human carcinogens."

To reduce dioxins, purchase recycled, chlorine-free paper. The Chlorine Free Products Association posts a list of products it endorses online at http://www.chlorinefreeproducts.org/endorsed.htm.

Recycled paper content

Increase the demand for recycled paper by purchasing paper products with recycled content. The higher the percentage of postconsumer recycled content, the better.

On a recent visit to an office supply store, Emma and I were pleased to see a whole display of environmentally friendly school supplies—notebooks, binders, journals, and loose-leaf paper. Invest in binders made from recycled materials, and reuse them year after year. Purchase notebooks with at least 80 percent postconsumer fiber. They are inexpensive and help reduce landfill waste. At the end of each semester, be sure to recycle paper after it has been used on both sides. If you purchase notebooks with wire binding, remember to remove the wire after using both sides of all the paper, and then recycle the wire and the paper separately.

Coming from Left Field

Because my daughter, Emma, is left-handed, she finds it difficult to write on the right-hand sides of notebooks—the binding, wire, or rings always get in the way. But that doesn't mean she can't use both sides of the paper. Emma takes notes for one class on the left-hand side of the paper. The next semester, she flips the notebook over to write on the backs, where she can again write on the left side.

When we bought school supplies this year, Emma opted for notebooks and a composition book made with bagasse, the plant fiber waste remaining after sugarcane is processed and crushed to make sugar. The bagasse content maximizes the use of all parts of renewable agriculture products rather than cutting down trees, and the quality is just as good as traditional tree-based paper.

To learn more about the 2,000 products made from recycled paper—saving 1.6 million trees per year and 5,000 acres of forest—visit http://www.staples.com/ecoeasy.

Posters

Paper-intensive projects seem to be the rage in schools, though I am less than convinced that their contribution to learning is commensurate with the amount of resources they consume—both in terms of time and paper. In many cases, parents (me included!) end up running from store to store trying to find the right poster board and supplies, and then end up "helping" with the project late into the night.

When possible, make or purchase a display board that can be

reused and handed down from child to child. If poster board is the only option, be sure to use the back side for another project. At a parent-teacher conference, you may want to gently share your concerns about the use of financial and environmental resources for school projects that have a very limited life—often just one day.

Going Native

School projects use lots of resources, and have become much more elaborate since I was a kid, yet I don't know if the increase in learning is commensurate with the increase in expense and materials consumed.

Our family's most intense school project happened during Emma's sixth-grade year. The assignment was on a Native American tribe, due immediately after February break. Emma, who can do nothing halfway, worked on that project throughout the vacation, creating a clay pot, handmade soap, a traditional weaving, an elaborate Native American recipe book and foods, and explanatory posters. Emma is happiest when she is making things, but I had not anticipated that her entire ten-day vacation would be so consumed with the project.

On the Monday after vacation, Emma asked me to drive her to school, as the project was too big to carry on the bus. When she came home, I asked how her presentation went. It hadn't.

Emma, who is dyslexic, had read the due date wrong. That year, February and March had the exact dates on the same days of the week. What Emma read as February 26 was really March 26. True, while the rest of her class toiled to finish their projects, Emma was resting easy—but then again, they (and their families) had probably enjoyed a more relaxed vacation.

Learn from my mistake: Set boundaries for how much money, time, and resources your family will spend on school projects, and stick with them. Don't allow school assignments to monopolize family life, or detract from the firstfruits, which should always belong to God. And use environmetally friendly supplies whenever possible.

Yes, excelling in school is important, but not at the expense of the health of the planet, or our relationships.

> **GO GREEN**
> In one year, the average school throws away 38 tons of paper. That's more than 8 million sheets! Your school could save 646 trees per year by recycling its paper.

Lighting

Replace standard lightbulbs with energy-efficient or LED ones. Implement a "lights off when leaving" policy, which also applies to computers, printers, and fax machines.

Because exit signs are on twenty-four hours per day, changing regular lightbulbs to LED bulbs will save money fast. Incandescent bulbs use ten times more energy than LED exit sign bulbs and burn out every few months.

> **GO GREEN**
> Concerned about what to do with your school's compact fluorescent lightbulbs once they burn out? Home Depot stores now collect used CFLs. Just take your used CFLs to the return desk, and the bulbs will be recycled responsibly.

LED bulbs cost just $4 per year to operate and don't have to be changed for ten or more years—saving energy, labor, and money. Your school can save as much as $450 over the life of the bulb for *every* exit sign.

Vending machines

Consider installing an energy-saving device called a vending miser on school vending machines. This device powers down the vending machine's lights when no one is around, while still keeping your drinks cool. Your school can save as much as $100 in electricity costs per year for each vending miser installed. Order online at http://www.vendingmiserstore.com.

Green cleaners

When I was a kid, I didn't know anyone in my school with asthma. Now nearly every student can tell you of a family member or friend with asthma.

One way to provide students with a healthier environment for learning is to switch to Green Seal–certified cleaners. Using less toxic chemical cleaners in schools can cut down on indoor air pollution and related health problems. Visit http://www.greenseal.org/find aproduct/index.cfm to view a list of certified products and services.

If you believe hazardous cleaning products are being used in your school, talk to someone on the school's custodial staff. If the cleaners they are using are not on the green list, ask to see the Material Safety Data Sheets (MSDS) for each product. Unhealthy ingredients commonly used in school cleaning products include 2-butoxyethanol, petroleum distillates, chlorine (sodium hypochlorite), ammonia, quaternary ammonium compounds, alkylphenol ethoxylates, and acids.

New York and Illinois were the first two states to require that school districts use environmentally sensitive cleaning products; more districts are taking initiatives to protect both their children and their custodial staffs from the health hazards associated with chemicals.

Air quality

Proper ventilation, dust and mold reduction, and eco-friendly building and cleaning products can all improve a school's indoor air quality. Live plants in classrooms also can improve air quality while adding beauty and color. In my classrooms, students enjoyed the plants we kept growing year-round along my south-facing windows.

Asthma Facts

- Asthma is the leading cause of school absenteeism, affecting one out of every eleven school-age students in the United States. Annually, children miss about 15 million school days due to asthma.

- Over 150,000 children are hospitalized from asthma each year. Indoor air pollution at school and home can exacerbate asthma.

- Twenty-four percent of children between the ages of five and seventeen have some limited activity due to respiratory impairment.

- While the rate of asthma among American schoolchildren ranges from 6 percent to 8 percent, prevalence in low-income, minority neighborhood asthma "hot spots" is as much as two to three times greater.

- African American children are more likely to be hospitalized due to asthma complications than Caucasian children and are four times as likely to die from asthma.

- More than 2 million children who suffer from asthma attacks live in areas of the United States that received a failing grade for ozone levels by the American Lung Association.

- For a child without asthma, the cost of medical expenses averages $618 a year; the annual cost of medical expenses for a child with asthma averages $1,042.

- The estimated annual cost for treating asthma in children younger than eighteen is $3.2 billion; 41 percent of families with asthmatic children have no primary health insurance.

Pesticides

Children are more sensitive than adults to pesticides and are often at higher risk for coming into contact with chemicals because of sitting on the floor and having hand-to-mouth contact. Instead of using hazardous pesticides at school, promote integrated pest management by reducing food sources, water supplies, and shelter for pests in and around your school. Integrated pest management is a safer and usually less costly option for schools. Talk to your local agriculture extension agent, or download a how-to guide from the Environmental Protection Agency at http://www.epa.gov/pesticides/ipm/schoolipm/index.html.

New buildings

Building a new facility or an addition for your school provides unique opportunities for integrating eco-friendly building practices and saving the school district money for decades to come. The Leadership in Energy and Environmental Design (LEED) Green Building Rating System provides clear guidelines for green building. Learn more at the U.S. Green Building Council's Web site (http://www.buildgreenschools.org).

IN THE CLASSROOM

Temperature

Turn the thermostat in classrooms down three degrees in the cooler months and up three degrees in the warmer months. Each degree of temperature saved per schoolroom equates to as much as a 3 percent cost savings on utility bills.

Pens and pencils

Look for pencils made from recycled materials and packed in lightweight or recyclable packaging. Pens are commonly thrown away and not recycled or reused, so purchase refillable pens. Although the initial cost is higher, they can be reused over a longer period of time, and refills are inexpensive.

Rewritable CDs

Choose rewritable compact discs that can be reused for data storage. Buy CDs packed on bulk spindles, avoiding individual packaging in plastic jewel cases. CDs are made of the recyclable materials

Ten Ways to Green Your Classroom

1. Appoint a student each week as the power ranger to make sure that lights, monitors, and printers are turned off when leaving the room and at the end of the day.

2. Remind students to turn off the faucet while lathering the soap during hand washing.

3. Encourage students to print work on paper that has been used on one side.

4. Rely on natural sunlight and turn off the lights when the sun shines in the room.

5. Collect used paper for students to use as scrap paper.

6. Ask students to bring reusable thermoses or water bottles.

7. Set your printer to double-sided default and assign fewer paper-intensive projects.

8. Hand out fewer worksheets.

9. Designate recycling bins for paper, plastics, and aluminum to encourage recycling in the classroom.

10. Bring in live houseplants, and assign a student each week to keep them watered.

polycarbonate and aluminum. If you have old CDs that can no longer be used for memory storage, contact a CD recycling center:

GreenDisk Services (800-305-3475)
NESAR Systems (724-827-8172)
Digital Audio Disc Corporation (812-462-8323)
Plastic Recycling Incorporated (317-780-6100)

Crayons and markers
Use nontoxic crayons made from soybean oil in place of standard, petroleum-derived paraffin wax crayons. A strong smell in markers means they contain toxic chemicals that can leak into the groundwater at the landfills. Instead, use water-based markers with nontoxic ink and refillable heads.

Plastics
School supplies like notebooks, binders, pencil cases, and backpacks contain polyvinyl chloride (PVC), the most environmentally hazardous plastic. PVC is extremely difficult to recycle and may contain toxins that are harmful to the immune system. Eliminate PVC and polycarbonate (PC) plastic from your school supplies, particularly avoiding items stamped with numbers three and seven in the triangular recycling symbol. You can purchase PVC-free supplies at http://www.treeco.com or http://www.mamasearth.com.

IN THE CAFETERIA
Pack smart
When your child takes lunch to school, pack sandwiches, fresh fruits and vegetables, and treats stored in reusable lunch containers. These foods can be purchased in larger quantities, saving money and packaging. Avoid using plastic bags and utensils, paper napkins, and brown paper bags. Instead, invest in a reusable lunchbox, thermos or other reusable drink containers, cloth napkins, and silverware.

A Whole Lot of Sandwiches

Our son, Clark, took his lunch to school every day throughout elementary school, except one. Noticing that Clark never bought lunch, his second grade teacher scheduled a date with him in the cafeteria. It was an extremely nice gesture, and Clark enjoyed the hot meal—but he continued to take his lunch.

I wish I could say that it was because I packed cookie cutter–shaped sandwiches and scrumptious treats, but the truth is that Clark didn't want to wait in line for hot lunch and waste valuable recess time. Our lunches were on the boring/healthful end of the scale when compared to the lunches his friends brought to school. Early on, I found a container that held a full-sized sandwich on one side. Flip the box over, and there were three compartments: one for carrots, one for fig bars, and one for pretzels. Add a piece of fruit, a water bottle, and a cloth napkin, and that's pretty much the lunch that Clark ate for seven years running.

Or, maybe I should say the lunch that Clark brought, but not necessarily ate. Only much later did I learn that one of his best friends loved fig bars, for which he would gladly trade an individually packaged cupcake or candy bar.

I don't blame Clark for bartering occasionally, but neither do I think he was deprived by bringing healthful, eco-friendly lunches. Clark likes good food. Habits formed at a young age have stuck.

As a twenty-year-old medical student, Clark now must fend for himself. Except for an occasional meal at the hospital cafeteria, Clark cooks his own—for the most part, healthful—meals.

A lot of sandwiches on whole grain bread. A lot of apples. Peas, chicken, and a starch for dinner. Soy milk or water to drink. An occasional dessert. Almost no snacks.

As a parent of young children, it can be hard to say no to junk food, especially when it's so convenient. But the Bible does not promise that parenting is easy. It's the seemingly small decisions, like saying no to junk food, that can help our children grow into healthy adults.

A disposable lunch generates 4 to 8 ounces of garbage. If your child takes lunch to school on a regular basis, he can produce as much as 100 pounds of garbage in a year. Instead, pack lunches in reusable containers.

Compost

Composting is a great way to teach kids about ecology, biology, and waste reduction. If your school is composting for the first time, start by composting leaves and grass clippings in an enclosed container.

Worms!

Vermicomposting uses earthworms to convert organic wastes into rich, high-quality compost. This method can reduce garbage by up to one-third and provide organic soil for houseplants and container gardens. Students add their snack scraps to a worm box, providing an ongoing, live science lesson.

Our children's third grade teacher kept a worm box in the classroom. It worked great. The worms thrived, and the compost they made was added to the school vegetable garden.

Our home worm bin didn't work out as well. It may have been because we kept our pantry too cool in winter, or because we didn't have enough food scraps to feed the worms, but eventually the worms stopped producing. We decided to return to outdoor composting.

If your first attempt at vermicomposting does not work, experiment with another bin, a different placement of the bin, or a fresh supply of worms. We didn't persevere because we live in an area where outdoor composting is easy. If you live in an apartment or in the city, worms could be the answer to your composting prayers!

For more on vermicomposting, visit http://www.journeytoforever.org/compost_worm.html.

Once you have had success with composting yard waste, the school might want to consider composting cafeteria waste. Before composting food scraps, seek advice from a local expert to help with placement, procedures, and maintenance of your composting bins. If you don't know where to find help, contact your local recycling center or cooperative extension office.

GO GREEN

A single elementary school can create 18,760 pounds of lunch waste per year. Only pack as much food as your child can eat, and encourage your child to take a reasonable amount from salad bars and self-serve lines. Studies have shown that food waste can be cut as much as 50 percent when all-you-can-eat cafeterias eliminate trays for carrying food.

Recycling

Make sure recycling bins are visible and easily accessible in the cafeteria. Your elementary school could save $6,000 this year in landfill disposal costs by recycling 90 percent of the waste that would normally go to a landfill.

Local foods

Talk to your cafeteria about buying local and organic foods. Partnerships with local farmers and community gardens can provide healthy foods for students while keeping the miles food must travel to a minimum. Encourage smart eating choices by offering healthy snacks and meal options.

Leftovers

Donate leftover perishable food such as produce, dairy products, and baked goods to a nonprofit organization. Your school can keep usable food out of the waste stream, lower disposal costs, and feed hungry people in your community. America's Second Harvest is a food bank network that can help you decide where to donate (http://www.secondharvest.org).

Disposables
Are your school lunches served on one-time-use plastic plates and paper cups? Reusable plates, cups, and serving utensils will save money in the long run and significantly reduce waste. Ask children to bring cloth napkins from home. If reusable plates are not an option, investigate biodegradable, compostable options, and make sure they end up in the compost bin, not the landfill.

Vending machines
Discourage your children from buying drinks and snacks from vending machines and school stores. Items purchased from these sources usually come heavily packaged, contributing to landfill waste. In addition, they are often empty-calorie foods sold at high prices.

OUTSIDE THE BUILDING
Green space
School green spaces can provide students with beautiful and engaging outdoor learning opportunities. Talk to your school about starting a flower or vegetable garden, creating a nature trail, or maintaining a small woodland area. Then build time into the schedule for outdoor learning and play. In these settings, students can observe wildlife and ecological systems, or plant and harvest their own organic produce.

Trees
If local schools in your community aren't surrounded by trees, volunteer to plant some. Trees provide shade, beauty, and clean air for generations to come.

One of my husband's most cherished memories is planting trees with his dad at the elementary school across the street from their house. Those trees are now more than 60 feet tall. When Matthew went back to preach a creation care sermon in his hometown, a young mom told him about the hours of outdoor fun her children now enjoy playing in the school's trees.

Pesticides and fertilizers

If there is any one place that pesticides and fertilizers should be avoided, it's on school grounds. Children run, roll, and tumble in the grass; such activities should be healthy, not hazardous. Young children also tend to put their hands in their mouths a lot. If we post signs saying that dogs should not be allowed out after fertilizers are applied, shouldn't we at least have the same concern for our children?

I will teach you the way that is good and right.
1 SAMUEL 12:23

Native plants are a wonderful teaching tool, designed by our Creator to grow well in local conditions without the use of fertilizers. Encourage the custodial staff to use natural methods for taking care of school grounds. You'll greatly improve your chances of success if you get personally involved: volunteer to organize a Saturday cleanup day in the spring and fall, with community members collecting litter, tending gardens, and planting trees and flowers.

EN ROUTE TO AND FROM SCHOOL

Taking the bus

Taking a bus rather than a car to school is a better choice for the planet. A student can travel over 5 miles on a full bus using the energy it would take to go just one mile in a car. Additionally, school buses account for fewer accidents than private transportation.

Walking or biking

Less than one-third of kids who live a mile or less from school walk there. To promote walking instead of using cars, map out safe biking and walking routes to school. Encouraging students to walk to school will provide regular exercise, reduce traffic congestion near the school, improve air quality, and save gas money for parents. Visit the U.S. Department of Transportation's Safe Routes to School site at http://www.nhtsa.dot.gov/people/injury/pedbimot/bike/Safe-Routes-2002.

Want to jump-start a program for walking to school? Promote International Walk to School Day in your community. Find out more at http://www.walktoschool.org.

GO GREEN

Among students who live within 2 miles of school, only 2.5 percent ride their bikes to school. Still, those 600,000 students save about 100,000 gallons of gasoline each day by not taking a bus or car.

Carpooling

The average mother of school-age children spends sixty-six minutes each day driving, covering about 29 miles and taking more than five trips to and from home.

Start a rideshare network and encourage car pools. Carpooling saves time, money, and gas while lowering stress levels and reducing congestion around the school.

SHARING THE MESSAGE
Greening your curriculum

Eco-friendly activities can be incorporated into science, arts and humanities, math, language arts, and electives. View sample environmental lessons online at http://www.teach-nology.com/teachers/lesson_plans.

Engage students in studies outside the classroom and bring conservation to life. A trip outside can stimulate journal writing or inspire poetry about nature. Schedule a field trip to a park, nature center, recycling center, water treatment plant, or local organic farm.

For ideas on environmental literature for children, visit http://www.dnr.state.wi.us/org/caer/ce/eek/teacher/childlit.htm. This list includes more than four hundred recommended books, both fiction and nonfiction, with short descriptions and recommended ages. Some of our family favorites include *Just a Dream*, *The Lorax*, *The Giving Tree*, *Planting a Rainbow*, *Owl Moon*, *Paddle to the Sea*, and many of the wonderfully wacky and informative Magic School Bus series. For older readers or read-alouds, we've enjoyed *Freckles*, *My Side of the Mountain*, and *Lost on a Mountain in Maine*. And then there was the year of *Little House on the Prairie* and *On the Banks of Plum Creek*, when Emma related everything to our favorite frontier girl, Laura Ingalls Wilder.

Educating everyone

Successful environmental education is not aimed just at students. Everyone from parents to school administrators to custodians to community members should be involved. Share what your school is doing with the local media, and encourage families to go green at home.

Celebrating Earth Day

On April 22, make caring for the environment fun with an Earth Day celebration at your child's school. Organize a cleanup event for a local highway, lake, trail, or park. Put up a communal pledge board and encourage students to write their environmental promise for the year, like "I will turn off the water while brushing my teeth," or "I will turn off the lights when I leave the room." Host a food festival with representatives from natural and organic food growers in your area. Organize a hike, or plant a tree.

To extend the environmental learning and fun, celebrate National Environmental Education Week. This is a full week of educational preparation and activities leading up to Earth Day. Find out more at http://www.eeweek.org.

From One Teen to Another: Twelve Steps toward a Greener Education

BY EMMA SLEETH, AUTHOR OF *IT'S EASY BEING GREEN*

1. Always write on both sides of the paper. Use college-ruled paper (skinnier lines, more words per page).

2. Use the back side of class handouts for printing out your papers. (Most teachers won't mind, as long as you cross out the irrelevant side.)

3. Use the draft mode on your printer, except on final drafts.

4. Use both sides of poster board—ask teachers if you can have their extra student posters at the end of the year when they clear out their classrooms, and use the clean sides next year.

5. Recycle all binder paper at the end of the year.

6. Walk or ride the bus to school. If neither is an option, carpool.

7. Bring your lunch in reusable containers. Instead of getting a throwaway carton of juice or milk, bring your drink in a water bottle. Wide-neck bottles are easier to keep clean.

8. Buy refillable pens instead of disposable ones, and use a couple of mechanical pencils that you really like.

9. Ask your homeroom teacher if you can bring in live plants for the classroom—and offer to take care of them. They will make the room more cheerful and cut down on indoor air pollution.

10. Recycle everything you can at school—paper, plastic, cans, cardboard. If there's no recycling program, start one.

11. Do some investigative work. Does your school use paper towels and toilet paper with recycled paper content? Do they use recycled paper in the copiers and printers? Is double-sided printing the default on the printers? Do all lights and computers get turned off at night? If not, work with your student government or environmental group to suggest changes.

12. Start a clothing exchange where students can drop off clothes in good condition that they no longer need, and others can pick some up. Do the same with binders, backpacks, and school supplies. When it comes time for prom and formal dances, ask girls to donate last year's dresses so someone else can go to school events without spending a fortune.

How to Save Money This Year

On average, families with school-age children spend $527 each year for back-to-school purchases, plus up to $600 per child for school lunches. By learning a few environmentally friendly practices, you can save a bundle throughout the year while helping the planet.

INSTEAD OF	DO THIS
Purchasing a new backpack each year	Reuse last year's pack; if you must buy another, look for one with a lifetime warranty that can be easily washed and reused. Stores like REI, Redwood Trading Post, and L.L. Bean offer canvas packs in many styles.
Using wood pencils and one-time-use pens	Invest in refillable pens and pencils
Packing lunches in disposable plastic and paper bags	Buy a lunchbox and fill it with reusable containers
Purchasing individually wrapped, single-serving snacks	Buy healthy snacks in bulk
Purchasing Lunchables and similar convenience foods marketed as a complete meal	Make fresh sandwiches
Buying regular paper and folders	Look for products made from recycled materials, preferably 80–100 percent postconsumer recycled content
Using a regular calculator that requires batteries	Consider a solar calculator
Purchasing new clothes	Find quality used clothing items at Goodwill, Salvation Army, or other local thrift stores
Driving alone	Carpooling, walking, biking, or taking the bus

. . . And Share It with Those in Need

- Educate a Haitian child in the Zunuzi School for one year, including one nutritious meal per day. (http://www.monafoundation.org/contribute.htm)

- Put sixty-six Braille books into the hands of a blind child, ready to read by touch. (http://www.seedlings.org)

- Donate one hundred and sixty books—ten new books (one for each checkup visit from six months to five years) for sixteen impoverished children. (http://www.reachoutandread.org)

- Bring talented and energetic young teachers to underserved school systems. (http://www.teachforamerica.org)

- Share books and educational resources with needy children in the Philippines. (http://www.booksforthebarrios.com)

- Donate to your local school:

  - 577 boxes of recycled facial tissue (http://www.reliablepaper.com)

  - 7,968 Paper Mate EarthWrite pencils made from recycled materials (right down to the lead and the eraser!)—$3.99 for a box of 48 at Office Depot

  - 97 reams of 100 percent recycled office paper (40,000 sheets of paper)—$6.79 for a ream or $46.99 for a case from Staples.com

  - 639 packs (50 sheets/pack) recycled construction paper (http://www.discountofficeitems.com)

  - 165 eco-friendly binders—$3.95 each from GreenLine Paper Company (http://www.greenlinepaper.com)

  - 31 gallons of all-purpose, nontoxic, biodegradable green cleaner like Simple Green (http://www.ecost.com)

  - 8,000 biodegradable bagasse cups (http://www.greenhome.com)

  - 100 indoor plants from your local nursery and community

Putting Your Faith into Action

Dear heavenly Father, thank you for teaching me about your character through trees, animals, lakes, flowers, and fields. Please increase my love for your creation, and help me to pass on the lessons of environmental stewardship to those who look to me for guidance. I pray that caring for the planet will become a natural part of my child's day-to-day routine, in and out of school. Please give everyone involved in my child's education the wisdom, will, and perseverance to teach healthy stewardship practices throughout the year.

Lord, help me *today* to:

- pack my child's lunch in reusable containers
- save paper used only on one side for my child's schoolwork
- borrow an age-appropriate library book with an environmental theme
- encourage my child to turn off the water while washing his or her hands
- take a nature walk with my child
- pray that everyone involved in my child's education, including me, learns to model healthier stewardship practices

Lord, help me *this week* to:

- call my utility company to find out about energy audits for schools
- pack a reusable thermos or water bottle for my child's drinks
- pack a cloth napkin in my child's lunch
- offer to bring in one or more live plants
- donate tissues made from recycled paper content
- ask friends about the possibility of carpooling to school and after-school activities
- read a book that has an environmental theme with my child
- talk to my children about their ideas on how their school can help care for the planet
- find out if my child's school uses green cleaning products

Lord, help me *this month* to:

- buy recycled, chlorine-free paper
- purchase refillable pens and pencils
- ask the school librarian if my child and I can help create an environmental display in one of the showcases
- encourage my child to carpool, walk, and bike to school more often
- initiate a green team at school
- encourage my school to conduct an energy audit
- find out if the printers in the school's computer lab are set to double-sided default
- investigate the possibility of donating leftover perishable cafeteria food to a nonprofit organization
- look for space on or near school property for starting a vegetable garden

Lord, help me *this year* to:

- purchase at least half of my child's clothes from secondhand and thrift stores, and develop a network for sharing clothes that my children have outgrown
- reuse backpacks instead of buying new ones
- ask teachers to save posters at the end of the year, so they can be used again on the other side
- help the green team develop a plan of action and enact recommendations
- plan a schoolwide Earth Day celebration
- plant trees, flowers, or a vegetable garden at school
- encourage my child's teacher to plan an environmental field trip to an organic farm, recycling center, or nature preserve, and volunteer to chaperone the trip

Summing It Up

Getting Started

I have:

- ○ packed healthy lunches and snacks in reusable containers
- ○ packed drinks in reusable containers; packed a cloth napkin
- ○ donated at least one live plant
- ○ talked to my child's teacher about how I can help green up the classroom
- ○ called my utility company and asked about energy audits
- ○ initiated a discussion about the formation of a schoolwide green team
- ○ encouraged my child to walk, bike, and carpool more

On the Journey

I have:

- ○ volunteered time or resources to green up my child's classroom
- ○ helped form a schoolwide green team
- ○ helped the school perform an energy audit
- ○ developed a carpooling network
- ○ donated clothes, school supplies, and books to others

Green Superstar

I have:

- ○ helped the green team develop a plan of action and act on recommendations
- ○ developed a network for sharing green ideas with other local schools
- ○ eliminated the use of hazardous cleaning products, pesticides, and fertilizers at school
- ○ planned an Earth Day celebration
- ○ donated money my family has saved to green efforts at my school or to a worthy cause

There is much work to be done if we are to hand our great-grandchildren a world as good as the one we got. It will take many changes and even sacrifices. Now that the church is taking up the biblical mandate for creation care, I have great optimism. I pray that we will all keep in mind what is important, and that we will carve "God is love" on the tablet of our hearts. We are commissioned to do *God's* will on earth through loving acts of faith. With God, all things are possible.

 —*Serve God, Save the Planet*

If our congregations can see that we really do believe in protecting the planet God created, that we really do think conservation is a biblical practice, I believe that they will respect and support us in our efforts. If we bring the passion and the dedication, they will help us with the finances, with the rides, and with the infrastructure needed for our ventures.

 —*It's Easy Being Green*

Church

Ministry That Makes Cents

*Now you are the body of Christ, and each
one of you is a part of it.*

1 CORINTHIANS 12:27

"AM I SUPPOSED TO SAY ANYTHING?" I whispered to the woman who had invited us to the meeting.

"That's why you're here!" she responded.

Yes, it was a setup—in the best sense. Matthew and I had been asked to lead a retreat on stewardship of God's creation. The church was in a period of transition and planning a major building project. The night before the retreat, we were asked to attend a presentation by the lead architect. Matthew and I immediately saw that little attention had been paid to solar orientation, green building materials, basic energy-saving principles, or the long-term environmental impact of the new building.

With my friend's permission, we started to ask some questions about energy use, waste reduction, and maintenance. That's when the surprise came: the architect was LEED (Leadership in Energy and Environmental Design) certified and only too delighted to make environmental impact a priority. Suddenly everything from green roofs (living plants on the roof) to water-saving toilets was on the drawing board. We talked about the financial and environmental stewardship reasons for selecting materials that will last a century or more, and how outside spaces could be designed to attract the community. The discussion flowed to how the building could be best used by providing space for a day care and offering teens a safe place to hang out.

> Christ wears "two shoes" in the world: Scripture and nature. Both are necessary to understand the Lord, and at no stage can creation be seen as a separation of things from God.
>
> —John Scotus Eriugena (810–877)

Like most major building projects, this one would take several years to complete. In the meantime, the church decided to change all the lightbulbs in the existing sanctuary, start a recycling program, offer a Sunday school series on creation care, and plan a yearlong series of public talks offering practical ways to conserve God's resources—a creative way to welcome new people into the church.

Such miraculous turnarounds are happening in churches all over the United States. One woman who attends a megachurch had a life-changing experience when she visited a park with her family. She felt called by God to help her church become a better steward of creation. This would not be an easy task: her pastor recently had made fun of recyclers—from the pulpit.

For the first year, she struggled alone, educating herself and diving deeply into creation care Scripture. The second year, she gathered a core group of four or five cobelievers. By the third year, the lead pastor had a conversion experience: he not only agreed to sponsor the group but also invited Matthew to preach to their seven thousand members. The church held a creation care fair around the sermons; their "small group" immediately had 250 members—including the lead pastor.

Such stories both encourage and inspire us. Once churches hear the biblical call to honor God by caring for his creation, they are capable of *big* changes—*fast*. That is why Matthew and I believe the church must get involved—first by cleaning up its own act, and then by reaching out to the world.

For encouragement, we remember the abolition and civil rights movements when the church provided the hands and feet necessary for seemingly impossible changes to become reality.

The same will be true in the environmental movement: people of faith can change hearts. Yes, government and science will be part of the solution, but the church must take on a leadership role. We offer something that is sorely missing from the environmental movement: hope.

With God, anything is possible.

GETTING STARTED

Matthew 7 tells us to take the plank out of our own eye before worrying about the speck in someone else's. As sons and daughters of God, we need to clean up our own churchyards first. Lessening our environmental impact, consuming less, sharing more, and taking care of those in poverty are all ways that we can enrich our church bodies while greening up America's 350,000 houses of worship.

The changes we make at church show the outside world that we honor the Lord not only in what we say but also in what we do. Encourage your church leadership to conduct an energy audit of the church building, switch to fair-trade, shade-grown coffee, and stock up on reusable mugs. Use the church lawn as a mission field by starting a garden that attracts birds and butterflies while providing fresh vegetables to low-income families in your community. Lead a creation care study during Sunday school, and support each other as you reduce your environmental footprint.

D. L. Moody once said, "There are many of us that are willing to do great things for the Lord, but few of us are willing to do the

> *To the Lord your God belong the heavens, even the highest heavens, the earth and everything in it.*
> Deuteronomy
> 10:14

little things." Seemingly small acts, like recycling used bulletins, really *do* make a difference.

SHARING THE MESSAGE

When we continue to increase our consumption and consequent abuse of the earth, we are impacting every segment of life—human relations, health, food sources, vegetation, water, air, wildlife, and natural disasters. The good news, however, is that we can make a

Let Your Light Shine

1. **Weigh in on your energy use.** Conduct an energy audit, either through your local utility or a performance contractor. Many church buildings can be made more efficient through simple changes, such as increased insulation, ceiling fans, LED bulbs in exit signs, and insulated curtains.

2. **Illuminate your church.** Change the lightbulbs in the church to energy-efficient ones. *We* are supposed to be a light to the world, not our sanctuary lamps.

3. **Recycle.** Recycle church bulletins. Encourage people to share their bulletins, and reduce the size of the bulletin to fewer pages. Print bulletins on recycled paper.

4. **Switch coffee.** Purchase organic, fair-trade coffee. Show your love for our neighbors across the globe by not polluting their water supplies with herbicides and pesticides, and not tearing down their forest canopies. Use ceramic mugs instead of disposable cups.

5. **Scatter seeds.** Organize a church garden. Soup kitchens, homeless shelters, and local after-school programs will welcome your fresh produce. A church garden is also a great way to engage people who normally don't go to church but are interested in gardening or community service.

6. **Share your stuff.** Start an exchange program. Set up a bulletin board for people to post items they need and items they want to give away. Consider starting a library for tools and toys, in addition to books, magazines, and videos.

7. **Teach.** Start a book study or small group on God-centered environmentalism and discuss how group members can reduce their impact on ecosystems.

difference. With God's love and direction, churches can help lead the way by making decisions that put God's ministry at the top of the list. In doing so, we are fulfilling part of God's command to go out into the world.

Any real change in our churches begins with prayer. Ask God to give you the ability to reach out to others. Pray for a core group of people who are committed to caring for God's creation. Share your ideas and strive to make small steps, starting today.

8. **Pray.** Hold prayer meetings for people affected by the environmental changes and natural disasters. Pray for wisdom to know how to help and the strength to carry out God's will.

9. **Plant trees.** Plant trees native to your region. Avoid using pesticides on church grounds.

10. **Rideshare.** Organize car pools to and from church. If you have many people coming from one area (such as college students or senior citizens), arrange for a van or bus to take them all to church instead of them driving separately.

11. **Share your space.** Share the church building with other organizations. Multiple church congregations can share one church building on Saturdays and Sundays. Soup kitchens and community groups can use the building during the week.

12. **Power off.** Turn off electronic devices in the church when they're not in use. Unplug empty refrigerators and prop them open to prevent the growth of fungi.

13. **Reduce waste.** Set up recycling bins in the church kitchen and throughout the building. Place boxes for cans, plastic, and paper, and bring them to the recycling center on a regular basis.

14. **Clean green.** Make sure that the cleaning products used at the church are not harmful for the environment and contain no phosphates.

15. **Curb clutter.** Hold a church yard sale. The fewer things we have, the less distraction in our lives and the more time we have to spend with God. Donate the money raised to church outreach, missions, and worthy charities.

Creation care Bible study

Changes in action begin with changes in the heart. Start a Sunday school class, book discussion group, or Bible study that helps make the connection between environmental stewardship and Jesus' command to love our neighbors. Many study groups use half their time each week discussing a creation care reading, and half their time sharing the stewardship changes that they are making in their lives. Encourage one another. Be honest about obstacles and struggles you are facing. Make personal changes before recommending changes at church. By removing the plank from your own eye first, you will gain practical experience and give credence to your message.

Serve God, Save the Planet includes an excellent discussion guide that hundreds of congregations have used to study creation care. Organizing a Sunday school class or book study will help identify and engage a core team committed to greening up the church. For more information, visit http://www.servegodsavetheplanet.org. You can access additional resources on the Internet through http://aeoe. org/resources/spiritual/index.html or the environmental stewardship section of your denominational Web site.

Movie night

For a community-building event, host a movie night at your church, followed by a discussion of how our choices impact the health of the planet. You may want to start with a film that links faith and the environment, such as *Renewal* (http://www.renewalproject.net), *Mountain Mourning* (http://www.christiansforthemountains.org), or the faith version of *The Great Warming* (http://www.thegreat-warming.com). Look for discussion guides on their Web sites. If you use *Renewal*, preview it in advance and select two or three of the short segments that would work best with your congregation.

Other films you might consider include *Affluenza* (http://www .bullfrogfilms.com), *Kilowatt Ours* (http://www.kilowattours.org), *The End of Suburbia* (http://www.endofsuburbia.com), and *What a Way to Go: Life at the End of Empire* (http://www.whatawayto

gomovie.com). You can also check your local library for films on related issues, such as *The Future of Food* (http://www.thefutureoffood.com), which exposes alarming facts about the genetically engineered foods that now fill our grocery store shelves, or *The Power of Community*, an inspiring film that shares how Cuba survived peak oil (http://www.power ofcommunity.org).

> *You alone are the Lord. You made the heavens, even the highest heavens, and all their starry host, the earth and all that is on it, the seas and all that is in them. You give life to everything, and the multitudes of heaven worship you.*
>
> NEHEMIAH 9:6

Prayer

Designate a weekly or monthly prayer focus for people around the world who are harmed by the effects of environmental degradation. Educate yourself about programs that address the interrelated issues of poverty and environmental restoration in countries such as Ethiopia, Sudan, Haiti, Madagascar, and Kenya (http://www.edenprojects.org; http://careofcreation.net).

Newsletter

Write a creation care column for your church newsletter or bulletin. Provide educational information on important local, regional, and global environmental issues and tips for personal action. For article ideas, sign up for the free, weekly Eco-Justice Notes (http://www.eco-justice.org/e-list.asp#forms), check out the monthly news capsules at http://www.nccecojustice.org/capsulessept08.html, or subscribe to *Creation Care* magazine (http://www.creationcare.org/magazine). Then spur your church into action!

Teaching kids to love creation

Make creation care a priority in your church by teaching kids to love God's creation. Consider choosing a creation-themed curriculum for vacation Bible school, like God's Big Backyard from

Standard Publishing (http://www.vacationbibleschool.com/vbs 2008). Reviews of other curricula can be found at http://www .eco-justice.org/CurricReview.asp.

Engage young people in action: keeping the community safe and healthy is a tangible way to love our neighbors. For teens, help plan and carry out an outreach project, like a park or streambed cleanup. Plant trees on the church grounds or in the community. Also, consider offering a creation care study with your youth group, using Emma's book *It's Easy Being Green* as a guide.

God's Hands

Last summer, Emma was asked to help with a vacation Bible school. Two of my friends shared the creation care message with the older kids, and Emma worked with the three- and four-year-olds. She told the parable of the Good Samaritan and then invited the children to act out the story. Of course, everyone wanted a part, so Emma had three innkeepers and several Good Samaritans.

One of Emma's favorite questions of the day was "What's an innkeeper?" Back to basics! The children learned that innkeepers take care of people who are hungry and tired, and that taking care of God's creation is one way of loving our neighbors.

Before the morning was over, all of the children made handprints, inscribed with a promise of what they would do to help care for the earth. Perhaps footprints would have been even more symbolic—representing their carbon footprints. Fortunately, however, Emma knows her audience. She's still young enough to remember that wet paint on little feet would have been a wee bit too tempting!

Earth Day Sunday

Psalm 24:1 declares, "The earth is the Lord's, and everything in it." Affirm this idea as a church body by celebrating Earth Day Sunday. Talk to your pastoral staff about planning a special service to highlight our responsibility as Christians to care for creation.

During the weeks leading up to Earth Day, display books and articles relating to creation care in the church library or lobby. Write creation care articles for the church newsletter. On Earth Day Sunday, worship outdoors. Sing hymns about nature, such as "This Is My Father's World" and "For the Beauty of the Earth." Incorporate praise songs, liturgies, and Scripture readings that celebrate nature and encourage stewardship. You can access resources through http://www.livinglightly24-1.org.uk/church.html; http://www.creationcare.org/resources/sunday/sermon.php; and http://www.webofcreation.org.

The Generation That Could

Last April, Emma was invited to give a sermon at a church in Louisville. The church combined an Earth Day celebration with their annual youth-led service. Chairs were set up outside, the youth sang songs glorifying God for his creation, and the young people acted out the story of creation in Genesis. They also dedicated a tree that the youth planted on the church grounds.

Before Emma started her sermon, the pastor warned her that every time he had preached outside, his talk had been interrupted by a train—Emma's podium was about 40 feet from the railroad tracks. He advised her not to get flustered, and to wait until the train passed before continuing.

Miraculously, the train did not come until the very end of Emma's sermon. The timing could not have been more perfect. Here's what Emma was saying just before the train arrived:

"When I was a child, one of my favorite books was *The Little Engine That Could*. The story is about a big train that breaks down while carrying a load of toys and other good things to children who live on the other side of a mountain. The broken-down engine asks several other passing trains for help, but they are either unable or unwilling. Finally, he sees a tiny blue engine and asks that much smaller engine if he'll pull the shipment of good things to the children on the other side of the mountain. The little train looks up at that huge mountain and isn't sure he's up to the task. But finally he decides to give it a go. And all the way up the hill, our little hero puffs, 'I think I can. I think I can. I think I can.'

"Like that little train, we may feel like there's a huge mountain standing between us and the greener world we long for. But Jesus had a few words for us about mountains. In Matthew 17:20, NIV, he says, 'If you have faith as small as a mustard seed, you can say to this mountain, "Move from here to there" and it will move. Nothing will be impossible for you.'

"With faith in God, nothing is impossible. Living a green life is within the reach of every one of us. I think you can. God thinks you can.

"When the children from the next 'valley,' from the next generation, see us and the world we pass on to them, my hope is that they'll see a generation that was green. My hope is that they'll see a generation that took its choices seriously, that placed its faith in God and found the strength to climb the highest mountain.

"My hope is that they'll see a little generation that did."

Right on cue, the train whistle blew—a reminder that God's timing is always perfect.

GO GREEN

Looking for a comprehensive guide for making changes at church? Consider ordering the *Greening Congregations Handbook: Stories, Ideas, and Resources for Cultivating Creation Awareness and Care in Your Congregation* (http://www.earthministry.org/Congregations/handbook.htm). This 225-page handbook will help you respond to the question, "Why should people of faith care for creation?" and develop an enduring, creation-honoring focus within all dimensions of congregational life.

CHANGES IN THE CHURCH BUILDING

Your church facility can become a tangible testimony of how we can steward resources for the glory of God. Small changes to conserve energy, save water, use land and building spaces wisely, reduce waste, and cut transportation pollution will save money while showing respect for God's creation.

Energy audit

One of the first steps your church should take is an energy audit. Talk to the leadership about assessing current energy use so you'll

Earth Stewardship Principles

Check your denomination's Web site to find out if your church has taken a leadership stance in creation care. Below are the guiding principles for the Ohio Council of Churches' policy on earth stewardship. Consider adopting similar principles for your church.

- The earth was made by God, and we are called to be faithful stewards of creation. We are inextricably linked to all creation, each element of which is worthy of our respect and care.

- As followers of Christ, humility, simplicity, sacrifice, service, and prophetic courage guide our decision making and our actions.

- We are individually and collectively responsible for the ecological impacts of our consumption, locally and globally.

- We are individually and collectively responsible to the entire human family, particularly "the least among us" and future generations who bear the cost of our excess.

know where to start making changes. Your local utility provider may perform this service for no charge or a small fee. You also can hire a performance contractor to help prioritize energy-saving projects and oversee the implementation process.

Alternatively, if you have environmental engineers, science teachers, or other knowledgeable adults in your congregation, ask them to help conduct an audit with your youth group. Encourage the youth group to present its results to the church, along with proposed changes to increase energy efficiency.

Lighting

One of the easiest ways to make your facility's lighting more efficient is to replace incandescent lightbulbs with compact fluorescent ones (CFLs). CFLs cost about 75 percent less to operate than their incandescent counterparts and last about ten times longer.

Make sure exit signs are lit with LED lights, or consider installing Energy Star–qualified exit signs. These signs drastically reduce maintenance requirements and save money in electricity costs.

Saving $ and Energy in the Church Office

- Turn off all office equipment at night. Install power strips to avoid phantom loads that keep equipment partially powered up 24-7.

- Use the power management software on computers so they switch to energy-saving mode when not in use.

- Set the office printer to double-sided default to save paper.

- Distribute documents electronically to church staff and members whenever possible.

- Purchase paper products with a high postconsumer recycled content. Paper that contains 30 percent postconsumer waste costs about the same as regular paper; 100 percent will cost more, but the extra expenditure can be offset by reducing the length of or eliminating weekly bulletins and printing documents on both sides.

Your church can save $10 per sign annually while preventing the release of up to 500 pounds of greenhouse gas emissions.

It makes little sense to light rooms and hallways when they aren't in use, yet sanctuaries are often kept fully lit with no one inside. Turn off lights when rooms are not occupied; a simple sign next to every switch can serve as a gentle reminder. Rely on natural light whenever possible. Go a step further by installing occupancy sensors for lights, and reduce the length of time your lights operate. When daylight savings time rolls around, make sure to adjust outdoor light timers appropriately.

In your church offices, focus on task light, such as lighting a desk rather than an entire room.

SAVE GREEN

Compact fluorescent lights cost about 75 percent less to operate than incandescent bulbs, and they last about ten times longer. Replacing a 100-watt incandescent bulb with a 32-watt CFL can save about $30 in energy costs over the bulb's life span.

Lighting the Way

A number of years ago, Matthew and I participated in an ecology class held at a local church. We enjoyed meeting people who shared our concerns and encouraging each other on the creation care journey.

Matthew and I wanted to give something back to the church that hosted the meetings, so we purchased a case of compact fluorescent bulbs on eBay. The following week, we asked the group—including the minister of the church—if they wanted to grab some ladders and help us change lightbulbs. Everyone chipped in, and in less than an hour we had replaced nearly all of the bulbs in the church. It was both a bonding and empowering experience for the group—and one of the most satisfying $54 investments Matthew and I have ever made!

Heating and AC

Clean furnace and air-conditioning filters frequently. During peak heating and cooling seasons, they should be changed every month. Consider installing programmable thermostats that automatically reduce heating and cooling when areas are unoccupied.

Each month, natural gas pilots use $5 to $10 worth of gas. When heating season ends in the spring, turn off furnaces or boilers that have a standing gas pilot, when feasible.

Embracing the sun

Make direct sunlight work with your heating and cooling plan, not against it. In hot weather, block the sun's rays from shining through the glass, especially on the east and west sides of your facility. Consider installing curtains or drapes and planting trees strategically to shade windows from the outside. In fall and winter, windows on the south side of the building can help create a warm and inviting climate in your church.

If lighting is needed for the parking lot, install solar-powered lights.

Fans

During the warm months of the year, use fans to reduce the need for air-conditioning. Ceiling fans, box fans in windows, and whole facility fans in the attic can all boost your congregation's comfort level while cutting energy costs.

Air leaks

Use weather stripping and caulking to plug leaks throughout your church building. One week during Sunday school time, arm everyone with caulking guns and get to work!

Indoor air quality

Carpeting, cleaning products, and other off-gassing materials can contribute to unhealthy indoor air. Use live plants throughout the building to improve air quality. For more ideas, visit the Environmental Protection Agency's Indoor Air Quality Web page at http://www.epa.gov/iaq.

Appliances

When the budget allows, consider replacing inefficient appliances around your church. Appliances that are used frequently or are on 24-7, like furnaces and refrigerators, have the biggest payback. Look for the bright yellow tags with information about annual energy usage and the Energy Star symbol, or visit http://www.energystar.gov/index.cfm?c=appliances.pr_appliances.

While you wait for more efficient replacements, use your current appliances wisely. Unplug any electronic devices that are not

The Church Kitchen

- For refrigerators, watercoolers, and freezers, maintain an air gap of at least 3 inches between the appliance and the wall.

- Check door seals for signs of cracking or hardening. You know it's time to replace the seal when you can easily pull a dollar bill out from between the seal and the frame on a closed door.

- Use dishwashers only when full. You'll save energy, water, and detergent. Or better yet, ask for volunteers to wash and dry dishes by hand.

- Set coffeemakers on a timer to ensure their heating elements are not operating longer than necessary.

- Avoid using the oven in summer.

- Unplug unused refrigerators and appliances.

According to the U.S. Environmental Protection Agency, congregations that practice environmental stewardship can save 30 percent on their utility bills.

in use to avoid phantom loads, or plug them into a power strip that can be turned completely off. Keep refrigerators around 37 degrees Fahrenheit (3 degrees Celsius), and freezers at zero degrees Fahrenheit (-18 degrees Celsius)—or the warmest setting that is feasible. To help maintain the correct temperature in your freezer, keep it full. If the freezer is partially empty, take up space with ice cream pails or milk jugs filled with water.

Water
Leaks
Even small leaks can waste many gallons of water each month—and money that could be used for other purposes. Schedule regular leak detection checks throughout the church and have leaks fixed as soon as possible.

In the summer, turn off water heaters that aren't used and drain the tank. Reduce the temperature on water heaters in use during warmer months. Heating water uses a tremendous amount of energy; an adjustment of even a few degrees can have a significant effect on your energy bills.

Sinks and toilets
Install faucet aerators on sinks to reduce splash and save water. Consider purchasing devices for your toilets that reduce the amount of

Each day, 6,000 children worldwide die from water-related diseases. Conserve water at church by fixing leaks, installing low-flow toilets, and landscaping with native plants. Use the money saved to help dig wells in Africa.

water used per flush. For an old-fashioned water-saving trick, place bricks or gallon jugs of water in toilet tanks to decrease the amount of water used during flushing. When toilets need to be replaced, purchase low-flow or dual-flush toilets.

Rainwater

Landscaping with native plants and those that require little water to thrive will reduce the amount of water your church requires for landscaping. Water plants in the early morning and use a drip irrigation system instead of sprinklers. Or better yet, install a rainwater collection system to use for landscape watering. You also can irrigate plants with water that has been used for other purposes, such as dishwashing.

> **GO GREEN**
>
> Flushing a toilet one time in the Western world takes the same amount of water that the average person in the developing world uses in a day for washing, drinking, cleaning, and cooking—10 liters.

Sharing your space

Is there another congregation that needs a place to meet? Show them Christ's love while fostering Christian community by sharing your facility. Many buildings are equipped with both a large and a small sanctuary, so it's possible for two groups to hold services simultaneously. If noise or space is an issue, consider staggering service times or days.

Church mergers, especially among churches with declining memberships, are often difficult, but can result in better stewardship of facilities and finite fossil fuels. Making neighborhood groups welcome—such as Scouts, recovery groups, food cooperatives, and homeschooling co-ops—will ensure that the building is used more frequently.

Where Two or Three Are Gathered

Emma and Clark attend a church that doesn't own a building. One reason they were attracted to the church was that a larger percentage of donations go toward relationship building and service rather than toward maintaining a physical structure.

The church started thirty years ago as an outreach to the university campus, with a focus on fellowship and sharing God's love with others. Their leadership believes that it's difficult to know each other deeply once the congregation grows beyond a hundred people, so every time they reach one hundred and forty, a few dozen people split off and start a sister church community.

The church rents space in a house of worship near the university campus. Because the church is active nearly every day of the week—leading a homeschool cooperative, organizing classes and prayer meetings, holding home groups, and extending fellowship to nonbelievers—they have had to shift spaces several times over the years; for some congregations such changes would be disconcerting, but this group seems to go with the flow.

Because they hold their weekly service on Saturday night, church sharing is not difficult. Emma and Clark also attend home groups once a week and a praise and worship service held on Thursday nights in a campus facility. On Friday nights, about seventy young people gather for a coffeehouse, hosted in the home of five guys who live in community.

When I hear the word *church*, my first image is usually a white steepled building. Jesus, however, made it clear that church is not a building—it is the people who make up the body of Christ. Wherever two or three are gathered, he is present.

Praise God for churches that are willing to share their beautiful—but often empty—houses of worship, and for congregations that focus on fellowship more than facilities.

New construction

All new construction uses energy and resources. Before embarking on an expansion or new building project, explore the possibility of using existing facilities within the community.

A friend recently told me about a church in Ohio that meets in the YMCA. The church believes it can reach new people in the community by integrating their ministries with the child-care, soccer league, after-school, and exercise activities that the Y offers. Church members have plenty of opportunities for service outreach through the Y, and Bible study classes are now offered in the facility. Three church plants in the area soon will be establishing partnerships with their local YMCAs, allowing the congregations to focus on community building and outreach rather than capital campaigns.

Greening Your Worship Space

- Schedule cleaning shifts and special events on days immediately preceding and following worship services so the building is warmed or cooled on consecutive days.

- Use natural light to your advantage. Windows and skylights can reduce the need for artificial lighting.

- If your church has a direct entrance to the sanctuary from outside, make sure doors are properly sealed to prevent heat loss. As a temporary alternative to installing new energy-efficient doors, use weather stripping and caulking to stop air leaks.

- Especially in sanctuaries with high ceilings, use ceiling fans to promote proper air circulation so your system doesn't have to work harder to keep the lower areas at a comfortable temperature. Ceiling fans can help with both cooling and heating.

- Turn the temperature up 3 degrees in summer and down 3 degrees in winter, and ask your congregation to dress accordingly.

- Install programmable thermostats that raise or lower temperatures an hour before the service starts to reduce energy use and promote a more comfortable environment.

- Recycle paper bulletins, use washable communion cups, and serve (fair-trade) coffee in ceramic mugs.

Community garden

Using your church's outdoor space to grow a garden will draw people to the church and allow you to donate produce to a homeless shelter or food bank. Start a gardening group at church, or encourage your youth group to lead the project. Church members, especially those who live in apartments, should be encouraged to adopt a plot for their own use or to share with others.

Start a compost heap for yard and kitchen scraps to reduce waste and eliminate the need for chemical fertilizers. In rural areas, the compost pile can be open; in the city, you should use a compost barrel or other enclosed system.

Pesticides

Instead of depending on harmful pesticides to rid your church of unwanted bugs and other critters, consider implementing an integrated pest management program. This is especially important if you have a vegetable garden or if children and youth spend time playing outdoors on your church's property.

People can unwittingly carry pesticides into the church on their shoes and clothes, spreading chemicals and contributing to poor

Building Green

If your church is planning to undertake a new building project, talk to the building committee about implementing energy-efficient design and construction. Work with the committee in the planning stages; you will save money and resources for years to come. Also consider renewable energy options, such as wind and solar power, and the possibility of geothermal heating and cooling.

One way to show your concern for the environment is to get your building certified under the LEED (Leadership in Energy and Environmental Design) rating system of the Green Building Council (http://www.usgbc.org). Your local chapter of the American Institute of Architects (http://www.aia.org) also has resources on environmentally responsible buildings, as does the Environmental Protection Agency (http://www.epa.gov/greenbuilding).

air quality. Sponsoring an educational program on chemical-free lawn and garden practices is a tangible way to show love for our neighbors and future generations.

Learn more about integrated pest management systems at http://www.epa.gov/opp00001/factsheets/ipm.htm.

> We shall awaken from our dullness and rise vigorously toward justice. If we fall in love with creation deeper and deeper, we will respond to its endangerment with passion.
> —Hildegard of Bingen (1098–1179)

Wildlife

Enlist youth and other nature lovers to transform your church grounds into a haven for birds, butterflies, and other wildlife. Plant berry bushes and hang bird feeders that will attract a variety of birds. Select native vegetation that draws butterflies and will require little maintenance. Maintain old trees and plant new ones to attract other wildlife. With a little bit of effort, you can provide a beautiful space for people to pray and experience the beauty of creation firsthand.

Cleaning products

Talk to your custodial staff about switching to nontoxic, biodegradable cleaning products that are not made from petroleum. Green cleaning supplies can now be purchased easily at office supply, grocery, and home improvement stores. Keep your church clean without damaging the planet, harming your custodial staff, or degrading indoor air quality.

The Prodigal Son

A few years ago, Matthew was asked to preach at the church where he grew up. For nearly three decades, Matthew had completely rejected organized religion, vowing never to step into a church again except for a wedding or a funeral or, in his words, "when someone is wed or dead." So when the lead pastor of this now very large and vibrant mainstream church asked Matthew to preach their first creation care sermon, it was like the Prodigal Son returning home—no bitterness, all sweetness.

Matthew preached once in the spring and then again the following fall. In the intervening time, the church formed five book groups to study *Serve God, Save the Planet*, using the discussion guide to apply stewardship principles to their daily lives at home, work, and church.

Out of these book studies, an ongoing creation care group was formed. The group recommended energy-saving actions throughout the church, including changing lightbulbs, making recycling bins readily available, and using nondisposable dishes.

One church member bought a dozen cases of lightbulbs to share at cost. They sold out immediately, with requests for more bulbs at the next service. The pastor and creation care group also encouraged their building committee to hire a green architect for their $3.4 million addition.

Now the group is reaching out to the community. The choir director and pastor have recorded a CD (they have a spectacular music program), and all proceeds are donated to a nonprofit that promotes earth stewardship at churches throughout the country. A member of the creation care group organized a sale of handcrafted pottery filled with meals prepared by the congregation. The pastor has recommended that creation care be designated as one of the church's ongoing missions. Like the work they do to support a hospital in Guatemala, earth stewardship is now recognized throughout the church as an opportunity to love their global neighbors.

WASTE REDUCTION
Disposables

Replace disposable plates, cups, and silverware with reusable dishware. If you are short on supplies, ask for donations from church members. Most people are glad to de-clutter their kitchen cabinets and share some infrequently used dishes with the church. Or purchase a large collection of compact, stackable dishes that do not take up a lot of storage space.

If paper products have to be used at times, purchase plates that can be composted and napkins made from recycled paper. Buying the products in bulk from office supply stores can significantly reduce costs. Check out the EcoEasy products now available from http://www.staples.com.

In the bathrooms and kitchen, use donated hand towels instead of paper towels. Set up a weekly rotation of volunteers to wash them.

Paper

E-mail newsletters and monthly calendars to parishioners when possible. Recycle bulletins or choose another method of making announcements and helping the congregation follow the service order. Many churches now project hymns, Bible readings, and announcements on screens during the church service, so there is less need for bulletins. Calendars with church events can be posted on Web sites and bulletin boards.

Recycling

Whether your weekly service attendance is 50 or 5,000, you have materials around your church that can and should be recycled on a regular basis. Recycling items like aluminum cans, glass and plastic bottles, old bulletins, cardboard, and paper from the church office keeps them from crowding the landfill. If your church does not already have a recycling program, talk to your building management about starting one; you might want to ask the youth program to help sort and collect the recyclables. For more information on recycling centers in your area, visit http://www.earth911 .org/recycling.

If your city or town doesn't have an official recycling program, work

The heavens declare the glory of God; the skies proclaim the work of his hands. Day after day they pour forth speech; night after night they display knowledge. There is no speech or language where their voice is not heard. Their voice goes out into all the earth, their words to the ends of the world.

PSALM 19:1-4

with other local churches to get one started. Recycle Bank (http://www.recyclebank.com) rewards recycling efforts with points that can be redeemed at hundreds of local and national businesses. Help your church become better stewards and get paid to recycle.

To offset green expenses in the church or fund a community-wide creation care project, ask church members to bring aluminum cans, electronics, cell phones, and ink cartridges to the church to redeem for cash.·

Leftovers

If your church hosts large meals that occasionally result in significant amounts of leftover food, don't throw it away; donate it to a local soup kitchen instead. Visit http://feedingamerica.org to learn more about food rescue organizations in your area.

CONTINUING THE JOURNEY
Local foods

The next time your church decides to share a meal, make it a local food potluck. Encourage members to bring dishes and vegetables purchased from local sources like the farmers' market or grown in their own gardens.

Create and distribute a directory of local food sources, and encourage people to purchase shares in CSAs (Community Supported Agriculture). Take orders for local butter, cheese, and eggs, and arrange for pickup on Sundays after church. Raise awareness among your congregation about eating seasonally and purchasing foods that traveled fewer miles to reach the table.

During vacation Bible school and other events for kids, serve healthy, locally grown snacks that involve little or no packaging, like cheese and apple slices. If there are people in the church who have farms, orchards, or gardens, arrange a field trip to increase awareness of where food comes from and the care needed to raise and harvest local produce.

Share board

Provide a bulletin board for church members to post messages about needed services and goods, or food, furniture, and equipment they want to give away.

The more church people share what they have, the stronger the church community becomes. A share board also will save money by avoiding the purchase of items people use only occasionally.

Fair-trade coffee

Trade in your standard coffee for shade-grown, fair-trade coffee. When your church brews fair-trade coffee, more of the money you spend reaches the farmers in developing countries who actually grow it. Moreover, their land is not left devastated by clear-cutting and the overuse of dangerous pesticides and herbicides required to grow coffee in unnatural conditions. Fair-trade coffee is a direct way in which our actions can show love for our global neighbors.

Consider asking your creation care group to designate part of their yearly tithe to covering the extra cost of fair-trade coffee.

Service

Look for a park or other area around your church that is littered with trash and plan an environmental service day for church members.

A Cleaner Getaway

Reduce your congregation's carbon footprint as you travel to and from church. Encourage members of your congregation to walk or bicycle to church when possible. Installing bike racks on church property will encourage people to bike to church events instead of hopping in the car. Remember, as far as we know, Jesus only rode once in his entire ministry, and that was on a borrowed colt.

To encourage carpooling, make a map that shows areas where parishioners live to help coordinate the effort or start a rideshare board—either in the church lobby or online.

Foster community in your church and inspire a deeper love for creation as you serve side-by-side with people in your congregation.

As your church decides where and how to serve, choose mission projects that empower needy people to become self-sufficient.

Web Resources for Green Congregations

- **http://www.creationcare.org.** Part of a growing movement among Christians to respond faithfully to the biblical mandate for stewarding God's creation, the Evangelical Environmental Network publishes *Creation Care* magazine, engages directly in advocacy, and produces helpful curricula and congregational resources.

- **http://www.earthministry.org.** An ecumenical, Christian nonprofit that helps individuals and congregations connect their faith with care for the planet, Earth Ministry has created many resources for congregations, including the *Greening Congregations Handbook: Stories, Ideas, and Resources for Creation Awareness and Care in Your Congregation*.

- **http://www.energystar.gov/index.cfm?c=small_business.sb_ congregations.** The Environmental Protection Agency's Energy Star Web site provides resources for cutting energy costs at church, including a downloadable congregations guide titled *Putting Energy into Stewardship*.

- **http://www.theregenerationproject.org.** Interfaith Power and Light helps congregations make environmentally wise choices and offers opportunities to purchase renewable power.

- **http://www.nccecojustice.org.** The National Council of Churches' Eco-Justice Working Group provides Earth Day liturgies, curricula, environmental justice resource lists, and various congregational programs. Check out their *Building a Firm Foundation: "Green" Building Tool Kit*.

- **http://www.webofcreation.org.** Web of Creation is a clearinghouse for congregations to develop earth-keeping practices as well as to learn about the theology and ethics of caring for creation. You'll find the *Training Manual for the Green Congregation Program*, worship resources like the "Seasons of Creation" liturgies, and a comprehensive set of links to other sites promoting environmental stewardship.

Many churches have mission programs that improve sewage systems, dig wells, improve crop diversity, prevent future environmental disasters, and offer loans for starting small businesses, such as vegetable stands.

Partnering with like-minded groups

Encourage the formation of local ecumenical environmental groups. In our town, a group of people formed a creation care group after Matthew spoke at a local church. Representatives from several churches attend the bimonthly gatherings. They quickly gained positive exposure by recycling at summer town concerts and a major Christian music festival. The group gave away hundreds of free trees to local citizens for Arbor Day and has become involved with city planners to discuss how to create a greener community.

The creation care group also sponsors a community garden, which is located on a church property. In addition to offering individual plots for a small fee to people who want to grow their own

Success Stories

- **Christ Church, Ontario, California.** Reduced its summer utility bills from $600 to $20 a month by installing solar panels on the roof and changing lighting.

- **Hebron Baptist Church, Dacula, Georgia.** Saved $32,000 and 450,000 kilowatt hours of energy in one year by revamping its lighting system and converting fixtures and exit signs.

- **All Saints Episcopal Church, Brookline, Massachusetts.** Saved $17,000 in one year by installing a new boiler with zoned heating, programmable thermostats, and more efficient lighting. They have invested 14 percent of the savings to buy 100 percent renewable energy, further reducing pollutants.

Be inspired by other energy- and money-saving success stories at http://www.energystar.gov/index.cfm?c=sb_success.sb_successstories_state.

vegetables in the garden, a large area is planted with vegetables to give to needy people. Planting, harvesting, and sharing the food creates a beautiful community spirit among the members of the group. People at a low-income housing development who receive the food are extremely grateful for fresh, organic produce.

Individuals in the group also write a green article for the town's monthly newsletter and invite the community to hear speakers on subjects such as native trees and plants, mountaintop removal, rain gardens, and meeting the material needs of refugees. They host potlucks, make local eggs available at meetings, and have plans to share other local foods.

Here's the most inspiring part: this group has only been in existence for a little over a year! It's amazing what God can do through a few faithful followers.

SAVE GREEN

Through energy efficiency and clean energy technologies, congregations can cut utility costs by 25 to 30 percent, saving on average $8,000 to $17,000 per year.

How to Save Money This Year

Shut down the computers in the church office when not in use	$219
Turn off the power strip when electronic devices are not in use	$200
Trade disposable coffee cups for reusable mugs	$400
Use cloth hand towels instead of paper towels in the bathroom	$390
Change exit sign lightbulbs to LED bulbs	$150
Replace incandescent bulbs with compact fluorescent bulbs	$210
Set office printers to double-sided default	$100
Turn off furnaces/gas boilers with standing pilots and dial back the temperature of water heaters after spring	$125
Weather-strip and caulk air leaks	$400
Host a churchwide garage sale	$2,000
Turn the thermostat up 3 or more degrees in summer and down 3 degrees in winter	$4,500
Rent space to another congregation	$12,000
TOTAL	**$20,694**

$AVE

. . . And Share It with Those in Need

- Donate money to purchase energy-saving bulbs for other congregations in your city.

- Select a sister church in a poorer neighborhood and retrofit with energy-saving insulation, windows, lighting, and heating and cooling systems.

- Provide land, seedlings, tools, and water for a community garden.

- Work with your denomination's missions department to partner with a church in a developing country and help fund an energy-efficient building project.

- Mobilize churches across the United States to become better stewards of God's creation through the Interfaith Power and Light campaign (http://www.theregenerationproject.org).

- Partner with us at http://www.blessed-earth.org to share the creation care message with hundreds of congregations around the country, inspiring churches to reduce energy consumption.

$HARE

Putting Your Faith into Action

Dear heavenly Father, you are the creator, the everlasting God. Thank you for entrusting me with the task of caring for your creation. Forgive me for the times I have neglected the things that are near to your heart. Take away any self-centeredness and apathy in my thoughts or actions, and help my church to make changes that will protect and preserve the planet. Increase my desire to serve you through caring for your creation.

Lord, help me *today* to:

- pray that my church gains a better understanding of your heart for creation
- look online to learn about my denomination's stance on earth stewardship
- make a list of people who might be interested in forming a creation care group at my church
- visit Web resources for green churches and download one of the energy-saving guides

Lord, help me *this week* to:

- give someone a ride to church to reduce transportation pollution
- make a list of little or no-cost changes my church could make to become better stewards
- see if my church serves fair-trade coffee
- pray for people affected by environmental degradation around the world

Lord, help me *this month* to:

- encourage my church to conduct an energy audit
- ask my pastor to preach a sermon on creation care or invite a guest speaker
- talk to the facilities manager at my church about recycling options
- ask the custodial staff about switching to eco-friendly cleaning products

- turn the heat down three degrees in winter and up three degrees in summer
- establish a bulletin board where church members can post goods or services
- start a creation care Bible study group or Sunday school class

Lord, help me *this year* to:

- form an ongoing creation care group in my church or community
- switch from disposable to reusable dishes at church
- plant trees on church property and in lower-income neighborhoods
- avoid use of pesticides and fertilizers on church property
- sponsor a series of creation care talks, open to the community
- start a sheet music exchange program with area churches
- help plan an Earth Day Sunday service and celebration
- start a community garden at my church
- install a rain collection system for harvesting water from the roof
- reduce energy usage at my church by at least 10 percent

Summing It Up

Getting Started

I have:

- ○ changed the incandescent lightbulbs in my church to compact fluorescent bulbs
- ○ switched to eco-friendly cleaning products at church
- ○ checked for water leaks and had them repaired
- ○ started a creation care Sunday school class
- ○ conducted an energy audit of church facilities

On the Journey

I have:

- ○ donated leftovers from church meals and special events to a local food bank
- ○ eliminated pesticides and chemical fertilizers from church grounds
- ○ stopped purchasing disposable paper towels and dinnerware for church events
- ○ planted trees on church property and in poor neighborhoods
- ○ started an ongoing creation care group

Green Superstar

I have:

- ○ helped my church start a community garden and donated produce to the needy
- ○ planned an environmental service day for church members
- ○ shared the church building with another congregation or organization
- ○ reused our gray water for irrigation
- ○ lowered the church's energy costs by at least 10 percent

All over New England where I live, thousands of canoes sit high and dry in garages and basements. I live on the Connecticut River—Canoe Central. During the summer months, a dozen canoes may pass by on a Saturday. This means that thousands of canoes are waiting for use in garages. If you don't own one and feel a desire to go for a paddle, borrow one. If you own one, make sure folks feel comfortable coming by and getting yours. If people don't feel comfortable borrowing your "stuff," you need to change. If you don't feel comfortable borrowing from your neighbor, maybe you need new neighbors. How are we going to live together forever in heaven if we can't even share a chain saw?

—*Serve God, Save the Planet*

[S]tart an exchange program. Just having a simple bulletin board where people can indicate what they need and what people have to give away or share can prevent a lot of unnecessary purchases. If possible, set up a way people can share tools. We don't all need to have our own personal lawnmower, weed whacker, table saw, bicycle pump, snow blower, and pickup truck. Even if just three families started sharing a single lawnmower, that would mean there are two fewer lawnmowers that need to be manufactured and purchased in this world.

—*It's Easy Being Green*

Community

Reconnecting, One Neighbor at a Time

All the believers were one in heart and mind.
No one claimed that any of his possessions was his own,
but they shared everything they had.

ACTS 4:32

WHEN WE FIRST DOWNSIZED and moved to a new community, I was fortunate to find a job that combined several of my passions: reading, kids, and service. My official job title was "community outreach coordinator," but I was mostly known as "Miss Nancy" or simply "the library lady" by my primary constituency of three- to five-year-olds.

One of the best parts of my job was bringing books to day care centers. Selecting my favorite picture books from the library shelves, I put together theme-related bags—gardens, trees, farm animals, the seasons, rain forests, the moon and stars, sharing, love, friendship, helping others—all the important things in life. Each week, I picked up books from the day care centers and dropped off a new bag. I stayed for about thirty minutes with each group, reading them stories and leading a literacy-related activity.

Talk about a fun job. And they paid me for this?

My position was partially funded through AmeriCorps—a

community service program that focuses on making a difference in poorer communities. AmeriCorps is also a great way to get to know your neighbors: I was practically a celebrity by the end of my first month. I couldn't go to the grocery store or post office without being hugged around the knees.

Anyone, then, who knows the good he ought to do and doesn't do it, sins.

JAMES 4:17

In the summer months, Clark—then in high school—joined me on my rounds. Clark is a gentle giant—well over six feet tall—and kids naturally gravitate toward him, especially rambunctious little boys. He's also a gifted artist, a talent he did not inherit from his mother: stick figures and the occasional cartoonish baby chick pretty much max out my drawing skills. It was hard to say good-bye each week, with all the little boys wanting a Clark-signed original sketch, and so many of them not having a consistent male figure in their lives.

When I started teaching at an independent boarding school a block from the library, I continued visiting some of the day care centers once a week with a group of high school students, including Emma. We called ourselves "reading buddies."

What could be cooler for a young child than having a teenager spend an hour each week reading books one-on-one and making art projects together?

What could be cooler for a teenager than to have a little kid rush to give a hug and a crayoned picture?

Reading with preschoolers taught me that, contrary to my preconceived notions, community outreach jobs aren't just for teens wanting to buff their college applications and twentysomethings who don't know what they want to do after they graduate; they're also for middle-aged, change-of-life folks like me who are still learning what we want to be when we grow up, as well as energetic retired people like my friend Fran, who volunteers with middle school kids—bless her heart!

I also learned that:

1. Day care providers have an important, difficult, and often lonely job.
2. Those who remain calm and patient with parents who are late picking their kids up—especially on Fridays—deserve an express ticket to heaven.
3. Little kids like to poke their neighbors and pick at scabs while you read books to them.
4. Some kids like to pick their neighbor's scabs while you read books to them.
5. *Always* carry a clean handkerchief to wipe away green "11" signs from a runny nose.
6. *Never* joke that a child's nose is leaking brain lubricant. They will believe you.
7. If you act out *The Very Hungry Caterpillar*, every child will want a chance to play the caterpillar.
8. There is nothing more precious than hearing a three-year-old pronounce "cal-a-pillar."
9. You will be forgiven if you find multiple occasions for a three-year-old to say "cal-a-pillar."
10. Handmade cards are priceless, especially when they are from a young boy with a lousy home life, and they say:

> "Dear Miss Nancy,
> I like your name.
> Love, James"

Most important, I learned that when you reach out, others will reach in. And when you love your neighbor, you will receive seventy times seven more than you give.

GETTING STARTED

Through the life of Christ, we see examples of community—people living together in unity and helping meet each other's needs. Although an independent, self-sufficient mind-set prevails in much of American culture, we can share God's love most readily in the context of community. Helping an elderly neighbor rake leaves, weeding the community garden, celebrating Earth Day with the people on your block—these are all opportunities to improve the environment and our neighborhoods.

Sharing and Caring

Jesus wasn't shy about getting involved in his community—he reached out to everyone, from the woman at the well to those who were blind or sick. Part of caring for the earth involves caring for our neighbors, and sharing the gifts that God has provided.

Talk to the bank clerk, the postal carrier, and the person beside you on the bus. Welcome a new neighbor with a gift of local produce or a helping hand. And don't be bashful about borrowing—or lending—tools. A neighbor with an extra shovel may also be a great source of gardening wisdom.

Caring for God's creation can be a central part of community building. Plant a neighborhood garden. Line your streets with trees. Work with your neighbors to adopt a highway, clean up a streambed, and reduce rainwater runoff. Promote bike paths, car pools, and safe sidewalks. Band together and adopt a refugee family that has recently moved to your area. As you give Christ control of every aspect of your life, including your community, you will notice positive changes in your neighborhood, your family, and yourself.

The apostles lived in close community, with Jesus at the center. Look at the distance between the example of Christ's life and yours, and start closing the gap. Enjoy the fellowship that comes with sharing and caring.

BUILDING COMMUNITY

With the click of a mouse, we connect in seconds to people across the globe—completing business transactions, corresponding with friends who live abroad, scanning prayer updates from missionaries. These days, it's not uncommon to communicate regularly with people who live hundreds—even thousands—of miles away. With connections like these, it's ironic that so many of us struggle to name the people who live on our street. The first step to honoring God's creation in your community is building relationships with the people outside your door.

Whether you moved to the area recently or have lived in your house for twenty years, now is the time to take action. Talk to your neighbors, find out what's going on around you, and get involved. It may sound obvious, but with busy schedules and commitments galore, keeping in touch with the community isn't always a priority. Be an agent of change: help foster networks of neighborly love and interdependence.

Finding like-minded people

Don't do it alone! For many, change doesn't come easily, especially when it involves altering deeply embedded habits. Finding like-minded people in your town will give you energy and encouragement to stay the course.

Does your community have a parks and recreation committee, eco-team, or creation care group? Attend their next meeting and volunteer to help. If a group doesn't already exist, start one. Talk with neighbors who are interested in learning more and form a green book club or monthly earth stewardship film night.

Having trouble connecting? Find people in your area with similar interests who want to take action at http://www.meetup.com.

Starting a creation care group

A creation care group usually consists of five to ten families who meet at least once a month to discuss, plan, and implement positive, environmental changes at home and in the neighborhood. Many in the group are motivated by their faith to live more simply and take action. To encourage each other, they usually share practical actions they are taking to reduce waste, use less water and energy, improve air and water quality, and invite additional neighbors to get involved. Working toward this common goal is almost guaranteed to build a sense of belonging and camaraderie among your group. And make sure you hold a potluck featuring local foods several times a year.

> " The first law of our being is that we are set in a delicate network of interdependence with our fellow human beings and with the rest of God's creation.
> —Archbishop Desmond Tutu (1931–), God Has a Dream "

Sometimes a little (eco-) friendly competition goes a long way. Challenge your neighbors to "out-green" a nearby town or community. Sites like http://www.18seconds.org allow visitors to view their town's CFL bulb purchases and compare their savings with other towns. Or use the Environmental Protection Agency's online tool to gauge the quality of your local air and nearby rivers and streams at http://www.epa.gov/epahome/whereyoulive.htm.

Common Ground

A little over a year ago, we helped start a local creation care group. At our first meeting I must admit that I felt a bit nervous. It's one thing to give a presentation to people at a one-day retreat; you plant some seeds, say a few prayers, and leave the rest up to God.

But it is quite another thing to speak before a group that you will see in Fitch's grocery store the next morning.

We opened in prayer. My British friend, Aureol, handed out cards with pictures of endangered species, and we used them to help introduce ourselves. More than two dozen people sat in a circle, from college students to retired ministers, from a five-month-old cooing on the floor to a middle-aged seminary graduate sitting in a wheelchair. One member came from a philanthropic family, another from a heritage of Christian writers. Two households were between jobs. What we shared was a common love of the Lord and of his creation.

Our discussion focused on community. My husband, Matthew, opened by telling about a Christian community in upstate New York that he recently visited where people share everything—meals, money, cars, housing, child care, livelihoods—much like the first-century church. I spoke of another Christian community here in Kentucky that shares gardens, homeschooling, and twice daily prayers. And then we got to the good part—how we, this group of twenty-some Christians from various denominations, could "share one heart and mind." Could we lend and borrow rototillers, chop saws, and pickup trucks? Could we find sources for local eggs, butter, and meat? Could we petition the mayor to improve the recycling program?

A year later, I can answer a resounding "yes" to these questions, plus a whole lot more. I have borrowed a rototiller, chop saw, and pickup truck, plus shovels, gloves, and hoes to help teach college students gardening skills. Matthew and I have lent recycling barrels for the town concerts, recommended environmental films for community events, and donated funds so the group could join a national Christian environmental organization, A Rocha (The Rock). We have plowed a 2-acre plot on church grounds and shared the produce. A woman sells local eggs at every meeting and is expanding her offerings. Soon, we hope to share a locally raised hog. We have invited community speakers to teach us about rain gardens, mountaintop removal, and native plant species. We have taken a field walk with a biologist who knows everything there is to know about indigenous trees. Together, we have recycled tens of thousands of plastic bottles at a major Christian concert. We have cleaned a streambed and planted more than a hundred saplings on Arbor Day. We have partnered with the college environmental group and with church creation care study groups. We have joined town committees and church boards to share our concerns and expand our influence.

We have had our disappointments, our frustrations, and

our failures. But we have also shared community, friendship, meals, and love.

We closed our first meeting by singing "Fairest Lord Jesus"—sharing hymnbooks from half a dozen different denominations. I know that the angels heard us singing: what a joyful sound, brimming with purpose and unity and hope!

Dear God, Let these words of worshipful song move our hearts and minds to right action: "Fairest Lord Jesus, Ruler of all nature . . . Fair are the meadows, fairer still the woodlands. . . . Fair is the sunshine, fairer still the moonlight, and all the twinkling starry host." Heavenly Father, grant us the power and the solace and the kinship of community, sharing a common love and a common purpose. Let us encourage and inspire one another to move toward the humble example set by Jesus. Help us to hold ourselves accountable to each other and to God. Please strengthen our ties as a community of believers through a loving connection with your glorious creation.

Fellowship and Support

Connect with like-minded folks in your area by joining a local environmental group or chapter of a national conservation organization. Many sponsor hikes and outings and give you a chance to find out how others are supporting green initiatives in your community.

A Rocha/Christians in Conservation	http://www.arocha.org
Buy Fresh, Buy Local	http://www.foodroutes.org
4-H Clubs (for young people)	http://www.4husa.org
The Garden Club of America	http://www.gcamerica.org
The Nature Conservancy	http://www.nature.org
OrganicAthlete	http://www.organicathlete.org
Sierra Club	http://www.sierraclub.com

GO GREEN

Initiate a creation care group in your community so that you can encourage one another, and work toward community-wide changes. Start a share board at the town hall or at church — people can list what they need, and you can list what you have to lend. Ask the recycling center if they can set aside space for a permanent swap area. If you don't have access to clean energy options, petition the local utility. If you need better public transportation or bike lanes, ask the town council. Start a bike share program by soliciting and repairing unused bikes, painting them a bright color, and making them available for public use.

Staying put

If you're like most Americans, you will move an average of 11.7 times during your life. Jumping from city to city—or even house to house—makes building community difficult and can put a strain on finances. Moving the contents of a three-bedroom home from Lexington, Kentucky, to Provo, Utah, using a national moving company could set you back almost $6,000.

Before your next major move, consider putting down roots in your current location. Although a higher-paying job or a bigger house in another community may sound enticing, staying put could bring greater satisfaction in the long run. You can't put a price tag on friendships with neighbors and community ties.

Dare to Care

Two of my dearest friends, Geoff and Sherry, bought a house in the poor section of Lexington, Kentucky. They are committed to staying in that neighborhood, in that very house, for the rest of their lives.

Both are deeply devoted to their neighbors. They've started an urban garden, served on the low-income housing board, and been extremely active in the neighborhood association. Geoff helps regularly with refugees who come to Lexington from war-torn countries with nothing—no furniture, no pots or pans, no warm clothes. Sherry is currently focusing her considerable energies on starting an urban orchard and outdoor classroom. Both are trying to build resilient neighborhoods that can flourish in economically difficult times.

Hospitality was a top priority in selecting their home, and they nearly always have at least one nonfamily member living with them. When Geoff, who is Australian, passed his U.S. citizenship test this past summer, the whole neighborhood came over to celebrate.

Sherry recently told me about a severely mentally challenged man who shows up at their door fairly regularly, often before most people are awake. He thinks he is the godfather of Isaac, their five-year-old son. Geoff and Sherry treat him as if he really is Isaac's godfather, inviting him in for a cup of tea before the birds are even awake.

This amazing couple is listed as the next of kin for several elderly neighbors, and they have been called to the hospital in the middle of the night to help make major health and end-of-life decisions.

I know we are not supposed to covet, but I do. I envy that commitment to stay in one place. To put down deep taproots. To dare to care, as our Lord Jesus did, for those who have been marginalized, ostracized, and abandoned.

The welcoming committee

You can foster a sense of community by greeting people who move to your neighborhood. Set a goal to welcome new neighbors within one week of their arrival; the longer you wait to say hello, the less likely you'll take action.

> *How good and pleasant it is when brothers live together in unity!*
> PSALM 133:1

Start by sharing food. Deliver a basket of homemade baked goods or vegetables from your garden, or invite your neighbors over for dinner. Also, be ready to share recommendations for helpful services they'll likely use—farmers' markets, locally owned

grocery stores, a gentle dentist, a dependable mechanic, bus schedules, and nearby playgrounds and area parks. Lend them items
they might need, and introduce them to other families in your
neighborhood.

Lawn Chairs, Step Stools, and Birthday Cakes

When we moved to Kentucky, Clark and I came down a week
before Emma and Matthew, who had stayed behind for a speaking engagement in New England. Clark and I painted the
entire interior of the house, primer plus two coats (with low
VOC paints—the kind that don't off-gas or smell). Besides a
few changes of clothes, we brought two sleeping bags, two pillows, two mugs, two plates, two sets of silverware, a pot and a
pan, and a few good books.

It was one of the best weeks of my life. We painted from
sunrise until sunset, talking about everything and nothing,
often falling into companionable silence. At night we read, then
collapsed—Clark gallantly giving his mom the air mattress a
friend had lent us.

The very first day we arrived, we went next door to borrow
a ladder. They invited us to come back for dinner. We became
immediate friends, with daily visits back and forth. Another
neighbor invited us out to lunch, then brought us two lawn
chairs. Heaven-sent! Clark and I thought we had reached the
ultimate in luxury—a place to sit while we read at night. A
third neighbor lent us a step stool; not long after we moved in,
their daughter came over to bake a surprise birthday cake for
her mom. She had never baked a cake before. I felt honored to
teach her.

When my beloved next-door neighbors moved away, I am
ashamed to say that I did not welcome the new family as quickly
as we were welcomed. It was winter, and we were cocooned in
our own world, traveling frequently. Pretty poor excuse. We
could have brought over a loaf of bread. Actually, that is what
we finally did. It was Matthew's idea. I had baked two loaves of
challah, a braided egg bread from the Jewish tradition. Matthew

suggested we give one to the new neighbors. We've since shared homemade salsa (the secret ingredient is local peaches—amazing stuff), apple butter, pickles, tomato sauce, and many loaves of bread. We exchange gardening advice nearly daily. (I'm mostly on the receiving end, since Hank is a walking botanical encyclopedia.) Their daughter recently came knocking on the door, looking for a job. I now hire her to work alongside me for an hour each week doing household chores. She's grateful for the work; I'm grateful for the help. We've exchanged books, borrowed eggs, and shared many a Friday night meal in the outdoor tent between our yards.

When a new neighbor moves to town, I think of the story of the rich man who invited everyone to the wedding celebration. Yes, some neighbors turned him down. But that's no excuse to quit extending ourselves. Jesus' story reminds us that we just need to reach out a little further. Jesus *is* the ultimate welcome wagon. He always has room at the table.

So what if I can only offer a few frozen fish fillets and some not-so-fresh bread? Miracles happen.

Meeting a need

Jesus talks more about serving the poor than he does about family values, being born again, and quiet time all put together. Yet most of our lives, including mine, don't reflect these scriptural priorities.

Jesus wants us to stop living in isolated silos and go beyond our comfort zone. Adopt an immigrant family and share holiday celebrations with them at your house. Team up with neighbors to purchase school supplies and new clothes for a child across town. Arrange meals for someone who has a loved one in the hospital. Instead of volunteering in your child's school where room mothers are plentiful, volunteer in a classroom where parents work double shifts to make ends meet. Gather with neighbors to pick up trash in the park or plant trees along your street. Meeting tangible needs in your community will result in intangible outcomes—including the gifts of compassion and friendship.

Planning an event

What better way to get to know people in your community than by spending time with them in a fun setting? This summer, organize a neighborhood-wide garage sale and make it an annual event. Coordinate a community block party in September to celebrate National Neighborhood Day (http://www.neighborhoodday.org). Or plant trees together on Arbor Day next spring.

GO GREEN

I have one friend who hosts neighborhood gatherings in her backyard the first Sunday of each month. Her house is one of the smallest in the neighborhood, but she and her husband have a big heart for hospitality. The gatherings keep getting bigger, as neighbors invite other neighbors. Over the last year, these Sunday potlucks have become a central part of their family ministry, and a focal point for neighborly sharing. Don't wait for someone else to initiate; if you plan it, they will come.

Lending and borrowing

Although our American hyper-independence makes many of us reluctant to borrow, sharing tools and equipment can create a strong feeling of belonging within a community while saving resources. Does every family on your block really need its own pressure cooker? What about a canoe or tent? Consider splitting costs with a neighbor and sharing power tools or other expensive equipment that's used infrequently.

If borrowing and lending isn't a common practice in your neighborhood, start a chain reaction. Consider asking your neighbors to borrow something, and make it known that you are willing to return the favor with your belongings.

Random acts of kindness

Never underestimate the power of a random act of kindness. Do something nice for your neighbors for no particular reason and see what happens. Shovel snow off their driveways and sidewalks. Volunteer to babysit so they can enjoy an evening out together. Pick up some vegetables for them if you go to the farmers' market. Offer to take them to the airport and mow their yards while they are out of town. Small gestures go a long way when it comes to establishing a community where people can count on each other.

> **GO GREEN**
>
> When we lived in New England, our local post office put out a sign-up sheet each November. Families volunteered to bring in a tray of holiday treats each day of December.

Turning trash into treasure

Our town recycling center in New England had a covered free-exchange area where people could drop off or pick up items. See if you can establish a similar drop site in your town, or designate a free exchange board where people can post items they no longer need. You can also create an e-mail-distribution list or visit Web sites like http://www.freecycle.org. That old printer or computer monitor in the basement might come in handy for someone just down the street.

Carpooling

When your to-do list requires a car ride, try to fill at least one other seat. I have three friends who rotate picking up milk, butter, and cheese from a local dairy. Another friend sends out an e-mail when

> **GO GREEN**
>
> Find a central gathering place and start your own community tradition: a shared produce table in late summer, a canned goods drive at Thanksgiving, handmade Valentine cards to give out in nursing homes, or a year-round board for posting free items.

he makes the trip to pick up local meat; he happily accepts meat orders from others in the neighborhood. My daughter drives to church events with at least two other friends from her college. Yes, it takes a bit more effort and planning, but carpooling saves gas and fosters relationships.

Do a bunch of moms from the same neighborhood all drive their kids to school? Consider sharing rides—you'll save time, money, and gasoline. Or even better, promote healthy living for kids by starting a walking school bus—a group of children walking to school with one or more adults. Visit http://www.walkingschool bus.org for details.

Community, Cross-Cultural Style

Emily, a close family friend, recently spent five months living in a primitive village in the Uluguru Mountains of Tanzania, teaching English to high school students.

Coming from the United States—where independence, personal space, and the rights of the individual are highly valued— Emily realized she needed a bit of an attitude adjustment. Privacy quickly became a foreign concept. Before long, every grandma and shop owner in the village could recite the details of her daily routine. Any kid at the soccer field would eagerly tell how many eggs she had purchased that week at the market. Even trips to the outdoor latrine were public events, as she was often greeted by elders along the way.

For the people in this small village, sharing life was as natural as breathing. They ate, worked, and celebrated together, meeting each others' needs regularly. Women seated on mats outside their huts talked as they sifted rice in search of small rocks. Friends and family lined up to comfort relatives who had lost a loved one, paying respect to the dead. When someone had a need—physical or emotional—people rallied to provide support, encouragement, and maybe a kilo of cornmeal. When a fallen tree blocked the road after a late-night storm, the villagers didn't wait for a road crew—they banded together to clear the wreckage.

Emily became accepted as an honorary village member.

Women next door taught her how to cook chipatis, a tortilla-like fried treat. Students led her on hikes to the nearby waterfall. Neighbors showed her how to plant seeds and till the soil. The school's headmaster even instructed Emily on the proper way to kill a chicken for a special dinner.

But it was a simple, selfless act performed by three little girls that touched Emily most deeply. One morning outside her house, she filled a bucket with soapy water and dirty clothes and started to scrub her laundry by hand. Before long, a tiny face peeked around the corner from behind the latrine. It was Anna, a neighbor, followed by Sabina and Winnie. Emily welcomed them into the yard with an enthusiastic "Karibu!" They crawled under the fence and hurried toward her. Seeing Emily's unpracticed attempt at washing clothes, the girls each grabbed a shirt from the bucket and began scrubbing, squeezing, and wringing it clean. No older than six or seven, these precious girls saw a need and quickly volunteered their skills to meet it, expecting nothing in return. In less than twenty minutes, the job was done, but Emily still gets misty-eyed when she describes the fellowship of working together.

Emily is now in the process of applying for a two-year appointment in Africa. Though richer materially, America now seems destitute when it comes to fellowship.

I guess that says something about where we store up our treasures.

As so often happens, my friend went to teach, but her young African students had something even more valuable to share: companionship, hospitality, and unconditional generosity.

ACTING LOCALLY
Buying local goods

Shopping locally not only decreases the number of miles food must travel to reach your dining room table but also gives you a chance to build relationships in your community. Locate people in your area who grow fruits and vegetables or sell meat and dairy products. Visit the chicken that lays your eggs and have a conversation with its owner. Sites like http://www.localharvest.org can help you find sources of sustainably grown foods in your area—including farmers' markets and family farms. The food will taste better and be healthier for you, and you'll have the opportunity to build new relationships with those who provide your food.

It's not only food that you can buy locally. When doing renovations at home, visit salvage shops and try to use locally harvested wood. Choose mom-and-pop businesses and independently owned stores over chains whenever possible. Patronize local companies that support environmental and social initiatives.

Not sure which businesses are looking out for the environment? Browse a directory of green businesses online at http://www.coopamerica.org/pubs/greenpages.

Recycling and composting

Many American towns still don't have curbside recycling programs. Our small town offers neighborhood recycling pickup, but that service does not include paper or plastics numbers 3 through 7. For those items, we coordinate neighborhood runs to the larger recycling centers.

If your city is behind the eco-times, check out http://www.earth911.org for an online directory of recycling and reuse centers near you. The site also offers advice about what to do with unwanted items such as electronics, cars, and batteries. Talk to your neighbors about establishing a plan for delivering recyclables to the center, and take turns hauling the goods.

SAVE GREEN

If your city or town doesn't have an official recycling program, take action to get one started. Talk to your local officials about asking Recycle Bank (http://www.recyclebank.com) to come to your town. This program rewards recycling efforts with points that can be redeemed at hundreds of local and national businesses. Just toss your recyclables into the bin. No sorting required. Help your community and get paid to recycle!

If you haven't tried composting, round up a few neighbors and start a community composting project. Composting with a group can be less intimidating and more fun. And you can reap the benefits of less waste and richer soil as a group. Visit http://www.communitycompost.org/info/index.htm to read a variety of helpful tips on getting started and to order the *Community Composting Guide*.

Volunteering

Building community starts with helping others. Find organizations in your area that are already bringing people together in positive ways and get involved. What skills could you put to work to meet someone's needs? Retirement homes, youth centers, soup kitchens, libraries, and animal shelters are just a few places where your help will be greatly appreciated. Find one or two that spark your interest and invest in them by volunteering a few hours every month.

If you have kids in school, next spring break, skip the beach, leave the overpriced tourist attractions behind, and make a difference in your community. Stay close to home and foster community by organizing a Habitat for Humanity volunteer project. Your children will long remember meeting a real need for a family in your area. Visit http://www.habitat.org/cd/local to find your local affiliate and learn how you can get involved.

SAVE GREEN

When the kids were young, I was amazed by the number of free events we could attend, and the talent that was right in our community. Libraries often sponsor free performances for children. Schools will allow you to attend concerts and plays if you check in at the front desk. Band concerts in the park and Veterans Day parades are a big deal to a young kid, as is the annual open house at the fire station. Sometimes the best things in life really are free.

Supporting local arts and culture

Get in sync with the rhythm of your town by celebrating local arts and culture. Visit summer arts festivals, and buy artwork from a local artist. Enjoy music with friends at concerts in the park. Attend local plays, school productions, and church events. You'll often spend less than you would at the movie theater and make meaningful connections with people who live in your area.

Two Powerful Words

A few years ago, I was checking out some books from the library. Gloria, the librarian, told me about an upcoming trip she was taking, mentioning that she could only be gone for two days because she had to get back to take care of her son, Mark. I knew that Mark was handicapped, but had never taken the time to ask about the history of his illness.

The librarian explained that Mark had been diagnosed with a brain tumor when he was five years old. The tumor caused terrible seizures, but the doctors had no medicines that could either treat or control his extremely rare illness. About five years ago, the seizures got so bad that his doctors had to remove a large portion of Mark's brain. The seizures ended, but Mark lost his ability to speak and is now bedridden and fed through a tube.

As she told the story, the librarian never expressed even a sliver of self-pity. Instead, she told me how grateful her whole family is for having Mark in their lives. Even though Mark can only communicate a few emotions, she thanks God every day for this beautiful twenty-five-year-old son who will never walk, never talk, never kiss his mother good morning, never go to college, never hold a job, and never have a family of his own.

She thanks God even though, in worldly terms, she has given her life for Mark.

The encounter reminded me of the story about Jesus healing the ten lepers. Leprosy is not only a physically deforming disease; it is a socially alienating disease. In Jesus' day, lepers were completely cut off from the community. They had to shout when approaching a town in order to warn others of their proximity.

After Jesus suddenly and completely healed the ten lepers, he told them to show themselves to the rabbis so they could be reinstated in their community. Imagine the joy of mingling with family, friends, and neighbors again—the delight of participating fully in ordinary chores, village exchanges, and productive work. Talk about being born again! Yet, only one of the lepers, a foreigner from a despised group called the Samaritans, glorified God and knelt at Jesus' feet, giving thanks. Jesus then asked, "Didn't I heal ten men? Where are the other nine? Has no one returned to give glory to God except this foreigner?" (Luke 17:17-18, NLT).

We've all felt like Jesus did at one time or another. We have extended ourselves for a friend or neighbor, and the recipient has not remembered to thank us.

More often, however, I've been like the nine lepers, those who have received a great kindness but have not taken a few moments to write a thank-you note, or bring some flowers from the garden, or share a loaf of freshly baked bread.

Too often I go through life in the "woe is me" mode. I grumble about someone who cut me off in traffic, or didn't respond to an e-mail, or tried to sell me something on the phone. I complain instead of appreciate. Despite the fact that one thousand people in the world die *every hour* from hunger, despite the fact that less than half the world's population enjoys the freedom to practice the faith of their choice, despite being blessed by two children with healthy bodies and intelligent minds, I tend to whine about my losses rather than rejoice in my gifts.

Why should I give thanks rather than gripe? The answer is simple: people who give thanks are happier. Yes, letting off steam may make me feel a little better—temporarily. But God is in the eternity business.

In the long run, the happiest people, young and old, have abandoned the "woe is me" attitude toward life. Instead, they have adopted the librarian's attitude, counting their blessings rather than their grievances.

These people are happier because they take the time to say thank you. They give thanks—frequently and openly—to something bigger than themselves. And they give thanks to the people around them—the sanitation worker sitting beside them in the pew and the preacher in front of them on the pulpit, brothers and sisters, friends and neighbors.

Gratitude is the balm of life in community. Gloria the librarian is the genius of gratitude. When others would despair, she has the courage and grace to give thanks. And she continues to say thank you every day.

Thank you, Gloria, for reminding me to be thankful.

RESTORATION AND BEAUTY

What do you see when you take a stroll down your street? Are fast-food bags and plastic bottles mucking up God's creation? Can you rest in the shade of a tree on a summer day? Do billboards scream their messages 24-7? The physical appearance of your community impacts how your neighborhood sees itself, and how you and your neighbors relate to each other. If you want people in your community to spend time together, you need to set the physical stage for relationship building.

Litter

Take bags with you on walks so you can pick up aluminum cans, discarded candy wrappers, and anything else that didn't make it to the trash can or recycling bin. If litter is a big problem in your community, expand your effort into a neighborhood-wide project. Consider planning an event in the spring. Ask local businesses to sponsor the event and offer gift certificates to kids who collect the most trash.

At one school in New England where I taught, we had a brown-up day each spring—brown because the grass would not turn green until late May or June. Just after the spring thaw, dozens of students met after school to pick up trash that had been hidden under piles of snow. It always amazed me how much litter we could pick up in just an hour or two. The resulting community pride and goodwill lasted all year.

Planting trees

As our towns and cities grow, forests and green spaces shrink. Planting trees around your neighborhood is a practical way to restore air quality and repair some of the damage of suburban sprawl.

In 1996, Florida native Dan Burden founded Walkable Communities, Inc. (http://www.walkable.org), an organization dedicated to helping neighborhoods, cities, and towns become more pedestrian-friendly. His research shows that tree-lined streets promote slower and safer traffic, lower crime rates, and improve business for local shops. They also significantly increase property values. Visit http://www.americanforests.org to find out which trees are best for planting in your community.

Community Green-Up Projects Increase the Value of Homes

- Improvements to streetscapes (street tree plantings, container plantings, small parks, parking lot screens, and median plantings) can add more than 25 percent to the value of a nearby home.

- Neighborhood commercial corridors in "excellent" condition are correlated with a more than 20 percent net rise in value for homes within one-quarter mile of a green corridor and 10 percent net rise for those within a half mile.

- Homes located in "business improvement districts" (BIDs)—neighborhood-based organizations that provide special services like trash pickup and greening—are valued 30 percent higher than comparable homes not located in BIDs.

- While proximity to a neglected vacant lot subtracts 20 percent from the base value of a nearby home, adjacency to a stabilized lot—one that has been improved through cleaning and greening—increases the home's base value by approximately 15 percent.

Trees can increase a home's value as much as 10 percent. If you have a $200,000 house on a lot with several mature trees, your house could be worth $20,000 more than the same house on a treeless lot. Each mature tree can add up to $5,000 in value.

Community gardens

Is there a vacant lot in your area that could be transformed into a garden? Community gardens have been shown to reduce crime, foster relationships, increase home values, and provide low-cost food. Rally your neighbors and contact local officials. Donate money for start-up costs, or hold fund-raisers to cover expenses. You might be able to find a neighborhood association or community development grant to help with initial expenses.

If there is no space available for a community garden, start a garden club with your neighbors. Buy seeds and other supplies in bulk with members and save money. Once fall comes, celebrate with a harvest party.

Want to save money on food year-round? Take a hint from your grandmother and preserve produce from the garden. Make it fun: can with an experienced friend or learn a new skill together.

Graffiti and billboards

Tired of graffiti defacing walls and bridges in your community? Organize a painting party to spruce up vandalized parts of town. Talk to city officials about purchasing the paint, and volunteer to donate the labor. Treat your neighborhood with the same care you give your own property.

Canning fruits and vegetables with a friend could save each of you $400 or more over the course of a year.

What about billboards? Four states—all known for their scenic beauty—currently ban billboards: Alaska, Hawaii, Maine, and Vermont. Visit http://www.scenic.org for information on billboard and sign control. You'll find a model community-level billboard ordinance and model statewide billboard legislation.

Earth Day

This April, gather a group of neighbors and plan an Earth Day party. Deliver invitations via e-mail or over the phone to eliminate paper waste. Or if you want to deliver invitations by hand, create your

Applying for Grants

I hesitate to write about grants because so often we put off doing *anything* until we get funding. My experience is that if you put in the effort, God will do the accounting.

The easiest and often quickest place to look for funding is within your community. When we needed a couple thousand dollars to purchase recycling barrels, a few of us sent e-mails to area churches. Within a week, we had the money.

I have a friend who works for a Catholic social service organization. When she had a vision to build a playground with recycled materials in a struggling neighborhood, she went straight to the manufacturer in a bordering state. Not only were the materials local but they were free. In exchange for positive publicity, the playground manufacturer donated everything she needed. A local structural engineer volunteered his time to do the site work, and she recruited church teens, supervised by volunteer construction workers, to provide labor.

Some major cities offer mini-grants for community greening projects. There are also national programs to involve kids in gardening. The National Gardening Association offers youth garden grants to actively engage kids in improving their communities by tending a garden. Your school or community group must organize with at least fifteen kids between the ages of three and eighteen. Visit http://www.kidsgardening.com/grants.asp for additional details.

To begin researching other grant opportunities in your area, visit http://www.foundationcenter.org.

own using old greeting cards or postcards cut from cereal boxes. Decorate your party site with flowers and other natural touches, and ask your neighbors to bring a dish using local ingredients. After the party, organize a community cleanup or plant a tree at a school or church.

GETTING INVOLVED
Speaking up
Trying to make national and international environmental changes can be overwhelming and frustrating. The best place to start is in your backyard. You have the power—and responsibility—to get involved with your local government. Write a letter to support eco-friendly legislation. Encourage your mayor to sign the U.S. Mayors Climate Protection Agreement and work toward greening your community. (Visit http://www.usmayors.org/climateprotection for more information.) Ask your local leaders if they have sustainability or environmental management offices. If these positions don't exist, lobby to see them created. Rally with friends and neighbors and make your voices heard.

Want to know what decisions your state is making about the environment? Consult the League of Conservation Voters at http://www.lcv.org. You'll find information about land use, energy efficiency, recycling, and conservation policies in your state.

Saving the Mountaintop—and More
Never underestimate the power of a few intelligent, passionate Christian women.

I met Pat Hudson, a writer, when she offered to put us up overnight in the cottage behind her house. We were giving a talk on creation care at some churches in Knoxville and needed a place to sleep. We've been back several times for several other speaking tours Pat has organized. Together with Dawn Cappock, an adoption attorney, and Thea, Pat's compassionate earth-mother neighbor, Pat supports a small nonprofit called LEAF, inspired by a friend and church member who died of cancer in 2005.

They had no idea what God had planned for their "little" nonprofit.

The initial idea was to equip area churches with tools to engage in creation care. They do this by offering free books and DVDs to interested churches through their Web site, http://www.tnleaf.org, and inviting speakers like us to give sermons and public talks.

Recently they went on a tour of mountains that were being blown up in Appalachia to mine small veins of coal. Here's how Dawn remembers the experience:

> "A small group of Christian clergy and lay leaders had gathered on a ridge overlooking a flattened mountain·that had once been higher than where they now stood. The ravage and rubble beneath them looked more like the surface of the moon than the lush Appalachian mountain it had been just weeks before. The group had just heard grim statistics and shocking stories of families whose faucets ran with poison water, whose children suffered from breathing disorders, and whose homes no one would buy. This desolate view brought tears and feelings of despair, as if at the funeral of a beautiful child. And like a funeral, these Christians leaned on their faith. Beholding this destruction, this forsaken piece of God's creation, they sang 'Amazing Grace.'"

As they looked over the destruction, one pastor said, "This is sin."

My friends asked, "How can we stop this?"

Mountaintop removal (MTR) coal mining is a method of mining that blasts off the tops of mountains, lowering them sometimes as much as 1,000 feet in order to get to the coal seams that lie within like thin layers of icing between thick slabs of a cake. It has been called strip mining on steroids. The practice permanently trades water quality, property values, tourism potential, and mountain communities for short-term gains for a few coal companies. MTR is cheaper than underground mining, which means that while coal companies make quick profits, fewer miners are employed.

As an adoption attorney who advocates for child welfare

laws, Dawn assumed that environmental welfare advocates would already have anti-MTR legislation in the pipeline, and she wanted to direct LEAF's energy to help the ongoing effort. However, when she searched the Web and made phone calls to traditional environmental groups, she found nothing. For too many years, environmentalists had their hands full working defense: maintaining and enforcing current law. No one had been working on offense against MTR: no one had been proposing new legislation.

Dawn was frustrated but didn't know what to do. LEAF was new and inexperienced—just a few moms who cared about the future of their children and their planet. Legislation, was not their primary mission. Other capable people had made mining issues their life's work. These women were still getting familiar with the lingo. Just two years earlier, they hadn't known a stream buffer zone from ozone.

All good reasons for inaction, but God spoke, as he sometimes will, in an unlikely voice. In the fall of 2007, at a child welfare meeting, Dawn met up with a Nashville lawyer and longtime colleague on child welfare issues. She told him about their mountaintop removal concerns. He said, "Legislatively, what is it that you want?" Before her brain engaged, Dawn replied, "A ban on mountaintop removal coal mining." She was a little embarrassed, afraid that she sounded naively optimistic, but instead he said, "We can do that!" It reminded her of God telling David, "Go choose five smooth stones."

These moms now had a powerful ally but still no legislation. None of them had the technical and scientific background to write effective legislation. But the blessings were just beginning. Later that same day, Dawn ran into the regional director of the National Parks and Conservation Association, an effective yet moderate environmental voice, widely recognized as a reliable source of technical information. Within two weeks, the first draft of the bill to ban mountaintop removal coal mining in Tennessee was completed.

The miracles just kept coming. As they reached out for support, the question was not, "What are you Christians doing here?" but "Where have you been?" Every time they needed something, they prayed, "Either that or something better, God." They keep getting a lot of something better.

As Christians, we all must work on God's timetable. Usually that requires patience, but in the case of creation care, God's timing appears to be right now. LEAF's legislation did not pass on the first round, but I have little doubt that it will. And soon.

All of these women are busy working mothers. Pat was finishing her first novel when LEAF was born. She acknowledged that a leadership role in the nonprofit set back her book considerably, but said, "There's not a book in this world, except Scripture, that's more important than a mountain."

When I first met Dawn, Pat, and Thea, I envied their close friendship. They raise their kids together. They pray together. They live in community.

C. S. Lewis says that when you aim at heaven you will get Earth thrown in.

When these women ascended a mountain, they gained a more sustainable planet.

Making your vote count

The next time you step inside the voting box and cast your ballot, make conservation issues a priority. Whether you're voting for the president or city council members, research candidates' positions and voting records on environmental policy. The League of Conservation Voters provides scorecards in most states for local representatives and governors; the national league provides scorecards for U.S. senators, members of the House of Representatives, and presidential candidates (http://www.lcv.org). Hundreds of U.S. cities have passed legislation to reduce smog and carbon emissions. Make sure you do your part to elect officials who share your concern for the future of the planet.

How to Save Money This Year

How are we going to share all things in common in heaven if we can't even share hedge clippers here on earth? Reduce the need for new goods and save money by purchasing infrequently used items with a friend. The more people who pitch in, the more money and resources saved.

ITEM	TOTAL COST	YOUR CONTRIBUTION	SAVINGS
Chain saw	$300	$150	$150
Hedge clippers	$30	$15	$15
Solar lawn mower	$500	$250	$250
Rototiller	$500	$250	$250
Tent (4-person)	$250	$125	$125
Canoe	$800	$400	$400
Hiking backpacks (2)	$330	$165	$165
Cross country skis and boots (2 sets)	$460	$230	$230
Croquet set	$170	$85	$85
Queen-size air mattress	$100	$50	$50
Pressure cooker	$230	$115	$115
Ice cream maker	$200	$100	$100
Food dehydrator	$70	$35	$35
Solar oven	$250	$125	$125
Pasta maker	$70	$35	$35
Table saw	$500	$250	$250
Miter box	$500	$250	$250
Orbital sander	$80	$40	$40
Generator	$500	$250	$250
Clamps (4)	$120	$60	$60
TOTAL SAVINGS			**$2,980**

. . . And Share It with Those in Need

- Help women, minorities, and immigrants receive loans to start small businesses and enrich their communities (http://www.accionusa.org).

- Help refugees resettle in your community. Support a local refugee ministry, or contact http://www.churchworldservice.org. You can also support refugee resettlement programs through organizations such as http://www.catholiccharitiesusa.org, http://www.ecusa.anglican.org, and http://www.ucc.org/refugees.

- Celebrate! Plant trees in your neighborhood (http://www.arborday.org), organize an Earth Day party (http://www.earthday.net/node/88), or start a community garden (http://www.communitygarden.org).

- Help establish strong communities, promote social and economic justice, and encourage environmental stewardship in rural areas across America. Assist new small rural businesses through a microloan program (http://www.cfra.org/rural).

- Help alleviate suffering, poverty, and oppression by helping people build secure, productive, and just communities throughout the world. Provide practical relief, such as rice, buckwheat, and baby food for Georgian refugees (http://www.mercycorps.org).

Putting Your Faith into Action

Dear heavenly Father, thank you for the gift of community and the joy of shared relationships. Fill my heart with gratitude for the beauty of your creation, and help me and my neighbors become better stewards of your resources. Teach me to cultivate a sense of inclusiveness and belonging among those around me. Help me to gladly share the resources you have given me and reach out to those in physical, emotional, and spiritual need. May you be the center of my community and my life.

Lord, help me *today* to:

- memorize one or more Bible verses about community, such as Philippians 2:3-4
- pick up trash I see on my street and in my neighborhood
- spend 15 minutes talking to a neighbor
- pray for the people on my street

Lord, help me *this week* to:

- coordinate an errand or shopping trip with at least one person in my neighborhood
- share produce from my garden or extra baked goods with a neighbor
- shop at a local business instead of a chain store, or shop at the farmers' market
- perform a random act of kindness for someone in my neighborhood, like offering to babysit so the parents can have a night out, or shoveling a sidewalk

Lord, help me *this month* to:

- invite a family in my neighborhood over for dinner
- borrow something from a neighbor rather than buying it
- advertise and give away an unwanted item on Craigslist or Freecycle
- volunteer at least four hours at a local soup kitchen, animal shelter, or other organization
- attend a local school play, art show, or concert in the park

- talk to my local officials to find out what my town is doing to protect the environment and how I can help
- learn more about relational tithing through http://www .relationaltithe.com and Christian medical noninsurance at http://www.medi-share.org.

Lord, help me *this year* to:

- start an eco-team in my neighborhood or join the local chapter of a national conservation group
- greet new families within a week of their arrival to the neighborhood
- help plan a community block party, garage sale, or celebration for National Neighborhood Day
- lend gladly to friends and neighbors when they ask to borrow something I own
- coordinate meals for someone in my neighborhood who has lost a loved one or is ill
- research political candidates' environmental records
- plan a community garden, start a garden club, or plant trees in my neighborhood
- talk to my neighbors about purchasing expensive, infrequently used items together

Summing It Up

Getting Started

I have:

- ○ initiated a relationship with one family in my neighborhood I did not know
- ○ shared or borrowed infrequently used items
- ○ picked up trash in the neighborhood
- ○ performed a random act of kindness
- ○ increased my patronage of local businesses

On the Journey

I have:

- ○ formed an eco-team of environmentally concerned friends and neighbors in my area
- ○ shopped at a farmers' market
- ○ made a greater effort to carpool and coordinate errands with neighbors
- ○ coordinated meals or rides for at least one person in my neighborhood going through a difficult time
- ○ invited new neighbors to my home

Green Superstar

I have:

- ○ shared tools and equipment with neighbors
- ○ beautified my neighborhood through gardens and tree planting
- ○ purchased at least one infrequently used item with a neighbor
- ○ coordinated a neighborhood block party or potluck dinner
- ○ done the majority of my shopping with local businesses
- ○ volunteered regularly for a community organization

Energy Audit Work Sheet

Use your most recent electricity and fuel bills to estimate the following:

Annual kWh of electricity _____ x .06 _____

Annual therms or ccf of natural gas _____ x .88 _____

Annual gallons of #2 fuel oil _____ x 1.23 _____

Annual gallons of propane _____ x .80 *or*

Annual pounds of propane _____ x .19 _____

Annual cords of wood _____ x 220 _____

Car 1:

_____ divided by _____ x 1 _____
miles driven annually   *mpg*

Car 2:

_____ divided by _____ x 1 _____
miles driven annually   *mpg*

Car 3:

_____ divided by _____ x 1 _____
miles driven annually   *mpg*

Diesel vehicle:

_____ divided by _____ x 1.23 _____
miles driven annually   *mpg*

Miles of airline travel _____ x .044 _____

Gallons of gasoline used annually
for boats, mowers, snowmobiles,
chain saws, ATVs, etc. _____ x 1 _____

Miles of bus travel _____ x .018 _____

Miles of train travel _____ x .013 _____

Total dollars spent annually
(*for goods, services, mortgage and
car payments, tuition, travel, etc.,
but not including contributions to charity*) _____ x .03 _____

TOTAL GALLONS (*in gasoline equivalents*) _____

Goal for next year _____

How to get there:

The Energy Audit Work Sheet is from *Serve God, Save the Planet*, and is used by permission of Chelsea Green Publishing, White River Junction, Vermont 05001.

Sample Energy Audit (Typical U.S. Family)

Use your most recent electricity and fuel bills to estimate the following:

Annual kWh of electricity _____ 12,340 _____ x .06 _____ 740 _____

Annual therms or ccf of natural gas _____ x .88 _____

Annual gallons of #2 fuel oil _____ 800 _____ x 1.23 _____ 984 _____

Annual gallons of propane _____ 120 _____ x .80 *or*

Annual pounds of propane _____ x .19 _____ 96 _____

Annual cords of wood _____ x 220 _____

Car 1:

_____ 18,120 _____ divided by _____ 24 _____ x 1 _____ 755 _____

miles driven annually   mpg

Car 2:

_____ 10,000 _____ divided by _____ 30 _____ x 1 _____ 333 _____

miles driven annually   mpg

Car 3:

_____ divided by _____ x 1 _____

miles driven annually   mpg

Diesel vehicle:

_____ divided by _____ x 1.23 _____

miles driven annually   mpg

Miles of airline travel _____ 6,900 _____ x .044 _____ 304 _____

Gallons of gasoline used annually
for boats, mowers, snowmobiles,
chainsaws, ATVs, etc. _____ 50 _____ x 1 _____ 50 _____

Miles of bus travel _____ x .018 _____

Miles of train travel _____ x .013 _____

Total dollars spent annually
(*for goods, services, mortgage and
car payments, tuition, travel, etc.,
but not including contributions to charity*) _____ 48,500 _____ x .03 _____ 1,455 _____

TOTAL GALLONS (*in gasoline equivalents*) _____ 4,717 _____

Goal for next year _____ 4,245 _____

How to get there:
- Change lightbulbs
- Vacation close to home next year
- Carpool to work
- Hang laundry on a clothesline in the summer

The Energy Audit Work Sheet is from *Serve God, Save the Planet*, and is used by permission of Chelsea Green Publishing, White River Junction, Vermont 05001.

Top Twenty Green Resources for Starting the Creation Care Journey

WEB SITES

http://www.arocha.org. Founded in 1983 in Portugal, A Rocha ("the rock") is an international Christian environmental group that now works in eighteen countries on six continents. A Rocha focuses on conservation, research, and education—helping to create a more sustainable world, one community at a time. Get involved by connecting with others and starting your own A Rocha local community group.

http://www.betterworldshopper.com. Want to purchase environmentally responsible products, but don't have time to do the research? Betterworldshopper.com does all the legwork for you. Ranking everything from cereal and cosmetics to fast food and gasoline, this site helps you use your buying power to make a difference.

http://www.blessed-earth.org. In response to God's calling, Matthew and I started Blessed Earth, an educational nonprofit that inspires and equips faith communities to become better stewards of the earth. Through outreach to churches, campuses, and media, we build bridges that promote measurable environmental change and meaningful spiritual growth. Our Web site keeps you current with our family's continuing journey and equips you with resources to create a more sustainable world—one community at a time.

http://www.creationcare.org. An environmental network that seeks to educate, inspire, and mobilize Christians to be faithful stewards of God's creation. Full of resources for both individuals and congregations. Check out their quarterly *Creation Care* magazine—the best Christian environmental publication I've seen.

http://www.thedailygreen.com. Inspiration for what you can do *today* to start making the world a better place. Includes current news, a comprehensive list of links to environmental blogs, and feature stories. Stewarding the earth is a marathon, not a sprint; this site is a great place to recharge your batteries along the creation care journey.

http://www.earthministry.org. Churches interested in becoming better stewards should check out the Earth Ministry Web site and publications, including *Greening Congregations Handbook: Stories, Ideas, and Resources for Cultivating Creation Awareness and Care in Your Congregation*—a "toolbox" for fostering creation awareness and care in congregations. Earth Ministry has a greening congregation process to help develop an enduring, creation-honoring focus within all dimensions of congregational life.

http://www.energystar.gov. Home of the Energy Star Program, this unbiased site provides guidance for purchasing energy-saving appliances, including online calculators and specific usage by make and model. You will also find helpful information on federal tax credits, rebates, energy audits, and green building. Produced by the EPA and DOE.

http://environment.about.com. Looking for a one-stop site for keeping up with the latest environmental events and research? About.com provides current, in-depth environmental news and information on renewable energy, conservation, green living and design, health, legislation, and other environmental issues.

http://www.thegreenguide.com. Sponsored by the National Geographic Society, this online magazine is full of tips and tools for green living, product reviews, and environmental health news. Also check out their book *True Green: 100 Everyday Ways You Can Contribute to a Healthier Planet* (Kim McKay and Jenny Bonnin, National Geographic Society, 2006).

http://www.nccecojustice.org. National Council of Churches of Christ Eco-Justice Programs. Believing that God calls us to be stewards of his creation, this organization seeks to make churches more environmentally friendly and help to protect God's creation for current and future generations. It places caring for the environment in the context of loving our global neighbors.

http://theregenerationproject.org. The Regeneration Project, an interfaith ministry devoted to deepening the connection between ecology and faith, is a great resource for congregations, with active chapters in twenty-eight states. Projects include the promotion of renewable energy, energy efficiency, and conservation.

http://www.treehugger.com. This site provides downloadable guides for going green in all aspects of life—from birth to burial. A great resource for families just starting on the journey as well as those who want practical information for digging deeper.

BOOKS

The Green Bible (Foreword by Desmond Tutu, Harper One, 2008). This green-letter edition includes over one thousand highlighted environmental verses, inspirational essays by creation care leaders, and a Green Bible Trail Guide for further study. It's the first environmentally friendly Bible printed with a linen cover, recycled paper, soy-based ink, and water-based coating.

It's Easy Being Green (Emma Sleeth, Zondervan, 2008). Written by a teen, for teens, this is a great read for any young person interested in making the world a better place. As Emma's mom (and former English teacher), of course I'm a wee bit biased, so here's what *Publishers Weekly* has to say about the book:

> Sleeth, now an Asbury College student, is a precocious advocate for environmental issues. She wrote this book when she was just 15. (And, no, she wasn't homeschooled, if that's what you're wondering.) She shares her passion for Jesus and for saving the planet, in roughly that order. Although the book is clearly aimed at teen and young adult readers, Sleeth is skillful enough at sermon illustrations that her anecdotes about babysitting, high school cliques and Mom's homemade meals help illuminate her points for older readers as well. Pull-out boxes offer concrete suggestions for young Christians who want to go green, but aren't sure how to go about it. (3 March 2008, PW)

(For more tools, visit http://www.itsezbeinggreen.org.)

Saving God's Green Earth (Tri Robinson, Ampelon Publishing, 2006). This book describes how the Boise Vineyard Church rediscovered its responsibility to environmental stewardship. A very accessible model for churches embarking on the creation care journey. (Visit http://www.letstendthegarden.org for more information.)

Serve God, Save the Planet (Matthew Sleeth, Zondervan, 2007). The author has been my husband for twenty-seven years, so I'm prejudiced, yet I know of no other book that has changed hearts like this one. I've found it to be the single best tool for starting a creation care group at churches; the discussion questions in the back have engaged and motivated hundreds of Sunday school classes. Here's what author and advocate for the poor Shane Claiborne has to say:

> *Creation is groaning. And Matthew Sleeth has responded.* Serve God, Save the Planet *is not an alarmist call of despair, but a hopeful invitation to reimagine the way we live. Sleeth's words have the urgency of an ER crisis coupled with the deep faith that the church is ready to join God in healing a wounded world.*

(Visit www.servegodsavetheplanet.org for more tools.)

FILMS

Kilowatt Ours. Filmmaker Jeff Barrie offers hope as he turns the camera on himself and asks, "How can I make a difference?" to save both the environment and money too.

Planet Earth (11-Part BBC Series, 2007). You can't love what you don't know: the unparalleled cinematography in this series filmed over five years will give you a deeper appreciation for the amazing diversity and interdependent ecosystems that God the Creator has entrusted into our care. Considered by many to be the greatest nature/wildlife series ever produced, Planet Earth presents magnificent sights and sounds from pole to pole.

Renewal. This documentary by Marty Ostrow and Terry Kay Rockefeller traces the rise in environmental activism among religious communities throughout America, including evangelical Christians, Muslims, Jews, Baptists, Buddhists, and others. All are striving to preserve what they see as God's creation, and all are increasingly working together as conscious stewards of the earth.

SERVICES

Energy audit from your local utility provider. The first step to reducing your energy costs! Call your utility provider today, and schedule a home energy audit (free or nominal fee). After inspecting your home, the auditor will provide a detailed list of inexpensive ways you can immediately start saving energy and money, as well as the costs and paybacks for long-term energy investments.

(For a comprehensive list of resources in all of the above-mentioned categories, visit http://www.gogreenthebook.com.)

Bibliography

Chapter 1: Home

Bach, David, and Hillary Rosner. *Go Green, Live Rich.* New York: Broadway Books, 2008.

Rogers, Elizabeth, and Thomas Kostigen. *The Green Book.* New York: Three Rivers Press, 2007.

Sleeth, J. Matthew. *Serve God, Save the Planet.* Grand Rapids, MI: Zondervan, 2007.

Various authors. Chelsea Green Guide series. White River Junction, VT: Chelsea Green Publishing, 2007.

http://www.builditsolar.com

http://www.census.gov

http://www.earth911.org

http://www.eere.energy.gov

http://www.eia.doe.gov

http://www.energystar.gov

http://www.epa.gov

http://www.grist.org

http://www.newdream.org

http://www.treehugger.com

Chapter 2: Lawn and Garden

Bach, David, and Hillary Rosner. *Go Green, Live Rich.* New York: Broadway Books, 2008.

Davis, Brangien, and Katharine Wroth. *Wake Up and Smell the Planet.* Seattle, WA: Skipstone, 2007.

Jones, Ellis. *The Better World Handbook*. Garbriola Island, BC, CAN: New Society
    Publishers, 2007.
McDilda, Diane Gow. *365 Ways to Live Green*. Avon, MA: Adams Media, 2008.
McKay, Kim, and Jenny Bonnin. *True Green: 100 Everyday Ways You Can Contribute to
    a Healthier Planet*. Washington, DC: National Geographic Society, 2006.
Rogers, Elizabeth, and Thomas Kostigen. *The Green Book*. New York: Three Rivers
    Press, 2007.
http://www.drycreekconservancy.org
http://www.harvesth2o.com
http://www.realmama.org
http://www.reelmowerguide.com
http://www.monolake.org/aboutwaterconservation
http://www.treehugger.com

Chapter 3: Work
McDilda, Diane Gow. *365 Ways to Live Green*. Avon, MA: Adams Media, 2008.
McKay, Kim, and Jenny Bonnin. *True Green: 100 Everyday Ways You Can Contribute to
    a Healthier Planet*. Washington, DC: National Geographic, 2006.
Rogers, Elizabeth, and Thomas Kostigen. *The Green Book*. New York: Three Rivers
    Press, 2007.
http://www.earth911.org
http://planetgreen.discovery.com
http://www.time.com
http://www.treehugger.com

Chapter 4: Transportation
Davis, Brangien, and Katharine Wroth. *Wake Up and Smell the Planet*. Seattle, WA:
    Skipstone, 2007.
Harrow, Lisa. *What Can I Do? An Alphabet for Living*. White River Junction, VT:
    Chelsea Green Publishing, 2004.
Jones, Ellis. *Better World Shopping Guide*. Gabriola Island, BC, CAN: New Society
    Publishers, 2006.
McKay, Kim, and Jenny Bonnin. *True Green: 100 Everyday Ways You Can Contribute to
    a Healthier Planet*. Washington, DC: National Geographic, 2006.
Rogers, Elizabeth, and Thomas Kostigen. *The Green Book*. New York: Three Rivers
    Press, 2007.
http://www.about.com
http://www.buses.org/files/ComparativeEnergy.pdf
http://www.geocities.com/dtmcbride/travel/train-plane-car
http://www.gliving.tv
http://www.nhtsa.dot.gov/people/injury/newdriver/SaveTeens
http://www.treehugger.com

Chapter 5: Food
Bach, David, and Hillary Rosner. *Go Green, Live Rich*. New York: Broadway Books, 2008.
Jones, Ellis. *Better World Shopping Guide*. Gabriola Island, BC, CAN: New Society
    Publishers, 2006.

Kingsolver, Barbara. *Animal, Vegetable, Miracle*. San Francisco: Harper Collins Publishers, 2007.

McKay, Kim, and Jenny Bonnin. *True Green: 100 Everyday Ways You Can Contribute to a Healthier Planet*. Washington, DC: National Geographic, 2006.

Rogers, Elizabeth,and Thomas Kostigen. *The Green Book*. New York: Three Rivers Press, 2007.

Schlosser, Eric. *Fast Food Nation*. New York: Houghton Mifflin, 2001.

http://www.ajc.com

Chapter 6: Sabbath

Dawn, Marva J. *Keeping the Sabbath Wholly: Ceasing, Resting, Embracing, Feasting*. Grand Rapids, MI: Wm. B. Eerdmans Publishing Company, 1989.

Hescehl, Abraham Joshua. *The Sabbath*. New York: Farrar Straus Giroux, 2005.

Muller, Wayne. Sabbath: *Finding Rest, Renewal, and Delight in Our Busy Lives*. New York: Bantam, 2000.

Muller, Wayne. *Sabbath: Restoring the Sacred Rhythm of Rest*. New York: Bantam, 1999.

Wirzba, Norman. *Living the Sabbath: Discovering the Rhythms of Rest and Delight*. Grand Rapids, MI: Brazos Press, 2006.

Chapter 7: Holidays and Special Events

Davis, Brangien, and Katharine Wroth. *Wake Up and Smell the Planet*. Seattle, WA: Skipstone, 2007.

Harrow, Lisa. *What Can I Do? An Alphabet for Living*. White River Junction, VT: Chelsea Green Publishing, 2004.

Jones, Ellis. *Better World Shopping Guide*. Gabriola Island, BC, CAN: New Society Publishers, 2006.

McDilda, Diane Gow. *365 Ways to Live Green*. Avon, MA: Adams Media, 2008.

McKay, Kim, and Jenny Bonnin. *True Green: 100 Everyday Ways You Can Contribute to a Healthier Planet*. Washington, DC: National Geographic, 2006.

Scott, Nicky. *Reduce, Reuse, Recycle: An Easy Household Guide*. White River Junction, VT: Chelsea Green Publishing, 2007.

Rogers, Elizabeth, and Thomas Kostigen. *The Green Book*. New York: Three Rivers Press, 2007.

Yarrow, Joanna. *1,001 Ways to Save the Earth*. San Francisco: Chronicle Books, 2007.

http://www.americanresearchgroup.com

http://www.environment.about.com

http://www.finance.yahoo.com/family-home/article/103771/halloween-by-the-numbers

http://www.freecycle.org

http://www.greenzer.com

http://www.hospitalitynet.org/news/4026341.search?query=average+holiday+travel+fa mily+spending+u

http://www.inhabitat.com

http://www.nationalgeographic.com

http://www.nrf.com/modules.php?name=News&op=viewlive&sp_id=235

http://www.sierraclub.org

http://www.thegreenguide.com

http://www.use-less-stuff.com

Chapter 8: Entertainment

Rogers, Elizabeth, and Thomas Kostigen. *The Green Book*. New York: Three Rivers Press, 2007.
http://www.allbusiness.com
http://www.cbn.com/health
http://www.destroydebt.com
http://www.energystar.gov
http://www.grist.org
http://www.lighterfootstep.com
http://www.make-stuff.com/recycling
http://www.treehugger.com
http://www.turnoffyourtv.com

Chapter 9: Schools

Rogers, Elizabeth, and Thomas Kostigen. *The Green Book*. New York: Three Rivers Press, 2007.
http://www.eco-schools.org
http://www.gogreeninitiative.org
http://www.greenschoolproject.com
http://www.greenschools.net
http://www.greenseal.org
http://www.grist.org
http://www.pediatricasthma.org
http://www.recycleworks.org

Chapter 10: Church

http://www.csmonitor.com
http://www.energystar.gov
http://www.greenguide.com
http://www.healthyfamiliesnow.org
http://www.nationalgeographic.com
http://www.nccecojustice.org/grbuilding.htm
http://www.ohcouncilchs.org
http://www.powerandlight.org
http://www.usgbc.org

Chapter 11: Community

Bach, David, and Hillary Rosner. *Go Green, Live Rich*. New York: Broadway Books, 2008.
Jones, Ellis. *Better World Shopping Guide*. Gabriola Island, BC, CAN: New Society Publishers, 2006.
Walljasper, Jay. *The Great Neighborhood Book*. Gabriola Island, BC, CAN: New Society Publishers, 2007.
http://www.econsciousmarket.com
http://planetgreen.discovery.com
http://www.treehugger.com